SEPARATION OF CHURCH AND STATE
IN THE UNITED STATES

SEPARATION OF CHURCH AND STATE
in the United States

by

ALVIN W. JOHNSON
President, Emmanuel Missionary College

and

FRANK H. YOST
Associate Secretary, Religious Liberty Association

GREENWOOD PRESS, PUBLISHERS
NEW YORK

Preface

EVER-INCREASING importance is being attached to a clearer understanding of the principles of separation of church and state. This volume seeks to set forth church-state relationships as they have developed in the principal areas of conflict and as they have been defined by the highest federal and state courts. Many of the conflicts which have called for an interpretation by our courts are found in the field of education. These involve such questions as Bible reading and religious instruction in the public schools, dismissed and released time for religious education, the allowing of credit for religious instruction, public aid to sectarian schools, the wearing of religious garb, furnishing of free textbooks, free transportation of pupils to other than public schools, and other related subjects. These are considered in their order.

Other controversial areas include such subjects as citizenship and the bearing of arms, saluting the flag, freedom of speech and of the press, and Sunday legislation.

These problems are obviously of special concern to school administrators, boards of education, school patrons, legislators, municipal authorities, and taxpayers.

The present volume is not only a revision of the earlier publication, *Legal Status of Church-State Relationships in the United States,* published in 1934, with much of the material completely rewritten and brought up to date, but it includes a number of chapters dealing with subjects which have gained prominence in recent years.

The materials used consist primarily of state constitutions, statutes, administrative orders, and court decisions. In selecting court decisions, with few exceptions only supreme court cases, federal and state, have been used.

No claim is made that this study is in any way a definitive treatise of the subject. It is rather a consideration of the principal controversial questions which have arisen. An effort has been made to examine those areas in which questions are frequently being raised. Those have been stressed which are of greatest concern and germain to the entire problem of separation of church and state in the United States and to the preservation of the guarantees of religious liberty.

Our indebtedness to individuals for aid in this study would constitute far too great a list to enumerate. However, we would be remiss if we failed to express appreciation to those who have not only encouraged the study but who have rendered valuable assistance in its preparation. To these belong much credit for what is meritorious without any responsibility for its shortcomings.

We are grateful for courtesies extended by the Law Division of the Library of Congress, and by the Law Libraries of the University of Minnesota and the University of Notre Dame, and for the use of the private law library of Judge M. C. Taft of the Orphans' Court of Montgomery County, Maryland. Especially would we express appreciation to the staff of the University of Minnesota Press for their courteous and efficient work in the publication of this study.

A. W. J.
F. H. Y.

Contents

CHAPTER I

The American Heritage

R ELIGIOUS liberty has been achieved out of misunderstanding and conflict. "Of all forms of persecution, religious persecution is the worst because it is enacted in the name of God. It violates the sacred rights of conscience, and it arouses the strongest passions." [1] So declared Philip Schaff, the church historian.

The separation of church and state has become one of the fundamental principles of government in the United States. By many it is considered to be the greatest contribution to civilization the people of the United States have made. This important principle has experienced a life span of only one hundred and fifty years in the United States. In many parts of the world it is still not an accepted principle, much less an assured fact. Separation of church and state is a minority view for a majority of the earth's population. It has indeed always been a minority view, and it took centuries for the development of the basic principles of religious liberty until they took permanent root in American soil.

In Pilgrim Hall in the old town of Plymouth, Massachusetts, there hangs a painting entitled "The Signing of the Compact in the Cabin of the Mayflower." The words written on that bleak November day in 1620 indicated that the signers were undertaking the enactment of just and equal laws by which they were to be governed, and that they were coming to a land where, in the words of the poet, they might find "freedom to worship God."

Other settlements followed. Then in 1636 the province of Rhode Island was settled by Roger Williams. Here for the first time in history was established upon American soil a republican form of government and religious liberty through the complete separation of church and state. Roger Williams had tasted the bitter dregs of religious persecution. He had been driven from England, then from Puritan Massachusetts; he finally sought a home in the wilderness

[1] *History of the Christian Church* (New York, 1882–1910, 7 vols. in 8), 3d ed., 7:693.

1

where he could work out his experiment in government, an experiment which proved to be a success from the start. In it he saw "mankind emancipated from the thralldom of priestcraft, from the blindness of bigotry, from the cruelties of intolerance."

Roger Williams contended that government should not interfere with or punish a breach of the first table of the law as represented in the first four commandments of the Decalogue, since these were the duties which man owed exclusively to his Creator. He contended that was why the Ten Commandments had been written upon two tables of stone, in order to distinguish between those duties which are purely religious and spiritual and those which are secular and civil.

In 1647 Roger Williams was granted a charter in England which recognized the separation of church and state in Rhode Island; and the same year the first General Assembly adopted a code of laws which granted freedom of conscience and included the words "All men may walk as conscience persuade them, every one in the name of his God." [2]

The colony of Rhode Island demonstrated to the world that a republican form of government granting to the individual the free exercise of the conscience in matters pertaining to religion was far superior to any known form of government in the world. George Bancroft, the American historian, says of Roger Williams:

At a time when Germany was desolated by the implacable wars of religion; when even Holland could not pacify vengeful sects; when France was still to go through the fearful struggle with bigotry; when England was gasping under the despotism of intolerance; almost half a century before William Penn became an American proprietary; and while Descartes was constructing modern philosophy of the method of free reflection — Roger Williams asserted the great doctrine of intellectual liberty, and made it the corner-stone of a political constitution. . . .

He was the first person in modern Christendom to establish civil government on the doctrine of liberty of conscience, the equality of opinions before the law . . .

Williams would permit persecution of no opinion, of no religion, leaving heresy unharmed by law, and orthodoxy unprotected by the terrors of penal statutes. . . . [3]

In the meantime the proprietary colony of Maryland had been

[2] Proceedings of the First General Assembly [of Rhode Island] . . . and the Code of Laws . . . 1647, p. 50.
[3] George Bancroft, *History of the United States of America, From the Discovery of the Continent* (New York, 1888), 1:254, 255.

settled (1634) as a place of refuge in the New World for Catholics by Cecil Calvert, Lord Baltimore, son of George Calvert, Baron Baltimore, a convert from Protestantism. This great estate of Maryland, granted to his father by James I, Calvert arranged to have peopled by men of any faith who would cooperate industriously in developing the Calvert property. With the growth of Maryland and the influence of Protestant immigrants, opposition to the Catholics increased. As a result the Maryland Assembly in self-defense passed the famous Toleration Act (1649), which provided that "no person in this province professing to believe in Jesus Christ shall be in any way troubled . . . for his religion . . . so that they be not unfaithful to the lord proprietary or conspire against the government established." This was the first act of religious toleration on American soil, but by excluding non-Christians it fell short of granting full religious freedom as established by Roger Williams. Later, when the province was taken away from the Baltimores and placed under a royal governor, the Anglican church was established, and the Catholics, who had become a minority group, were deprived of their political rights in the colony.

Neither in Maryland nor elsewhere, except in Rhode Island, could the Friends, the "Quakers" of historical slang, find asylum; and so West New Jersey, Pennsylvania, and then Delaware were settled. Pennsylvania became the haven of Quakers under the leadership of William Penn. Penn's Colony, as it was known, proved to be another "noble experiment" in government. Liberal terms of a proprietary government were established, invoking a degree of self-government unusual for those times. Here religious liberty was granted to all who would acknowledge God, though only those professing Christ as the Saviour of the world and promising allegiance to the king and the proprietor were allowed to take part in the government. Under these liberal provisions Pennsylvania prospered.

Both the Quakers and the Baptists had suffered severely in Congregational New England. Connecticut Baptists converted from Congregationalism moved into northern North Carolina, where they soon established a growing Baptist community. They spread with astonishing rapidity both toward the south and the north into Virginia. But there again they met with difficulty. The laws of Virginia recognized only licensed religion. The Episcopal Church was the established church in that colony. Other churches were denied official permission to conduct the rites of their faith. The Baptists, Quakers, and Presbyterians became active in their opposition.

Presently there began to pour into the Virginia House of Burgesses petitions for the recognition of inherent religious rights. Increasing talk was in the air about liberty because of resentment against English colonial policy. Such Virginians as Thomas Jefferson, James Madison, and George Mason took up the cause of the petitioners.

Twenty-two days before the adoption of the Declaration of Independence on June 12, 1776, the Virginia House of Burgesses adopted a Declaration of Rights, consisting of sixteen sections, the last of which read: "That the religion, or the duty which we owe to our Creator, and the manner of discharging it, can be directed only by reason and conviction, not by force or violence; and therefore all men are equally entitled to the free exercise of religion, according to the dictates of conscience." Thus in Virginia steps were being taken to divorce religion from the state.

As soon as independence had been declared, the Presbytery of Hanover presented a memorial to the General Assembly of the Commonwealth of Virginia asking for the abolition of the establishment, which had involved, among other things, the payment of state funds to the Episcopal clergy. The memorialists said:

In this enlightened age, and in a land where all of every denomination are united in most strenuous efforts to be free, we hope and expect our representatives will cheerfully concur in removing every species of religious as well as civil bondage. Certain it is, that every argument for civil liberty gains additional strength when applied in the concerns of religion; and there is no argument in favor of establishing the Christian religion but what may be pleaded with equal propriety for establishing the tenets of Mahomet by those who believe in the Alkoran; or if this be not true, it is at least impossible for the magistrate to adjudge the right of preference among the various sects that profess the Christian faith, without erecting a chair of infallibility, which would lead us back to the church of Rome.[4]

The memorialists further pointed out what they deemed the proper function of government and declared that they desired no state aid in religious affairs:

We would also humbly represent that the only proper objects of civil government are the happiness and protection of men in their present state of existence, the security of the life, liberty, and the property of the

[4] This petition was presented on October 24, 1776. Several other petitions were presented by the Presbyterians in subsequent years. William Addison Blakely, *American State Papers Bearing on Sunday Legislation* (Washington, 1911), pp. 92ff.

citizens, and to restrain the vicious and to encourage the virtuous, by wholesome laws equally extending to every individual; but that the duty which we owe to our Creator, and the manner of discharging it, can only be directed by reason or conviction, and is nowhere cognizable but at the tribunal of the Universal Judge.

Therefore we ask no ecclesiastical establishment for ourselves, neither can we approve of them and grant it to others: this, indeed, would be giving exclusive or separate emoluments or privileges to one set (or sect) of men, without any special public services, to the common reproach or injury of every other denomination. And, for the reasons recited, we are induced earnestly to entreat that all laws now in force in this commonwealth which countenance religious domination may be speedily repealed —that all of every religious sect may be protected in the full exercise of their several modes of worship, and exempted from all taxes for the support of any church whatsoever, further than what may be agreeable to their own private choice or voluntary obligation. This being done, all partial and invidious distinctions will be abolished, to the great honor and interest of the state, and every one be left to stand or fall according to merit, which can never be the case so long as any one denomination is established in preference to others.[5]

The Baptists and Quakers joined the Presbyterians in opposing the establishing of the Episcopal church. However, a motion was put before the Virginia Assembly to levy a tax for the support of not only the Episcopalians but all denominations. Though the proposed measure was defeated in 1779, it appeared again in 1784 in the form of "A Bill Establishing a Provision for Teachers of the Christian Religion." This bill allowed every person to pay his money to his own denomination, or if he did not wish to help support any denomination, his money would go for the maintenance of a school in the county.[6]

In general the bill was very liberal. The objection to it, however, was that it gave the Christian religion a preference over other beliefs, and therefore was opposed to real equality. It was on this basis that Madison declared the bill to be "chiefly obnoxious on account of its dishonorable principle and dangerous tendency."[7] The bill was championed by Patrick Henry.

Madison succeeded in having the vote on the measure postponed and immediately wrote and circulated his famous pamphlet, *A Memorial and Remonstrance*. In this pamphlet, among other objections to the bill, he made the following statement, which is as applicable

[5] *Ibid.*, p. 94.
[6] *Ibid.*, p. 119.
[7] *The Letters and Other Writings of James Madison* (New York, 1884), 1:130, 131.

today as it was then, however innocent the intrusion of religion into matters pertaining to the state may seem to be:

It is proper to take alarm at the first experiment upon our liberties. We hold this prudent jealousy to be the first duty of citizens, and one of the noblest characteristics of the late Revolution. The freemen of America did not wait till usurped power had strengthened itself by exercise, and entangled the question in precedents. They saw all the consequences in the principle, and they avoided the consequences by denying the principle. We revere this lesson too much soon to forget it. *Who does not see that the same authority which can establish Christianity, in exclusion of all other religions, may establish with the same ease, any particular sect of Christians,* in exclusion of all other sects? that the same authority which can force a citizen to contribute three pence only of his property for the support of any one establishment, may force him to conform to any other establishment in all cases whatsoever? [8]

Madison's remonstrance aroused such sentiment against the bill that not only was it defeated but there was passed in its stead the "Virginia Act for Establishing Religious Freedom," written by Thomas Jefferson, as a declaration of religious independence applicable to all situations growing out of a union of state with religion, or to any project which would involve such union:

Well aware that Almighty God hath created the mind free; that all attempts to influence it by temporal punishments or burdens, or by civil incapacitations, tend only to beget habits of hypocrisy and meanness, and are a departure from the plan of the holy Author of our religion, who being Lord both of body and mind, yet chose not to propagate it by coercions on either, as was in his almighty power to do; that the impious presumption of legislators and rulers, civil as well as ecclesiastical who being themselves but fallible and uninspired men, have assumed dominion over the faith of others, setting up their own opinions and modes of thinking as the only true and infallible, and as such endeavoring to impose them on others, hath established and maintained false religions over the greatest part of the world, and through all time; that to compel a man to furnish contributions of money for the propagation of opinions which he disbelieves, is sinful and tyrannical; that even the forcing him to support this or that teacher of his own religious persuasion, is depriving him of the comfortable liberty of giving his contributions to the particular pastor whose morals he would make his pattern, and whose powers he feels most persuasive to righteousness, and is withdrawing from the ministry those temporal rewards, which proceeding from an approbation of their personal conduct, are an additional incitement to earnest and unremitting labors

[8] *Ibid.*, pp. 163, 164. The italics have been supplied.

for the instruction of mankind; that our civil rights have no dependence on our religious opinions, more than our opinions in physics or geometry; that, therefore, the proscribing any citizen as unworthy the public confidence by laying upon him an incapacity of being called to the offices of trust and emolument, unless he profess or renounce this or that religious opinion, is depriving him unjuriously of those privileges and advantages to which in common with his fellow citizens he has a natural right; that it tends also to corrupt the principles of that very religion it is meant to encourage, by bribing, with a monopoly of worldly honors and emoluments, those who will externally profess and conform to it; that though indeed these are criminal who do not withstand such temptation, yet neither are those innocent who lay the bait in their way; that to suffer the civil magistrate to intrude his powers into the field of opinion and to restrain the profession or propagation of principles, on the supposition of their ill tendency, is a dangerous fallacy, which at once destroys all religious liberty, because he being of course judge of that tendency, will make his opinions the rule of judgment, and approve or condemn the sentiments of others only as they shall square with or differ from his own; that it is time enough for the rightful purposes of civil government, for its officers to interfere when principles break out into overt actions against peace and good order; and, finally, that truth is great, and will prevail if left to herself, that she is the proper and sufficient antagonist to error, and has nothing to fear from the conflict, unless by human interposition disarmed of her natural weapons, free argument and debate, errors ceasing to be dangerous when it is permitted freely to contradict them.

Be it therefore enacted by the General Assembly, That no man shall be compelled to frequent or support any religious worship, place, or ministry whatsoever, nor shall be enforced, restrained, molested, or burthened in his body or goods, nor shall otherwise suffer on account of his religious opinions or belief; but that all men shall be free to profess, and by argument to maintain, their opinions in matters of religion, and that the same shall in nowise diminish, enlarge, or affect their civil capacities.[9]

This resulted in the disestablishment of the Episcopal church in Virginia.

In the meantime Thomas Jefferson had drafted the Declaration of Independence. There was set forth in that document the doctrine of equality of man, that men are endowed by their Creator with certain inalienable rights, that among these are life, liberty, and the pursuit of happiness.

It has been said:

Thus in a single sentence the Declaration of Independence annihilated

[9] This act was passed on December 16, 1785. H. A. Washington, ed., *The Writings of Thomas Jefferson* (New York, 1861), 8:454ff.

the ancient despotic order of the divine right of kings to rule the people without their consent. By implication it denied the right of a spiritual hierarchy to sit in the place of God, to set up and pull down kings, to bestow kingdoms and empires at its will, and to control the consciences of men in spiritual matters by the power of the state. In the very nature of things under the new order, men's consciences were set free to worship, or not to worship God, to contribute to the support of religion or to refuse to do so, and to voluntarily serve or refuse to serve the functions of religion without being molested by the government. The equality of all men before the law and the bar of justice and the possession of certain inalienable rights on the part of each individual struck a death blow to the old despotic theory that the individual possessed no rights which the government could not invade or abridge, and that the state could exercise absolute power and sovereignty to rule in all things both human and divine; and that an infallible hierarchy could command unquestioned obedience to its edicts and decrees in violation of the dictates of the conscience of the individual.[10]

While the Declaration of Independence did not have any force as a legal enactment in protecting the rights of the individual, it announced an all-important principle, the spirit of which was to pervade future acts in the establishment and development of the new government.

Before the Federal Convention in 1787, each of the colonies had established a government of its own, based upon Anglo-Saxon political traditions, which included recognition for its citizens of certain inalienable rights. In addition, the thirteen colonies had united themselves under the Articles of Confederation into what they termed a "perpetual union," to be known as the "United States of America."

The first enactment of national importance guaranteeing religious freedom was included in the Ordinance of 1787, passed by Congress under the Articles of Confederation. This ordinance effecting the organization of the Northwest Territory provided that "no person demeaning himself in a peaceable and orderly manner shall ever be molested on account of his mode of worship or religious sentiments, in the said territory." [11] This ordinance has been regarded by many as second in importance only to the Constitution of the United States.

The principle of religious liberty was also set forth in our treaties with other countries from the beginning of our existence as a nation.

---

[10] C. W. Longacre, "What Constitutes a Union of Church and State?" *Liberty*, Third Quarter, 1944, p. 11.

[11] Henry Steele Commager, ed., "The Northwest Ordinance," *Documents of American History* (New York, 1934), p. 130.

The "Treaty of Amity and Commerce" is assumed to be the oldest treaty on record involving the Western Hemisphere. This treaty was entered into with the Netherlands and was approved by the Continental Congress of the United States on January 22, 1783. It contained the following provision:

There shall be an entire and perfect liberty of conscience allowed to the subjects and inhabitants of each party, and to their families; and no one shall be molested in regard to his worship, provided he submits, as to the public demonstration of it, to the laws of the country.

Under the Articles of Confederation the United States in her treaty with Prussia on May 17, 1786, provided that "the most perfect freedom of conscience and of worship is granted to the citizens or subjects of either party within the jurisdiction of the other, without being liable to molestation in that respect for any cause other than an insult on the religion of others."

Likewise with the adoption of our Constitution and the setting up of our national government, the "Treaty of Peace and Friendship" with Tripoli, made and framed under the administration of George Washington, was signed and sealed at Tripoli November 4, 1796. Article 11 contains this significant statement:

As the government of the United States of America is not, in any sense, founded on the Christian religion, as it has in itself no character of enmity against the laws, religion, or tranquillity, of Mussulmans; and, as the said States never entered into any war, or act of hostility against any Mohametan nation, it is declared by the parties, that no pretext, arising from religious opinions, shall ever produce an interruption of the harmony existing between the two countries.[12]

Subsequent treaties were to contain similar provisions with respect to freedom of religion.[13]

With the accumulating evidences of dissatisfaction with the gov-

[12] *American State Papers:* Documents, "Legislative and Executive, of the Congress of the United States," Class I, Foreign Relations, Vol. II, p. 18; also United States Statutes at Large, 8:155.

Article 6 of the Constitution of the United States states: "this constitution, and the laws of the United States which shall be made in the pursuance thereof; and all treaties made, or which shall be made, under the authority of the United States, shall be the supreme law of the land; and the judges in every state shall be bound thereby, anything in the constitution or laws of any state to the contrary notwithstanding." Here was declared the supremacy of the Constitution, its laws and treaties.

[13] The following nations are among those having signed treaties with the United States in the years indicated containing provisions granting religious liberty: Algiers, 1795, 1815, 1816, Argentine Republic, 1853, Austria, 1928, Bolivia, 1858, Central American Federation, 1825, Chile, 1832, China, 1844, 1858, 1868, 1903, Colombia, 1824, 1846, Congo, 1891, Costa Rica, 1851, Denmark, 1916, Dominican Republic, 1867, Ecuador, 1839, Estonia, 1925,

ernment under the Articles of Confederation, there assembled in Philadelphia in 1787 those fifty-five men who were to frame the Constitution of the United States. In the Convention the experience of the colonies, the new state constitutions, the Articles of Confederation, and the teaching of European writers like Montesquieu and Locke were the precedents and materials out of which our Federal Constitution took form. The substance of the constitution was, therefore, the embodiment of a nation's political philosophy, a philosophy resulting from a consideration of the problems relating to church and state and from vivid observation of what had happened to human rights and human responses under the widely varying situations that had existed under colonial governments.

While a close compact of church and state had been regarded by other governments as a necessity, the United States' government deliberately deprived itself of all legislative control over religion and refused to sectaries any jurisdiction in state prerogatives. This was an untrammeled independence in both the spiritual and civil realm. The nation's leaders felt that any interference with religion by the government would be an impious encroachment upon the prerogative of God, that every religion should maintain itself by the excellence of its own doctrines, and that any pretense of alliance between church and state would be dangerous to the safety of the new government. For these reasons a government was formed which provided for the complete separation of church and state.

With very little debate the Federal Convention adopted the provision "but no religious test shall ever be required as a qualification to any office of public trust under the United States." [14] The elimination of a religious test as a qualification for public office *implied* the right of worship according to the dictates of one's own conscience, but the Constitution was otherwise silent on the question of religious liberty. There was no mention made of religion or of power conferred upon the government to legislate in the field of religion. Some of the stanch friends of religious liberty were not satisfied, however, with negative declaration. They demanded a positive pronouncement upon the religious liberties guaranteed by the Constitution, thus assuring the separation of church and state. Some of the

France, 1803, Germany, 1923, Great Britain, 1924, 1930, Guatemala, 1849, Haiti, 1864, Hawaii, 1849, Honduras, 1864, Hungary, 1925, Japan, 1858, 1894, Latvia, 1928, Madagascar, 1867, 1881, Mexico, 1831, 1848, 1853, Netherlands, 1782, Nicaragua, 1867, Paraguay, 1859, Peru-Bolivian Confederation, 1836, Peru, 1851, 1870, 1887, Prussia, 1785, 1799, Russia, 1867, Salvador, 1850, Siam, 1856, 1920, Spain, 1819, 1898, 1902, Sweden, 1783, Tonga, 1886, Tripoli, 1796, 1805, Venezuela, 1836, 1860.

[14] Constitution of the United States, Article 6.

states refused to ratify the Constitution until they were assured that ample provision should be made in the form of a "Bill of Rights" safeguarding the inalienable rights of man.[15]

Five of the states, while adopting the constitution, proposed amendments. New Hampshire, Virginia, and New York proposed, among other changes, a declaration of religious freedom. North Carolina declined to ratify until she was given assurance that an amendment guaranteeing religious liberty would be added. Accordingly, at the first session of the first Congress seventeen amendments were proposed by the House, of which twelve were endorsed by the Senate and sent to state legislatures for ratification. Of the twelve, ten received approval of three fourths of the states and became a part of the Constitution on November 3, 1791. The first amendment dealt with the subject of religious liberty: "Congress shall make no law respecting an establishment of religion, or prohibiting the free exercise thereof; or abridging the freedom of speech, or of the press; or the right of the people peaceably to assemble and to petition the government for redress of grievances."[16]

In regard to this amendment and the purpose of it, the United States Supreme Court has said:

The first amendment to the constitution . . . was intended to allow everyone under the jurisdiction of the United States to entertain such notions respecting his relations to his Maker and the duties they impose as may be approved by his judgment and conscience, and to exhibit his sentiments in such form of worship as he may think proper, not injurious to the equal rights of others, and to prohibit legislation for the support of any religious tenets, or the modes of worship of any sect.[17]

This first amendment accorded with the views of the advocates of religious freedom as expressed in the words of Jefferson:

Believing with you that religion is a matter which lies solely between man and his God; that he owes account to none other for his faith or his worship; that the legislative powers of the government reach actions only, and not opinions — I contemplate with sovereign reverence that act of the whole American people which declares that their legislature should "make no law respecting an establishment of religion or prohibiting the free

[15] When Thomas Jefferson saw a draft of the constitution proposed for adoption he expressed in a letter to a friend his disappointment that there was no express declaration establishing freedom of religion. He was willing to accept it, trusting, as he said, "that the good sense and honest intentions of our citizens" would bring about the necessary alterations. Washington, ed., *Writings of Thomas Jefferson* (Philadelphia, 1871), 1:79; 2:355.

[16] Constitution of the United States, First Amendment.

[17] Davis v. Beason, 133 U.S. 333 (1890).

exercise thereof," thus building a wall of separation between church and state.[18]

Bryce, in his *American Commonwealth,* in speaking of reverence for the Constitution, said that it "is itself one of the most wholesome and hopeful elements in the character of the American people."[19]

The First Amendment insures not merely toleration but religious equality and liberty as a political right. Before the adoption of the Fourteenth Amendment some contended that the First Amendment prevented the states from passing legislation affecting religion. But it meant only what it says. It stipulates that "congress shall make no law" and thus it is not in itself a restriction upon the action of the state legislatures.[20]

In 1845, in the case of Permodi v. Municipality, the court made the following statement:

The constitution makes no provision for protecting the citizens of the respective states in their religious liberties; this is left to the state constitutions and laws: nor is there any inhibition imposed by the constitution of the United States in this respect on the states.[21]

The Fourteenth Amendment was the first to interfere between the state and the individual in matters of religious freedom. It declared that "no state shall make or enforce any laws which shall abridge the privileges or immunities of citizens of the United States; nor shall any state deprive any person of life, liberty, or property, without due process of the law; nor deny to any person within its jurisdiction the equal protection of the laws."

The United States Supreme Court observed that "the word religion is not defined in the constitution"[22] but in the case of Davis v. Beason, the court said the "term 'religion' has reference to one's views of his relations to his Creator, and to the obligations they impose. . . ."[23] The Virginia Declaration of Rights gives a definition of religion in the following language:

The duty which we owe our Creator, and the manner of discharging it, can be directed only by reason and conviction, not by force or violence;

[18] Reynolds v. U.S., 98 U.S. 145 (1878).
[19] Second ed. (London and New York, 1889), 1:29.
[20] The restrictions bearing upon religious legislation and the guarantees of religious liberty so far as the state legislatures are concerned are to be found in the state constitutions. Spies v. Illinois, 123 U.S. 131; in re Kimmler, 136 U.S. 436 (1890); Reynolds v. U.S., 98 U.S. 145 (1878).
[21] 3 Howard (U.S.) 588 (1845).
[22] Reynolds v. U.S., 98 U.S. 145 (1878).
[23] 133 U.S. 333 (1890).

and therefore all men are equally entitled to the free exercise of religion, according to the dictates of conscience.[24]

Thomas Jefferson defines the term religion as used in the early documents to comprehend "all believers or unbelievers of the Bible. Religion is the alpha and omega of our moral law." [25]

Schaff, in his *Church and State in the United States,* points out an important distinction between "liberty of religion" and "toleration," when he says that "toleration is a concession, which may be withdrawn . . . In our country we ask no toleration for religion and its free exercise, but we claim it as an inalienable right." [26]

Judge Cooley declared that the American constitutions have not merely established religious toleration but religious equality.[27]

The United States Supreme Court said:

In this country the full and free right to entertain any religious belief, to practice any religious principle, and to teach any religious doctrine which does not violate the laws of morality and property, and which does not infringe personal rights, is conceded to all. The law knows no heresy, and is committed to the support of no dogma, the establishment of no sect.[28]

Absolute separation of church and state is guaranteed by the Constitution and by judicial interpretations, "unrestrained as to religious practices, subject only to the conditions that the public peace must not be disturbed nor others obstructed in their religious worship or the general obligations of good citizenship violated." [29]

In recent decisions of the United States Supreme Court in connection with the so-called Jehovah's Witnesses Cases, the principle of religious liberty, including that of free speech and free press, has been greatly extended.[30] These cases have done much to define the scope and degree of protection accorded the individual by the due process clause of the Fourteenth Amendment.

Even after the adoption of the Fourteenth Amendment the Supreme Court was slow to place its restraint upon the states in the field of religious liberty.[31] As late as 1907, Mr. Justice Holmes in Patterson v. Colorado, said:

[24] Section 16.
[25] Paul Leicested Ford, ed., *Works of Thomas Jefferson* (New York and London, 1904), 1:545.
[26] P. 14.
[27] Thomas M. Cooley, *Constitutional Limitations* (5th ed., Boston, 1883), p. 577.
[28] Watson v. Jones, 13 Wall. 679 (1871).
[29] In re Opinion of the Justices, 214 Mass. 599, 102 N.E. 464 (1913).
[30] On May 3, 1943, thirteen cases involving the beliefs and activities of Jehovah's Witnesses were decided; with but one exception all were decided in their favor.
[31] Spies v. Illinois, 123 U.S. 131 (1887).

We leave undecided the question whether there is to be found in the Fourteenth Amendment a prohibition similar to that in the first. But even if we were to assume that freedom of speech and freedom of the press were protected from abridgements not only on the part of the United States but also of the states, still we should be far from the conclusion that the plaintiff in error would have us reach.[32]

The dissent in this case by Mr. Justice Harlan, in which he contended that the Fourteenth Amendment placed the restrictions of the First Amendment upon the states, is more nearly in harmony with recent decisions of the court, more specifically prohibiting a state from depriving a person of liberty without due process of law.

In 1925 in the case of Gitlow v. New York, Mr. Justice Sanford, speaking for the court, said:

For the present purposes we may and do assume that freedom of speech and of the press — which are protected by the First Amendment from abridgement by Congress — are among the fundamental personal rights and liberties protected by the due process clause of the Fourteenth Amendment from impairment by the states.[33]

Again in De Jonge v. State of Oregon, decided in 1937, the court ruled that "freedom of speech and of the press are fundamental rights which are safeguarded by the due process clause of the Fourteenth Amendment of the Federal Constitution." [34]

"This interpretation of the scope of that provision," says Judge Waite, "has since been recognized in numerous decisions, and is now settled law beyond dispute." [35]

A long succession of cases since 1937 makes it clear that the restriction placed upon Congress in the First Amendment is placed upon the states by the Fourteenth Amendment, and its sphere of protection is being more clearly defined.[36]

[32] 205 U.S. 454 (1907).
[33] 268 U.S. 652 (1925).
[34] 299 U.S. 353.
[35] *Minnesota Law Review*, Vol. 28, No. 4 (March 1944), p. 215; see also Palko v. Connecticut, 302 U.S. 319 (1937). State constitutions also contain similar provisions to those found in the First Amendment.
[36] Among these are Lovell v. City of Griffin, Ga., 303 U.S. 444 (1938); Hague, Mayor, et al. v. Committee for Industrial Organization et al. New Jersey, 307 U.S. 496 (1939); Schneider v. State of New Jersey (Town of Irvington) and three other cases, 308 U.S. 147 (1939); Cantwell et al. v. State of Connecticut, 310 U.S. 396 (1940); Chaplinsky v. State of New Hampshire, 315 U.S. 568 (1942); Jones v. City of Opelika, Ala., and two other cases, 316 U.S. 584 (1942); Murdock v. Commonwealth of Pennsylvania and seven other cases, 319 U.S. 105 (1943); Douglas et al. v. City of Jeanette, Pa., 319 U.S. 157 (1943); Martin v. City of Struthers, Ohio, 319 U.S. 141 (1943); West Virginia State Board of Education et al. v. Barnette et al., 319 U.S. 624 (1943); U.S. v. Ballard, 322 U.S. 78 (1944); Marsh v. State of Alabama, 326 U.S. 501 (1945).

The record of court decisions tends to indicate progress toward greater security of freedom of religious conscience. The federal Constitution and all state constitutions prohibit any law respecting an establishment of religion. They prohibit compulsory support of religion through taxation or otherwise, restraints upon expressions of religious belief or the free exercise of religion according to the dictates of conscience, and compulsory attendance at worship.

A careful examination of the federal and state constitutions discloses that nothing is more plainly expressed than the determination of their authors to preserve religious liberty and to guard against the slightest infringement of such rights. Nor did they fail to perceive that a union of church and state like that which existed in other countries was, if not wholly impractical in America, certainly opposed to the very spirit of her laws.

In some respects this struggle for religious freedom carried on during and after the Revolutionary War may be said to have been even more important than the war itself; for to the principles of religious liberty here established, more than to its national independence and its stand for civil liberty, may undoubtedly be traced much of the real greatness and influence of this nation in the world. A new nation with the old religious despotism still clinging to it would have been no great addition to the world's assets, but a nation founded upon the true principles of both civil and religious liberty was indeed a noteworthy achievement.

Thus in this country the individual has the full right to entertain any religious belief that he may choose and to teach any doctrine, so long as he does not violate the laws of property or infringe upon the personal rights conceded to all. Such a law knows neither heresy nor orthodoxy. It is not committed to the opinion of any dogma nor to the establishment of any sect. Our law does not depend upon the leniency of government or upon the liberality of any class of people, but upon the natural, indefeasible rights of conscience of the individual, which are beyond the control or interference of any secular authority. It is not a principle of toleration but of religious liberty, in which all religions are placed on an absolute equality before the law. In the words of Governor Pollard:

This was America's greatest and most distinctive gift to the science of government. Acts of toleration had before been passed, but never before had any government put all religions on a footing of perfect equality.

To the minds of some, religious liberty means liberty to Christian denominations only, and to other religions simply toleration; but the word "toleration" has no place in our political vocabulary, for it carries the implication that we, by our grace, may extend to others the privilege of worshiping God as they may please, while as a matter of fact men do not worship God according to the dictates of conscience by virtue of any man-given right. The gift is direct from God. It is born with us.[37]

[37] Speech of Governor Pollard of Virginia delivered at the National Celebration Commemorative of the Religious Character of George Washington and the Separation of Church and State, held in Fredericksburg, Virginia, on October 16, 1932. *Liberty,* Vol. 28, No. 1, 1933, p. 3.

CHAPTER II

The Religious Element in America's First Schools

W ITH the superconscientious Puritans, religious questions had an important place in education; with them the primary business of a school, as of any intellectual enterprise, was religion. A review of their history and literature, particularly that of the seventeenth and early eighteenth centuries, reveals that church affairs, moral beliefs, and religious conduct were particularly woven into the entire fabric of government. They were a people forever conscious of the imminence of impending doom and of the responsibility of every man for his neighbor's fate.

Their attitude toward education, like that of most of the other American colonists, was similar to that prevailing in England and in the continental countries. Education was considered the responsibility and the function not of the state but of the family and the church. In England school teachers were required to hold a license from the bishop or other church authorities. Dissenters from the English church were not permitted to participate in educational work. Our early colonies, save Rhode Island, were a long time in breaking away from the old theory of the union of church and state and much longer in actually relinquishing the traditions associated with that union.

In Virginia the parish institutions transported from England were the earliest educational agencies.[1] Although much of the teaching took place in the home and with the aid of tutors, every minister had a school, and it was the duty of the vestry to see that all the poor

[1] James Truslow Adams says, "The early Virginia settlers were, at first, indeed, as solicitous as the New Englanders about education, but the results of the geographic environment were felt as strongly in this as in the other matters on which we have already touched. With the bad roads and the scattered life of the plantations, it was impossible for the common school to take root as it did in the compact little villages of New England. But if the common schooling was somewhat less diffused, the culture of the educated class was wider, and the private libraries of the Virginians offer to the booklover a refreshing contrast to the dead weight of theology on the New England shelves." *The Founding of New England* (Boston, 1927), 1:369.

17

children were taught to read and write. County courts supervised the vestries, and every year there was held an "orphans' court" to provide for the education and material needs of all orphans.

In secondary education an early attempt was made in Virginia to establish a Latin grammar school. Here again European traditions were accepted and followed. At the beginning of the seventeenth century the Latin grammar school of one kind or another was commonly the institution in which children were taught in the principal countries of Europe. These schools had grown out of the monastic and cathedral schools of the Middle Ages. They had been enriched greatly by the literary influence of the Renaissance, which encouraged the study of the humanities. It was natural that colonies should establish similar schools in America. In the Virginia colony a plan was developed for the establishment of such a school, to be known as the "east Indy School." [2] It was to be located in Charles City, was to be a free school, and was to serve as a preparatory school for the college Virginia hoped soon to establish. Funds were collected for its endowment, and land was set apart for its use. But the Indian massacre of 1622, in which more than three hundred of the colonists lost their lives, took place before the school was actually established, and this was followed by the fall of the Virginia Company in 1624. The project seems to have been abandoned; at any rate, there is no evidence that the school was ever opened.

In New England, where Calvinism was at its height, the attempt of the Massachusetts Bay Colony to establish a free school was more successful. The Boston Latin school established in 1635 was the outcome of a Boston town meeting held on April 23, when it was voted "that our brother Philemon Pormont, shall be entreated to become scholemaster, for the teaching and nourtering of children with us." [3] The first record we have of a provision for the support of this school is an action of a meeting held on August 12, 1636.[4] This act is frequently called the progenitor of our public school system, inasmuch as the town was undertaking the education of its children. Charles A. Beard, in his *Rise of American Civilization,* questions this position, however, on the ground that the primary schools at the bottom of the system of formal education were inspired, as were the colleges, by the religious motive. He says

[2] The first benefactor of the East Indy School was the Reverend Patrick Copeland, who had spent a number of years in India, and the school was named in his honor.
[3] Quoted by John Franklin Brown, *The American High School* (New York, 1910), p. 7.
[4] Elmer Ellsworth Brown, *The Making of our Middle Schools* (New York, 1914), p. 35.

The idea of elementary schools supported by taxation, freed from clerical control and offering instruction to children of all classes, found no expression in colonial America. Indeed it was foreign to the experience of the Greeks, Romans, and Europeans of the Middle Ages, whose psychology still dominated the West.[5]

The Latin grammar school of Boston served as a preparatory school for Harvard College. Harvard, the "School of the Prophets," [6] was established in 1636, six years after the settlement of Boston, when the general court voted four hundred pounds toward the erection of a "public school or college." In September 1638 the school received its first and most important gift upon the death of John Harvard, a clergyman of Charlestown, who had resided in the country only a year. He bequeathed his entire library and half his property, worth seven hundred pounds. The college at once took the name of its principal benefactor.[7]

Other Massachusetts towns followed Boston's example in establishing a grammar school, and within a few years several such schools had been established, though there was great variation in regard to rules and the conditions of establishment.

The second college to be founded in America was William and Mary in Virginia, chartered by the crown in 1693. As Harvard opened under Puritan auspices, so the latter was launched under Anglican control. Yale, the third college to be founded, was a Puritan institution chartered by the legislature of Connecticut to fit the youth "for publick employment both in Church and Civil State." The five other colleges established before the middle of the eighteenth century were also organized under religious leadership. Princeton was Presbyterian; King's College (now Columbia University) was Anglican; Brown was Baptist; Rutgers was Dutch Reformed. Dartmouth College, which originated in Moor's Indian Charity School, though not established by any one denomination, was missionary in purpose, having for its ostensible object the education and conversion of the Indians.

That the religious impulse was the chief motive in establishing elementary schools as well as secondary schools and colleges is evident from the language of the legislative acts and articles establishing such institutions. In 1647 Massachusetts passed what has now become her famous law requiring the establishment of an elementary school

---

[5] Beard, *The Rise of American Civilization* (New York, 1927), 1:177.

[6] The school was variously referred to as a "seminary," as a "college," and as the "School of the Prophets."

[7] John Stetson Barry. *History of Massachusetts* (Boston, 1855), 1:310–13.

in every town containing fifty families and a grammar school wherever there were one hundred families.[8] The law reads:

It being one cheife piect of yt ould deluder, Satan, to keep men from the knowledge of ye Scriptures, as in formr times by keeping ym in an unknowne tongue, so in these latr times by pswading from ye use of tongues, yt so at least ye true sence & meaning of ye originall might be clouded by false glosses of saint seeming deceivers, yt learning may not be buried in ye grave of or fathrs in ye church & commonwealth, the Lord assisting or endeavors,—

It is therefore ordred, yet evry towneship in this iurisdiction, aftr ye Lord hath increased ym to ye number of 50 householdrs, shall then forthwth appoint one within their towne to teach all such children as such resort to him to write and reade, whose wages shall be paid eithr by ye parents or mastrs of such children, or by ye inhabitants in generll, by way of supply, as ye maior pt of those yt ordr ye prudentials of ye towne shall appoint; pvided, those yt send their children by not oppressed by paying much more yn they can have ym taught for in othr townes; & it is furthr ordered, yt where any towne shall increase to ye numbr of 100 families or householdr, they shall set up a gramer schoole, ye mr thereof being able to instruct youth so farr as they may be fited for ye university, pvided, y if any towne neglect ye pformance hereof above one yeare, yt every such towne shall pay 5£ to ye next schole till they shall pforme this order.[9]

This law, which really established a school system, is noteworthy in that it is distinctly civil in character. From the days of the Roman Empire, in which education had been considered a civil function, to the time when Massachusetts passed this famous law, education in the Western world had been in the hands of the church and church orders, the only exceptions being a few occasional and scattered projects under civil authority. The control of education was now gradually to come back to the civil power, but with a vigorous survival of church atmosphere and ecclesiastical intrusion.

Religion was bound up with education especially among the Puritans. The function of the school was primarily to train theologians, and only incidentally men to direct affairs of state. Frequently the church was put first, or church and state were considered one. In connection with "The Free Schoole in Roxburie" we read: "Whereas, the Inhabitants of Roxburie, in consideration of their relligeous care

---

[8] By an act of 1642 Massachusetts charged the selectmen in all of the towns to see that parents and masters provided for the education of their children. They were to teach them *to read and to understand the principles of religion*, the laws of the land, and to engage in some suitable employment.

[9] J. F. Brown, *The American High School*, p. 8.

of posteritie, have taken into consideration how necessarie the education of theire children in Literature will be to fitt them for public service, both in Churche and Commonwealthe, in succeeding ages . . ."[10]

The rules that governed the New Haven Grammar School, conforming to the "Orders of ye Committee," included the following requirements:

That the Schollars being called together the Mr shall every morning begin his work with a short Prayer for a blessing on his labours & theire Learning.

That ye Schollars behave themselves at all tymes, especially in Schoole tyme with due Reverence to theire Master, & with Sobriety & quietness among themselvs, without fighting. Quarreling or calling one anothr or any others, bad names, or useing bad words in Cursing, takeing the name of God in vaine, or other prophane, obscene, or Corrupt speeches which is any doe, that ye Mr Forthwith give them due Correction . . .

That if any of ye Schoole Boyes be observed to play, sleep, or behave themselves rudely, or irreverently, or be any way disorderly att meeting on ye Saboath Dayes or any other tymes of ye Publiqe worships of God That upon informacion or Complaint thereof to ye due Conviccion of the offender or offenders, the Master shall give them the Correccion to ye degree of ye Offence. And yt all Correccions be with Moderacion.

That all the Lattin Schollars, & all other of ye Boyes of Competent age and Capacity give the Mr an accompt of one passage or sentence at least of ye sermons the foregoing Saboth on ye 2d day morning. And that from 1 to 3 in ye afternoons of every last day of ye week be Improved by ye Mr in Catechizing of his Schollars yt are Capeable.[11]

Among the requirements of the grammar school connected with William and Mary College was this one: "Let the Master take special Care, that if the Author is never so well approved on other Accounts, he teach no such Part of him to his Scholars, as insinuates any Thing against Religion or good Morals."[12]

In the selection of teachers as much attention was given to their piety and religious standing as to their scholarship — perhaps more. As Professor Reisner points out, the town schools established by the Massachusetts Bay colony were schools of the Puritan religion. No one could vote who was not a church member. Affairs of the church and affairs of civil government were directed by the same group of persons. "The pastors of the churches were supervisors of the schools

---

[10] E. E. Brown, *The Making of Our Middle Schools*, p. 40.
[11] *American Journal of Education*, 4:710.
[12] Quoted by E. E. Brown in *The Making of Our Middle Schools*, p. 130.

and the main materials of instruction were the Bible and the tenets of the Calvinistic religion." [13]

Educational policies similar to those of Massachusetts were adopted by New Hampshire. Inasmuch as New Hampshire was a part of Massachusetts when the law of 1647, to which we have already referred, was adopted, the law applied also to New Hampshire. Penalties were attached for the failure of the selectmen of the towns to maintain or establish such schools in conformity with the Massachusetts act.

The Connecticut code of 1650 was virtually a verbatim copy of the Massachusetts act establishing a system of schools in that colony. Many of these laws were still in force at the time of the Revolution. In both New York and Maryland, education was fostered under the patronage of royal governors, largely under the Episcopal plan.

The patroons and colonists of New Netherlands were required by an order issued by the West India Company in 1629 to "endeavor to find out ways and means whereby they may supply a minister and school master." An elementary school was established in 1633 in connection with the church at New Amsterdam. This school, which is still in existence as a preparatory school for boys, probably has the distinction of being the oldest school in America. Other elementary schools were established, and some rather unsuccessful attempts were made to establish Latin grammar schools. The New York Latin grammar school, established by Catholic Jesuits, came to an end with the close of the reign of James II and the administration of the Roman Catholic governor in 1688. No other Roman Catholic schools appear to have been established in New York until after the Revolution.

The "Frame of Government" which Penn drew up for the colony he established upon the tract granted him in 1681 by Charles II provided for freedom of religion, except for atheists and malefactors. Large powers were granted to an elective legislature, and provision was made for a system of education under civil control. The governor and the provincial council were given orders to erect and order all public schools, and to encourage and reward authors of "useful sciences and laudable inventions in the said province." The first legislature of Pennsylvania, meeting in 1682, passed a statute directing that the laws of the province be taught in the schools of the province. The second legislature, which met in 1683, passed an act requiring parents and guardians to have their children taught reading and

[13] Edward H. Reisner, *The Evolution of the Common School* (New York, 1930), pp. 44, 45.

writing and "some useful trade or skill, that the poor may work to live, and the rich, if they become poor, may not want."

Thus in Pennsylvania, as to some extent in Maryland and Rhode Island, the provincial government took advanced steps in the matter of public control of education. With the close of the seventeenth century we find in Maryland, Pennsylvania, and especially in Rhode Island, what was virtually an experiment in religious liberty. Much of this ground was lost, however, in the early years of the eighteenth century. In Penn's final Frame of Government (1701) the earlier provisions for education were omitted, and public instruction was left to the several religious denominations in the colony. In Maryland five years earlier an act proposed a system of education that was a mixture of civil, ecclesiastical, and private endeavor.

Puritanism, or Congregationalism, in its various phases was established in Massachusetts and Connecticut, and the Church of England was officially recognized in Virginia and the Carolinas. In the other colonies ecclesiastical functions were more or less confused, no definite policy or organization being in control.

Upon the accession of William and Mary, the Church of England developed greater interest in the American colonies and entered upon extensive missionary operations. This Anglican influence was soon felt in the colonies and had an important bearing on educational movements. Notable Episcopal gains were made even in Puritan New England. While the first concern of the Society for the Propagation of the Gospel in Foreign Parts, the official extension agent for the Church of England, was to establish Anglican ministers in colonial parishes, their second concern was the establishment of schools, which were largely of the elementary grades. They not only established the elementary school of Trinity Church in New York, which still exists, but gave substantial support to King's College (now Columbia University), established in 1754, which was the second Episcopal college in the colonies.

The effort to extend Episcopalianism produced incidentally a bitter feeling on the part of sectarian groups, which by the middle of the eighteenth century had developed into heated controversy. While the leaders of the day were working for church unity, the existing differences became more evident; unintentionally the demands for religious freedom were strengthened, and the desire for a complete separation of church and state, which found expression in certain statements in the Declaration of Independence, increased. This movement toward separation went on slowly during the eighteenth century. Along with it developed that "positive civic and secular spirit" which was so evident during the Revolutionary period. Channing puts it thus:

Before the Revolutionary epoch, religion had been closely connected with the government except in those colonies where the Quakers had impressed their ideas upon legislation. Even in them, the policy of the English government had made it necessary for many officers to take oaths or subscribe tests that were contrary to the scruples of Roman Catholics and Jews. Everywhere dissent was growing and toleration increasing.[14]

As the idea of religious equality was taking shape, America came to be looked upon as a land in which the oppressed might find shelter under a government that welcomed all to its shores. Among the immigrants were the Presbyterians from northern Ireland, who began coming in 1718, and a similar group from Scotland. Public education was greatly emphasized by these people, and, believing as they did in an educated ministry, they laid great emphasis upon a college education. Their experience with the Anglican church system of Ireland and the established Presbyterianism of Scotland impelled them to oppose state-controlled church establishments in this country. Their influence was readily felt throughout the middle and southern colonies in their efforts to effect the separation of church and state and to remove from the domain of the churches education furnished by the states. The European Baptists and the Huguenots, who settled in the Carolinas, also promoted the secularization of education.

When we study the Revolutionary era of constitution making, we find that only the constitutions of Massachusetts and Connecticut required a system of universal public education that was recognized as an important element in civil life. Pennsylvania required that provision be made "to instruct youth at low prices." According to Bancroft, seven of the state constitutions established some sort of religious test as a qualification for civil office:

Maryland and Massachusetts required "belief in the Christian religion"; South Carolina and Georgia, in "the Protestant religion, and the divine authority of the Old and of the New Testament"; Pennsylvania, "a belief in God, the creator and governor of the good and punisher of the wicked," with a further acknowledging "the scriptures of the Old and New Testament to be given by divine inspiration"; Delaware, a profession of "faith in God the Father, Jesus Christ his only Son, and the Holy Ghost, one God, blessed for evermore."

[14] Edward Channing, *History of the United States* (New York, 1918), 8:560–61.

These restrictions were but incidental reminiscences of ancient usages and dearly cherished creeds, not vital elements of the constitutions; and they were opposed to the bent of the American mind.[15]

For more than two centuries the humbler Protestant sects had sent up the cry to heaven for freedom to worship God. To the panting for this freedom half the American states owed their existence, and all but one or two their increase in free population. The immense majority of the inhabitants of the thirteen colonies were Protestant dissenters; and, from end to end of their continent, from the rivers of Maine and the hills of New Hampshire to the mountain valleys of Tennessee and the borders of Georgia, one voice called to the other, that there should be no connection of the church with the state, no establishment of any one form of religion by the civil power; that "all men have a natural and unalienable right to worship God according to the dictates of their own consciences and understandings." With this great idea the colonies had travailed for a century and a half; and now, not as revolutionary, not as destructive, but simply as giving utterance to the thought of the nation, the states stood up in succession, in the presence of one another and before God and the world, to bear their witness in favor of restoring independence to conscience and the mind.[16]

Several of the states did not enfranchise the Catholics or Jews. The Catholics were permitted to hold office in Rhode Island, New York, New Jersey, Virginia, Massachusetts, Pennsylvania, Delaware, Maryland, and, with some restriction, in Connecticut. The Jews might hold office only in Rhode Island, New York, New Jersey, and Virginia.

In some states—Maryland, for example—the legislature might at its discretion lay a general tax for the support of the Christian religion. Massachusetts required "the support of public Protestant teachers of piety, religion, and morality." In Massachusetts and Connecticut the Puritan worship was still closely connected with the state. South Carolina, in her attempt to preserve the union of church and state, went so far in her legislation on religion as to declare the "Christian Protestant religion" to be the established religion of the state.

But gradually constitutional provisions and legislative acts designating an established religion came to have no meaning. The struggle in the Virginia legislature which resulted in the disestablishment of the Anglican church and the civil equality of every denomination in that state has been described in Chapter I. The principle of sepa-

[15] George Bancroft, *History of the United States* (New York, 1888), 5:121.
[16] *Ibid.*, p. 119.

ration of church and state carried over into the field of education. The same spirit that opposed state control or support of religion likewise opposed state support of sectarian schools. If education was to be religious it must be carried on by the churches and without the support of the state. With the demand for an educational system supported by the state came a similar demand that such an education be nonsectarian.

As we have seen, the Latin grammar school emphasized religious training because it prepared men for the two learned professions of the time — the law and the ministry; Latin, Greek, Hebrew, and the study of the Scriptures held a large place in its curriculum. Now, however, there arose a popular clamor for a different kind of school — a school in which theological discussions would be given less room, a school that would emphasize less its preparatory training for the college and more the ideals of general culture and a practical preparation for life. This demand gave birth to the academies.

The first American academy was the Public Academy in Philadelphia, founded by Benjamin Franklin in 1751, which later grew into the University of Pennsylvania. The organization of this school was largely the result of agitation carried on by Franklin and his friends, in the course of which he printed and distributed *Proposals Relating to the Education of Youth in Pennsylvania*. It received its support partly from public subscription and partly from the government. The subscribers chose a board of twenty-four trustees, who organized and conducted the affairs of the school. The work of the school is set forth by Franklin in the following words:

As to their studies, it would be well if they could be taught everything that is useful, and everything that is ornamental. But art is long and their time is short. It is therefore proposed, that they learn those things that are likely to be most useful and most ornamental; regard being had to the several professions for which they are intended. All interested for divinity, should be taught the Latin and Greek; for physic, the Latin, Greek, and French; for law, the Latin and French; merchants, the French, German, and Spanish; and, though all should not be compelled to learn Latin, Greek, or the modern foreign languages, yet none that have an ardent desire to learn them should be refused; their English, arithmetic, and other studies absolutely necessary, being at the same time not neglected.[17]

Though the spirit of the academy was obviously religious, it was more liberal than that which had prevailed in colonial schools and

[17] Jared Sparks, *Works of Franklin* (Philadelphia, 1840), 1:572, 574.

which still survived in the grammar schools. Most of the activities were nonsectarian, though many academies were established and controlled by individual denominations. Their control was generally vested in a self-perpetuating body. They were dependent upon individual contributions and church grants, though frequently they were liberally endowed. Sometimes they received financial assistance from the state or city, as did the Philadelphia Academy, for instance, though control remained in the hands of the corporation.

The academies were attended by more mature students than the grammar schools and were open to both boys and girls. Though they were broader, freer, and more democratic, the fact that they were under private control and that they charged tuition fees made them more or less exclusive. In many cases they served as an elementary as well as a finishing school, though their training early took on the college preparatory aspect, exerting a liberalizing influence upon the colleges of the day. They wielded a powerful influence in American education through their training of teachers for the elementary schools. As has been said, they were in a sense the predecessors of our present normal schools.

Many of the academies were taken over by the city or town and supported by taxation, and thus they were really the precursors of the public high schools of a later date. Roughly speaking, the academy was the chief secondary school from the American Revolution to the Civil War, just as the grammar school had been the principal school up to the Revolution.

The first high school in the United States was founded in Boston. By 1818, Boston had extended its public school system to include the elementary as well as the grammar schools. In 1821 the English Classical School was established as a free school for the boys of Boston who could not continue their education in an academy because of the expense. In general, the high school, which became the most important school after the Civil War, took the place of the academy. The grammar schools, as we have seen, did not meet the demand of the common people, for these schools looked to the college. Their course of study was designed to prepare students for positions in the state or in the church. The academy, while it offered a wider course of study and was practical in that it trained students for the practical needs of life, was controlled by a closed corporation, and, being expensive, was open only to the few. In response to the new demand for equality of opportunity, and in harmony with the growing spirit of freedom and democracy, the American high school was set up —

a free institution, under public control, which was to offer a practical as well as a cultural course of study, and which was to be open to all at public expense. Thus was established what was to become the connecting link between the public elementary schools and the colleges or, more particularly, the state universities.

The constitutional right of a community to levy taxes for the support of high schools was carried to the courts in 1872 in a suit brought by Stuart et al. v. School District No. 1 of the Village of Kalamazoo, Michigan,[18] in which an attempt was made to prevent the collection of taxes voted for the support of the high school and for payment of the school superintendent's salary. The Supreme Court of the state said:

> Neither in our state policy, in our constitution, or in our laws, do we find the primary school districts restricted in the branches of knowledge which their officers may cause to be taught, or the grade of instruction that may be given, if their voters consent in regular form to bear the expense and raise the taxes for the purpose.[19]

Everyone is familiar with the phenomenal growth of the public high school since 1860, but the desire for a free, nonsectarian public school system began long before this. Great strides were taken in the thirties and forties of the nineteenth century, a period during which the doctrine of equal rights was being spread by the Jacksonian democracy. In the words of Beard, "For a nation of farmers and mechanics, bent on self-government and possessed of the ballot, there was only one kind of an educational program in keeping with self-respect, namely, a free and open public school system supported by taxation and nonsectarian in its control."[20]

Organized labor now began to demand from the legislators the establishment of free common schools. With the development of factories in the early nineteenth century, new social problems arose. Aroused by the unwholesome conditions and injustice that existed, the workers formed labor unions. The spokesmen of labor interests frequently made demands for general public education. While changes came slowly, before the middle of the century many significant reforms sought by labor had been accomplished. "Laws for the protection of the life and health of the factory hands were enacted, imprisonment for debt disappeared, and the effort to establish schools supported by public taxes and controlled by the public will finally

[18] 30 Mich. 69.
[19] Ibid.
[20] Beard, American Civilization, 1:810.

succeeded." [21] Labor objected to charity education, demanding in its place a system of public education "not as charity but as the right of every child," an education that should be open and free to all. John R. Commons, in his *History of Labor in the United States,* says that in 1830 education was the "paramount issue in the Working Men's party. 'All history,' it was said, 'corroborates the melancholy fact, that in proportion as the mass of the people becomes ignorant, misrule and anarchy ensue — their liberties are subverted, and tyrannic ambition has never failed to take advantage of their helpless condition. . . .' " [22] Thus more and more education came to be looked upon not only as a function of government but as a duty to its citizens; an intelligent citizenry was considered indispensable to a successful democracy.

As the spirit of natural science wrought a transformation upon the minds of the intellectual classes, making for a secularization of social processes, so the multiplication of religious sects and their ceaseless rivalry tended to accelerate the movement for a more definite separation of church and state.

The increasing numbers of Irish and other immigrants from Europe, who, it was feared, were likely to fall under Catholic instruction if educated in charity schools, influenced Protestants to accept "secularism rather than papal authority." Such secularization of schools made its greatest strides in the frontier states, where there were fewer vested sectarian interests. In the eastern states private academies and universities had made more progress, with the result that property rights were involved to a greater extent.

The spirit of Jacksonian democracy was determined to destroy favoritism in education as well as privilege in politics. Thus the educational movement of the third, fourth, and fifth decades of the nineteenth century developed into a political force that served as a great impetus to education in both the elementary and the secondary field. Appropriations were increased. Teachers' salaries were raised. Better school buildings, textbooks, and general equipment were sought. The school year was lengthened and state supervision was introduced. District, county, and state organizations were set up in turn. Technical schools were developed, and finally the Morrill Act of 1862, which served as the great stimulus to the promotion of mechanical and agricultural education, was enacted.

The completely secularized university was represented by the Uni-

[21] Edgar Wallace Knight, *Education in the United States* (Boston, 1929), p. 179.
[22] John R. Commons, *History of Labor in the United States* (New York, 1918), 1:227.

versity of Virginia, established in 1825, and the University of Michigan, established in 1837. But more particularly the public elementary schools had become secularized. The tendency toward secularization in secondary education found expression in the public high school. It was demanded that all forms of religious practices be kept out of the public school system. In 1872 the supreme court of Ohio handed down by unanimous vote its famous decision in which it upheld the refusal of the Board of Education to permit the reading of the Bible in the public schools of Cincinnati, declaring:

Legal Christianity is a solecism, a contradiction of terms. When Christianity asks the aid of government beyond mere impartial protection, it denies itself. Its laws are divine, and not human. Its essential interests lie beyond the reach and range of human governments. United with government, religion never rises above the merest superstition; united with religion, government never rises above the merest despotism; and all history shows us that the more widely and completely they are separated, the better it is for both.[23]

President Grant enunciated this principle when he said, "Let us . . . leave the matter of religious teaching to the family altar, the church, and the private school, supported entirely by private contributions."[24]

This movement for the secularization of public schools reached its greatest height, perhaps, with the proposed federal constitutional amendment presented by James G. Blaine on December 14, 1875, which reads as follows:

No state shall make any law respecting an establishment of religion, or prohibiting the free exercise thereof; and no money raised by school taxation in any State, for the support of public schools, or derived from any public fund therefor, nor any public lands devoted thereto, shall ever be under the control of any religious sect; nor shall any money so raised, or lands so devoted, be divided between religious sects or denominations.[25]

The amendment passed the House by a vote of 180 to 7. In the Senate it received a vote of 28 for and 16 against, thus failing to receive the necessary two-thirds vote. In the same year, 1876, both the Republican and Democratic platforms included a declaration on the subject of religious freedom and public schools.

Since that time there have been various manifestations of a move-

[23] Board of Education of Cincinnati v. Minor et al., 23 Ohio St. 211.

[24] Speech made to G.A.R. veterans at Des Moines, Iowa, in December 1875, quoted in the *Catholic World*, 22:434, 435 (January 1876).

[25] William Addison Blakely, *American State Papers Bearing on Sunday Legislation* (Washington, 1911), p. 349.

ment on the part of certain individuals and organizations not only to stem the tide of complete separation but to reverse the movement and bring in a closer union of church and state.[26] As some have stated their aims, they would "capture the public schools" for Christianity. They have termed the public schools "godless" and would give Christ what they assert to be "His rightful place" in our public school system.

This attitude was expressed also in renewed agitation for Sunday legislation throughout the states and in the petitions and bills for religious legislation and religious amendments to the Constitution with which Congress was besieged. It accounts for the proposed "Religious Educational Amendment" introduced by Senator Blair on May 25, 1888, of which section 2 reads:

> Each state in this union shall establish and maintain a system of free public schools, adequate for the education of all the children therein, between the ages of six and sixteen years inclusive, in the common branches of knowledge, and in virtue, morality, and the principles of the Christian religion.

[26] From time to time efforts have been made to put what has been termed "God into our Federal Constitution." An amendment was proposed to that effect in 1844. Again in 1865 President Lincoln had a delegation of ministers representing a number of different denominations call upon him in a similar effort. The National Reform Association has been instrumental in spearheading such attempts on various occasions. In an effort to recognize the Christian religion and Jesus Christ as its author, religious amendments were introduced in Congress in 1894, 1895, 1896, 1908, 1909, and in 1910.

It appears that no attempts have been made since then until July 15, 1947, when in the House of Representatives, Representative Louis E. Graham of Pennsylvania proposed that the United States acknowledge Jesus Christ as Saviour and King by an amendment to the Constitution of the United States. On July 18 of the same year, Senator Arthur Capper of Kansas proposed a similar amendment. These two resolutions, House Joint Resolution 239 and Senate Joint Resolution 150, introduced in the Eightieth Congress, are identical and read as follows:

"Resolved by the Senate and House of Representatives of the United States of America assembled, (two-thirds of each House concurring therein), That the following article is hereby proposed as an amendment to the Constitution of the United States, which shall be valid to all intents and purposes as part of the Constitution when ratified by conventions in three-fourths of the several States:

'ARTICLE—
'Sec. 1. The Preamble of this Constitution shall hereafter read: "We, the People of the United States, DEVOUTLY RECOGNIZING THE AUTHORITY AND LAW OF JESUS CHRIST, THE SAVIOUR AND KING OF NATONS, in order to form a more perfect Union, establish Justice . . . do ordain and establish this Constitution for the United States of America.

'Sec. 2. This article shall not be interpreted as abridging the present rights of religious freedom, freedom of speech and press, and peaceful assemblage, guaranteed by the first article of amendment to this Constitution.

'SEC. 3. The Congress shall have power, in cases as it may deem proper, to provide a modified oath or affirmation for citizens whose religious scruples prevent them from giving unqualified allegiance to the Constitution as herein amended.' "

The Christian Amendment Movement, 914 Clay Street, Topeka, Kansas, has been organized in an effort to secure the adoption of the above amendment. A paper entitled "The Christian Patriot" is being published and individuals as well as organizations are being solicited throughout the country in a nationwide drive to change the preamble to the Constitution of the United States.

It appears that the purpose here was to establish the "Christian religion" throughout the public school system by teaching the "principles of the Christian religion." The proposed amendment died with the Fifty-first Congress. In many places this spirit is re-asserting itself in a movement fostered by those who would require some form of religious instruction in the public schools and are seeking to enact other forms of religious legislation.

CHAPTER III

Bible Reading in the Public Schools

D URING the nineteenth century it appears that only one state, Massachusetts, enacted a statute requiring Bible reading in the public schools.[1] However, in the twentieth century a number of states placed similar statutes upon their books. Pennsylvania passed a law requiring Bible reading in the public schools in 1913, Delaware and Tennessee followed with similar laws in 1915, New Jersey in 1916, Alabama in 1919, Georgia in 1921, Maine in 1923, Kentucky in 1924, Florida and Idaho in 1925, Arkansas in 1930. Other states have followed similar practices since then. In the year 1926 the board of education of the District of Columbia passed a ruling requiring the Bible to be read daily in the public schools.

This type of legislation has called forth considerable opposition, with the result that parties involved have appealed to the courts for interpretation of various constitutional and statutory provisions. Some of the legal questions that have been most often raised are: Does the reading of the Bible constitute sectarian instruction? Is the Bible a sectarian book? Does time spent in its reading or study by teachers constitute an appropriation of public funds for sectarian purposes? Does the reading of the Bible, the singing of religious hymns and the saying of the Lord's Prayer or other prayers constitute a religious service? Is compulsory attendance during such reading a violation of religious liberty granted in the federal and state constitutions? Shall the Protestant, Catholic, or Jewish Bible be read?

These and other perplexing questions have aroused a great deal of anxiety among many people who disapprove of required Bible reading in the public schools. They have deemed the question of sufficient importance to manifest their disapproval by calling upon the courts to invoke whatever constitutional and statutory provisions might prevent such practice.

[1] The Massachusetts statute was passed in 1826.

Statutes requiring the Bible to be read daily in the public schools vary somewhat in their details but in principle they are the same.[2] Alabama, for example, requires the teacher to read once every school day "readings from the Holy Bible." In Delaware the law requires that "at least five verses from the Holy Bible shall be read . . . at the opening of such school"; in Pennsylvania that "at least ten verses from the Holy Bible" be read every day; in Georgia that the "Bible, including the Old and the New Testament," shall be read, and that not less than one chapter is to be read every day at some appropriate time; and in Idaho that the readings be taken from a selected list of passages from the standard American version of the Bible, furnished from time to time by the state board of education, and that from twenty to thirty verses are to read each day. The Maine statute requires, in addition to the reading of the Scriptures, special emphasis upon the "Ten Commandments, the Psalms of David, the Proverbs of Solomon, the Sermon on the Mount, and the Lord's Prayer." That of Tennessee stipulates that "the same selection shall not be read more than twice a month."

Of the states having statutes requiring Bible reading, Arkansas, Florida, Kentucky, Maine, Massachusetts, New Jersey, and Pennsylvania require that no comments be made. The Idaho statute stipulates that if a pupil raises a question calling for comment or explanation, the teacher must, without comment, refer the inquirer to his parents or guardians for reply.[3] Alabama, Delaware, Florida, Maine, and Pennsylvania have no provision for excusing pupils during the Bible reading period. Georgia, Idaho, New Jersey, and Tennessee have made statutory provision for excusing pupils during reading at the request of parents or guardians. In Kentucky and Massachusetts pupils who have conscientious scruples against reading may, upon the request of parent or guardian, be excused from taking any personal part in the reading.[4] In Maine pupils must give respectful attention but may be free in their own forms of worship.[5]

The penalties for failure to comply with these statutes consist of making the teacher who fails to comply subject to revocation of his certificate and thus to dismissal, or in other cases makes the school

[2] Alabama Laws, 1919, Act 459, Section 1; Delaware Laws, 1923, Chapter 182, Section 2; Purdon's Pennsylvania Statutes, 1931, Title 24, Section 1555; Georgia Political Code, 1926, Section 1551; Revised Statutes of the State of Maine, 1930, Chapter 19, Section 125; Code of Tennessee, 1932, Section 2343 (Law of 1925).
[3] Compiled Statutes of Idaho, Section 3 (Laws of 1925, Chapter 35).
[4] The statutes of Kentucky and Massachusetts do not make provision for excusing the children during such reading but simply excuse them from taking part in the reading.
[5] Revised Statutes of the State of Maine, 1930, Chapter 19, Section 125.

ineligible to draw on the public school funds because of the teacher's failure to comply with the law.

In all cases where the constitutionality of statutes requiring Bible reading in the public schools have been challenged, the highest court in the states concerned have upheld them.

Indiana, Iowa, Kansas, Mississippi, North Dakota, Oklahoma, and South Dakota have statutes specifically permitting the reading of the Bible in the public schools. These statutes are practically identical, the common wording being that any prohibitions set up in the law shall not be construed to "deny the reading of the Holy Scriptures in the public schools." In all these states the reading of the Bible is optional either with the teachers or with the school board. Two of them, Iowa and North Dakota, have statutory provisions excusing pupils during such reading upon the request of parents or guardians.

North Dakota requires that any school supported by public taxes shall display a placard containing the "Ten Commandments of the Christian religion in a conspicuous place" in every classroom.[6] The department of public instruction has the authority to have such placards printed and may charge for their printing and distribution among the schools of the state.

Mississippi has a statute requiring "a suitable course of instruction in the principles of morality and good manners, prepared by the state board of education," which must be used in all the public schools of the state. The course must "include what is known as the Mosaic Ten Commandments and may be so graded with the idea that a certain amount of time will be devoted to it in each grade." [7] The statute stipulates further that no pupil may be required to take the course if his parent or guardian requests the superintendent or teacher in writing that the child be excused.

Whereas a number of states do not permit the reading of the Bible in the public schools, no state has any constitutional provision or statutory law that specifically prohibits it in the terms "Bible" or "Bible reading." The question is whether it is permitted by state constitution and the statutory stipulations that no money raised for the support of public schools shall be appropriated for the support of any "sectarian" or "denominational" doctrine, that education may not be "sectarian" in character, that no "religious test shall be required," that no one shall be "compelled to attend any religious worship," that the "rights of conscience" shall be respected, that there

[6] Laws of North Dakota, 1927, Chapter 247, Section I.
[7] Mississippi Code, 1930, Section 6646.

shall be no restrictions of the "free exercise and enjoyment of religious profession," and that "no discrimination shall be made against any church, sect, or creed of religion." That the question is debatable is evident from the number of cases that have been carried to the courts in an effort to interpret these provisions and from the fact that the courts have by no means been in agreement in their decisions.

The first case that appears to have found its way into an American court in connection with this question is Donahoe v. Richards,[8] which was tried in Maine in 1854. It was followed by a similar case in Massachusetts in 1866.[9]

Other cases were brought before the supreme courts of Ohio in 1872, of Iowa in 1884, of Wisconsin in 1890, and of Michigan in 1898.[10] With the turn of the century, the number of cases that have been appealed to the high courts have greatly increased.[11]

The power to regulate education does not appear among the list of powers delegated to the federal government by the Constitution of the United States. The Constitution provides only that "no religious test shall ever be required as a qualification to any office or public trust under the United States"[12] and that "Congress shall make no law respecting an establishment of religion, or prohibiting the free exercise thereof . . ."[13] The First Amendment, which places this latter restriction upon religious legislation, could not be

[8] 38 Me. 376.
[9] Spiller v. Inhabitants of Woburn, 94 Mass. 127 (1866).
[10] Board of Education of Cincinnati v. Minor et al., 23 Ohio St. 211; Moore v. Monroe, 64 Ia. 367; Weiss v. District Board, 76 Wis. 177, 44 N.W. 967; Pfeiffer v. Board of Education of Detroit, 118 Mich. 560.
[11] The following are among the most important of these cases that have been appealed to the highest courts in our states since the turn of the century: State v. Scheve, 65 Nebr. 853, 91 N.W. 846 (1902); Billard v. Board of Education, 69 Kans. 53 (1904); Hackett v. Brooksville Graded School District, 120 Ky. 608, 87 S.W. 792 (1905); Dorner v. School District No. 5, 137 Wis. 147, 118 N.W. 353 (1908); People v. Board of Education, 245 Ill. 334 (1910); Herold v. Parish Board of School Directors, 136 La. 1034, 68 So. 116 (1915); Knowlton v. Baumhover, 182 Ia. 691 (1918); State ex rel. Dearle v. Frazier, 102 Wash. 369 (1918); Wilkerson v. City of Rome, 20 A.L.R. 1535, 152 Ga. 763 (1921); Evans v. Selma Union High School District of Fresno County, 222 Pac. 801, 31 A.L.R. 1121 (1924); People v. Stanley, 81 Colo. 276, 255 Pac. 610 (1927); Kaplan v. Independent School District of Virginia, 214 N.W. 18 (1927); State ex rel. Finger v. Weedman et al., School District Board, 226 N.W. 348 (1929); Clithero v. Showalter, 159 Wash. 519, 293 Pac. 1000 (1930); People ex rel. Ring et al. v. Board of Education of Dist. 24, 245 Ill. 334, 92 N.E. 251 (1910); Lewis v. Board of Education of the City of New York, 157 Misc. 520, 285 N.Y.S. 164 (1935). Modified in other respects in 247 App. Div. 106, 286 N.Y.S. 174 (1936), rehearing denied in 247 App. Div. 873, 288 N.Y.S. 751 (1936), appeal dismissed in 276 N.Y. 490, 12 N.E. (2d) 172 (1937).
[12] Article 6, Clause 3.
[13] First Amendment.

invoked to protect the citizens of the respective states.[14] The protection of the religious liberty of citizens was, therefore, before the adoption of the Fourteenth Amendment, left largely to the states.[15] As Justice Story said,

it was under a solemn consciousness of the dangers from ecclesiastical ambition, the bigotry of spiritual pride, and the intolerance of sects, thus exemplified in our domestic as well as in foreign annals, that it was deemed advisable to exclude from the national government all power to act upon the subject.[16]

Whereas the First Amendment forbids the federal government to establish religion or prohibit the free exercise thereof, the Fourteenth Amendment places within its province the power to protect the liberties of the individual against state encroachment. It reads in part, "No state shall . . . deprive any person of life, liberty, or property, without due process of law." [17] There has been considerable dispute as to whether these words confer upon the federal government jurisdiction with respect to religious liberty. The decisions rendered in earlier cases would seem to be contrary to such an interpretation. In 1898, however, the Supreme Court of the United States, in defining the word "liberty" as used in the Fourteenth Amendment, said in the case of Allgeyer v. Louisiana:

The liberty mentioned in that amendment means not only the right of the citizen to be free from the mere physical restraint of his person, as by incarceration, but the term is deemed to embrace the right of the citizen to be free in the enjoyment of all his faculties; to be free to use them in all lawful ways; to live and work where he will; to earn his livelihood by any lawful calling; to pursue any livelihood or avocation, and for that purpose to enter into all contracts which may be proper, necessary and essential to his carrying out to a successful conclusion the purposes above mentioned.[18]

Again, in 1923, in the case of Meyer v. Nebraska the Supreme Court held that a state law forbidding the teaching in any private school of any modern language other than English to any child who

[14] Permoli v. Orleans, 3 Howard, U.S. 589 (1845).
[15] The right to worship according to the dictates of conscience was placed in the state constitutions beyond the power of legislatures to restrain. Thomas M. Cooley, *Constitutional Limitations* (8th ed., Boston, 1927), p. 960; Joseph Bondy, *How Religious Liberty Was Written into the American Constitution* (Syracuse, New York, 1927).
[16] Joseph Story, *Commentaries on the Constitution* (5th ed., 2 vols., Boston, 1891), Section 1879.
[17] Article 14, Section 1.
[18] 165 U.S. Rep. 578 (1898).

has not passed the eighth grade invades the liberty guaranteed by the Fourteenth Amendment and exceeds the power of the states:

The problem for our determination is whether the statute . . . infringes the liberty guaranteed to the plaintiff . . . by the fourteenth amendment. "No state . . . shall deprive any person of life, liberty, or property, without due process of law."

While this court has not attempted to define with exactness the liberties thus guaranteed, the term has received much consideration and some of the included things have been definitely stated. Without doubt, it denotes not merely freedom from bodily restraint but also the right of the individual to contract, to engage in any of the common occupations of life, to acquire useful knowledge, to marry, establish a home and bring up children, to worship God according to the dictates of his own conscience, and generally to enjoy those privileges long recognized at common law as essential to the orderly pursuit of happiness by free men.[19]

In Pierce et al. v. Society of Sisters the Supreme Court of the United States held that the act of 1922 requiring parents to send their children between the ages of eight and sixteen years to the public school "unreasonably interferes with the liberty of parents and guardians to direct the upbringing and education of children under their control."[20]

On October 19, 1931, there was appealed to the Supreme Court the case of George I. Clithero et al. v. N. D. Showalter as State Superintendent et al., from the supreme court of the state of Washington, where an attempt was made to force the state board of education to require the teaching and the reading of the Bible in the public schools of that state.

The constitution of Washington provides:

No public money or property shall be appropriated for or applied to any religious worship, exercise, or instruction, or the support of any religious establishment.

All schools maintained or supported wholly or in part by the public funds shall be forever free from sectarian control or influence.[21]

The supreme court of Washington construed the above provisions to forbid religious worship, exercise, or instruction in the public school system and denied the petition of the appellants for a writ of mandamus to compel the state board of education to arrange the

---

[19] 262 U.S. 390 (1923).
[20] 268 U.S. 510 (1925).
[21] Article 1, Section 11; Article 9, Section 4.

curriculum of the public schools to provide for Bible reading and instruction.

The petition, which was filed with the board on September 9, 1930, by George I. Clithero and thirty-six others who are described in the record as "parents and school-age children of the state of Washington," demanded that the superintendent and the state board of education require the teaching and reading of the Bible in the public school system of that state. By this "teaching and reading of the Bible" was meant that the Bible must be read at least once on every school day in every common school, high school, and other schools of the public school system, that instruction must be "given in the Holy Scriptures . . . on at least two school days each school week" [22] in all the schools, and that the said reading and teaching of the Bible was to be compulsory.

On September 26, 1930, the state board of education passed a motion that the petition be returned to Mr. Clithero on the grounds that it raised a constitutional question on which the board had no jurisdiction or authority. Thereupon the petitioners asked the supreme court of Washington to issue a writ of mandamus requiring the board to change its action and to receive and grant the petition. The supreme court ruled that the questions presented by Mr. Clithero were answered in the case of State ex rel. Dearle v. Frazier,[23] where a full discussion of the question was entered into and in which the state constitution of Washington was held to forbid everything that Mr. Clithero demanded.

In the petition for appeal to the United States Supreme Court, Mr. Clithero contended that "a denial of the things demanded would be a denial to petitioners of their rights and privileges guaranteed under the laws and constitution of the United States." [24]

Appellees pointed out that no federal question was involved.[25] The state supreme court had denied the appellants the order sought to require appellees as members of the board of education of the state of Washington to make Bible reading and religious instruction compulsory in the public schools of the state, on the grounds that the court cannot by mandamus control the discretion of an administrative board of officers in whom has been vested discretionary

[22] From Transcript of Record, Supreme Court of the United States, State of Washington ex rel. George I. Clithero et al. v. N. D. Showalter, etc., et al., No. 80; 159 Wash. 519; 293 Pac. 1000 (1930).

[23] 102 Wash. 369 (1918).

[24] George I. Clithero et al. v. N. D. Showalter as State Superintendent et al., No. 80, 284 U.S. 573.

[25] Appellees' Statement against Jurisdiction, Clithero v. Showalter, *ibid.*

power, and on the grcunds that Article 1, Section 11, of the state constitution forbids religious worship, exercise, or instruction in the public school system. It would thus be impossible, they held, for the board to make Bible reading and instruction a part of the public school curriculum even should they so choose.

The Supreme Court of the United States dismissed the case for lack of a substantial federal question.

This case is unique in that it was not only appealed to the Supreme Court of the United States but was the first time an attempt had been made to compel the reading of the Bible. As we shall see, in other cases litigation has been carried on in an effort to prevent Bible reading on the grounds that it constituted an infringement of religious liberty.

CHAPTER IV

Litigation Resulting from Bible Reading in the Public Schools

I N GENERAL litigation over the subject of Bible reading in the public schools seems to fall pretty well into three categories: (1) Bible reading in the schools required by statute or administrative order; (2) Bible reading specifically permitted by statute, or by court decisions in the absence of statutes, or by administrative discretion; (3) Bible reading prohibited by statute or constitutional provisions as interpreted by state courts.

BIBLE READING REQUIRED BY STATUTE OR ADMINISTRATIVE ORDER

The following cases have arisen in states that have statutory provisions requiring the daily reading of the Bible in the public schools.

Maine. One Donahoe brought suit against the superintendent of the school committee of Ellsworth for expelling his daughter from school for her refusal to read a Protestant version of the Bible as ordered by her teacher, such reading being a part of the general course of instruction.[1]

The court held that the regulation adopting the King James version of the Bible as a textbook was constitutional and did not infringe upon the right of conscience or the right of freedom of worship and that it was binding on all the members of the school even though they were of different religious faiths. In this case the constitutionality of Bible reading hinged upon the claim that it was being used as a textbook for reading. The court upheld the legislation placing the power of book selection in the hands of a committee, saying:

The power of selection is general and unlimited. It is vested in the committee of each town. It was neither expected nor intended that there

[1] Donahoe v. Richards, 38 Me. 376 (1854).

should be entire uniformity in the course of instruction or in the books to be used in the several towns in the state.

The court pointed out that a committee might for the time being prefer one version of the Bible to another; that any version might be used in the schools or excluded; that one committee might direct the use of one version, and another of a different version, according to their "respective views of expediency"; and that the adoption of any particular version by the committee did not place a sanction of "purity" of text or accuracy of translation upon that version.

Massachusetts. The school committee of Woburn required that the schools be opened each morning with reading from the Bible and prayer, and that during the prayer the students should bow their heads. The plaintiff in a supreme court case, a student named Ella R. Spiller, objected to the latter portion of this order.[2] The committee thereupon modified the order by directing that any pupil might be excused from bowing the head upon request from his parents. Her father declined to make such a request, whereupon his daughter was dismissed from school.

The court held that the committee of the town might lawfully pass an order requiring schools to be opened each morning by Bible reading and prayer, and that during prayer each pupil should bow his head unless his parents requested that he be excused. The court said, however, that it would not be within the power of a school committee to pass an order or regulation requiring pupils to conform to any religious rite or observance or to participate in any religious forms or ceremonies that were contrary to their religious beliefs or conscientious scruples. To do so would violate the spirit of the religious liberty clause of the constitution of Massachusetts, which states that "no subject shall be hurt, molested, or restrained, in his person, liberty, or estate, for worshipping God in the manner and season most agreeable to the dictates of his own conscience, or for his religious profession or sentiments . . ."[3]

The girl had persisted in her refusal to bow her head during prayer, and it was under these circumstances that she was dismissed until she should comply or her parents should make request that she be excused from participation. The position was taken that the act prescribed was not necessarily one of devotional or religious ceremony, and that it went no farther than to require the observance of

---

[2] Spiller v. Inhabitants of Woburn, 94 Mass. 127 (1866).
[3] Constitution of Massachusetts, Part 1, Article 2.

quiet and decorum during the religious exercises at the opening of school. It did not compel a pupil to join in prayer but only to assume an attitude calculated to prevent interruption and general disturbance, and the child might be excused from even this limited participation upon the request of the parent. Under these circumstances the court felt that the exclusion of the child from school was justifiable and furnished no ground for action.

Kentucky. Thomas Hackett, a Roman Catholic school patron, complained of the religious services required of children during school hours. These services consisted of prayers, denominational hymn singing, and reading from the King James Bible.[4] It was contended that these exercises constituted an appropriation of public funds in aid of sectarian schools and in violation of the following provisions in the constitution and the statute:

nor shall any person be compelled to attend any place of worship, to contribute to the erection or maintenance of any such place . . . nor shall any man be compelled to send his child to any school to which he may be conscientiously opposed . . . No human authority shall . . . interfere with the right of conscience.

No portion of any fund or tax now existing or that may hereafter be raised or levied for educational purposes, shall be appropriated to, or used by, or in aid of, any church, sectarian or denominational school.[5]

It was further contended that the exercises violated the statutory provision that "No books or other publications of a sectarian . . . character shall be used or distributed in any common school; nor shall any sectarian . . . doctrine be taught therein." [6]

The reading of the Bible by the teacher was without comment, in compliance with the state statute, and no child was required to read the Bible against the wish of his parent or guardian. The prayer offered by the teacher which, it was urged, made the school sectarian was reported as follows:

Our Father, who art in Heaven, we ask Thy aid in our day's work. Be with us in all we do and say. Give us wisdom and strength and patience to teach these children as they should be taught. May teacher and pupil have mutual love and respect. Watch over these children both in the schoolroom and on the playground. Keep them from being hurt in any way, and at last when we come to die may none of our number be

[4] Hackett v. Brooksville Graded School District, 120 Ky. 608, 87 S.W. 792 (1905).

[5] Constitution of Kentucky, Bill of Rights, Sections 5, 189.

[6] Kentucky Statutes, 1930, Section 4368.

missing around Thy Throne. These things we ask for Christ's sake. Amen.

Although the court conceded that any prayer is worship and that public prayer is public worship, it held that the prayer offered and the reading of the Bible were not sectarian within the meaning of the constitution or the statutes, that the appellant's children were not compelled to attend the place where the worshiping was done during prayer, that the school was not "a place of worship" nor its teachers "ministers of religion" within the meaning of the constitution as quoted above, and that the Bible is not a sectarian book when read without comment.[7] According to the Kentucky court, a book is not sectarian unless it teaches the peculiar dogmas of a sect as such; it cannot be regarded as sectarian simply because it is so comprehensive as to include the partial interpretation of the adherents of certain sects, because it is edited or compiled by persons of a particular sect, or because it has been adopted by certain denominations as authentic, or even because it has been accepted by them as being inspired. "It is not the authorship nor mechanical composition of the book, nor the use of it, but its contents that give it its character," said the court.

Georgia. The city commission of the city of Rome, Georgia, passed an ordinance requiring some portion of either the Old or the New Testament of the King James version to be read without comment, and prayer to be offered in the presence of the students during the regular school session. Readings and prayers were to be conducted daily by the principal or by some other person appointed by him to take charge of such services. Pupils might be excused, on the ground of conscientious objections, from hearing the Bible read or from prayer upon the written request of parent or guardian to the superintendent of schools. A mandamus was sought to require the board of education of Rome to enforce this ordinance.[8] The question of the constitutionality of the city ordinance was raised.

The issue here was whether or not Bible reading and prayer in the public schools is a violation of the rights of conscience within the meaning of the constitutional provision, "All men have the natural and inalienable right to worship God, each according to the dictates of his own conscience, and no human authority should in any case control or interfere with such right of conscience." Does it constitute

[7] Constitution of Kentucky, Bill of Rights, Section 5.
[8] Wilkerson v. City of Rome, 152 Ga. 763, 20 A.L.R. 1535 (1921).

sectarian use of public funds in violation of the constitutional provision, "No money shall ever be taken from the public treasury, directly or indirectly, in aid of any church, sect, or denomination of religionists, or of any sectarian institution"? [9]

The court held that the ordinance requiring Bible reading and prayer is not in conflict with the constitution of Georgia, nor does this practice constitute the sectarian use of public funds. To the contention that the enforcement of the ordinance would be to give the school children instruction in the teachings of the Bible that was contrary to the beliefs of Roman Catholics and Jews, the court said:

> It would require a strained and unreasonable construction to find anything in the ordinance which interferes with the natural and inalienable right to worship God according to the dictates of one's own conscience. The mere listening to the reading of an extract from the Bible and a brief prayer at the opening of school exercises would seem far remote from such interference.

It was further argued that "an insignificant fraction of their [the principals'] time would be consumed in the reading." The court declared that in Georgia, as in other colonies, church and state were not completely separated, nor was it intended by the founders that they should be.

Mr. Justice Hines dissented from the majority opinion in this case. "Being committed," he said, "with my whole soul to the doctrine of religious freedom, including freedom from molestation in matters of conscience, I feel in duty bound to give vent to my inability to agree to the conclusion reached by my able associates." He contended that the ordinance violates the right secured by the above-quoted constitutional provisions; that the constitution pledges the government to defend the "natural and inalienable right of the individual to worship God according to the dictates of his own conscience"; and "that no human authority, not even the board of commissioners of the City of Rome, shall in any case control or interfere with such right of conscience." He pointed out that the ordinance in question establishes a system of worship for the schools of Rome and in so doing controls or interferes with the individual worship of God, that religious freedom includes the right not to worship at all, and that even the exemption of certain classes does not make the ordinance constitutional. The reading of the King James version offends Catholics and Jews, the reading of certain texts is out of har-

[9] Constitution of Georgia, Article 1, Paragraphs 12, 14.

mony with the beliefs of some sects of Protestants, and the system of worship provided offends deists, atheists, and agnostics. "We cannot disguise the fact," said Justice Hines, "that making the reading of the King James version of the Bible a part of the worship of the public schools puts municipal approval upon that version, and thus discriminates in favor of and aids the Protestant sects of the Christian religion."

District of Columbia. In the District of Columbia reading of the Bible is required by the following administrative order issued by the board of education for the district:

Each Teacher shall, as a part of the opening exercises, read, without note or comment, a portion of the Bible, repeat the Lord's Prayer, and conduct appropriate singing by the pupils.[10]

The ruling contains no provision for exusing pupils during the reading of the Bible, singing, or prayer, but it does provide that the Bible must be read without comment. The board of education authorizes the excusing of pupils to observe church holy days.[11]

BIBLE READING SPECIFICALLY PERMITTED BY STATUTE, OR BY COURT
DECISIONS IN THE ABSENCE OF STATUTE, OR BY ADMINISTRATIVE DISCRETION

Kansas. In the case brought before the supreme court of Kansas [12] a public school teacher, for the stated purpose of quieting the pupils and preparing them for their regular studies, repeated the Lord's Prayer and the Twenty-third Psalm without comment or remark as a morning exercise.[13] Pupils were not required to participate. A pupil was expelled, however, for refusing to refrain from regular work, because it was believed to be legal and proper to preserve order during the exercises. The constitution of Kansas requires that

No religious sect or sects shall ever control any part of the common school or university funds of the state.[14]

No money shall ever be given by law to any religion . . . nor to any particular creed, mode of worship, or system of ecclesiastical policy nor shall any person by law be compelled to attend any place of worship, to contribute to the erection or maintenance of any such place . . . nor

[10] By-Laws and Laws of the District of Columbia Board of Education, 1926, Chapter 6, Section 4.
[11] *Ibid.*, Chapter 8, Section 14.
[12] Billard v. Board of Education of Topeka, 69 Kans. 53 (1904).
[13] Comments on the statement that the "repetition of the Lord's Prayer and the Twenty-third Psalm was intended merely to quiet the children" are found in an article on "The Bible in Public Schools," in *Law Notes,* September 1930, p. 119.
[14] Constitution of Kansas, Bill of Rights, Article 6, Section 8.

shall any man be compelled to send his child to a school to which he
may be conscientiously opposed. . . . No portion of any public fund shall
be appropriated to, or used by or in aid of any church, sectarian or denominational school.[15]

A statute provides that

No sectarian or religious doctrine shall be taught or inculcated in any
of the public schools . . . but nothing in this section shall be construed
to prohibit reading of the Holy Scriptures.[16]

The court held that the teacher was not conducting a form of
religious worship nor teaching sectarian or religious doctrine, and
that the exercises in question did not constitute a misuse of public
funds. It took the position that there was not the slightest effort on
the part of the teacher to inculcate any religious dogma. It held that
though the constitution and the statutes of Kansas prohibit all forms
of religious worship and the teaching of sectarian or religious doctrine in the public schools, there is nothing in either the constitution
or the laws that can be interpreted as intended to exclude the Bible
from the public schools. The constitution imposes upon the legislature the duty to "encourage the promotion of intellectual, moral,
scientific, and agricultural improvement by establishing a uniform
system of public schools." [17] The Bible, it was contended, contains
the "noblest ideals of moral character. . . . To emulate these is the
supreme conception of citizenship."

South Dakota. In a case tried in 1929 action was brought against
the school board of District 8 of Meade County, which had ordered
that the Bible be read or the Lord's Prayer repeated.[18] No sectarian
comment was to be made. Pursuant to this order, passages from the
King James version were read or the Lord's Prayer was repeated as
an opening exercise. Some twelve or fifteen Catholic children refused
to attend the opening exercises, whereupon they were expelled and
were not allowed to return without signing a written apology. South
Dakota has a statute permitting the reading of the Bible without
sectarian comment. No statutory provision is made, however, for
excusing children during such exercises. The constitution provides
that

[15] *Ibid.,* Section 5.
[16] Revised Statutes of Kansas, 1923, Chapter 72, Section 1722.
[17] *Ibid.,* Article 6, Section 20.
[18] State ex rel. Finger v. Weedman et al., School District Board, 226 N.W. 348 (supreme
court, S.D., June 27, 1929).

The right to worship God according to the dictates of conscience shall never be infringed. No person shall be denied any civil or political right, privilege or position on account of his religious opinions . . . No person shall be compelled to attend or support any ministry or place of worship against his consent nor shall any preference be given by law to any religious establishment or mode or worship. No money or property of the state shall be given or appropriated for the benefit of any sectarian or religious society or institution.[19]

Not only was the King James version being read, which offended the Catholic pupils and their parents, but the Catholic children were compelled to attend such reading under penalty of expulsion.

The supreme court of South Dakota ordered that a mandamus be issued to compel the school board to readmit the children without apology and thereafter to permit them to be absent during the reading of the King James version.

The court emphasized that the primary object was to insure personal freedom of conscience and to prevent the support of any religious organization or sect of the state by public taxes. The evidence disclosed that the reading of the Bible in this case was not for a secular purpose but for the purpose of "increasing, improving, and inculcating morality, patriotism, reverence, and the developing of religious and Christian character of the pupils."

The court declared that the Bible did not lend itself to use in secular instruction without comment and analysis; that no other book is read to the pupils of the public school under similar circumstances; that the legitimate function of our public schools is to impart secular knowledge to the pupils; and that comment in connection with such instruction is not only unrestricted but is necessary. The very limitation placed on comment in connection with the reading of the Bible "discloses the purpose of the order of the school board to enter the field of religious instruction, but not into sectarian controversy."

As soon as public education enters the field of religion, differences arise among the several sects as to the authenticity of the Scriptures. The various versions of the Bible are challenged, and one organization begins quarreling with another. Questions arise as to modes of worship and the construction to be placed on certain passages in the Bible. The primary object of the religious liberty provisions in our constitutions is to prevent the persecution that might arise from

[19] Constitution of South Dakota, Article 6, Section 3.

an arbitrary answer to such questions. In this South Dakota case, not only was the King James version read but Catholic children were compelled to attend such reading under penalty of expulsion. Thus the question was whether such reading, by forcing attention on the religious beliefs of these children, violated the pledge of liberty of conscience as stated in the constitutional provision that "the right to worship God according to the dictates of conscience shall never be infringed." [20]

The relief sought in this case was the reinstatement of the relator's son in school with liberty to absent himself during the reading of the Bible. The desired relief was granted, and that was all that was settled, though the whole tenor of the case is decidedly adverse to Bible reading in the public schools.

The court said:

It may be argued that the peace and safety of the state is enhanced by the teaching of our youth morality, reverence, and wholesome religious beliefs. Speaking for myself, I think it is; but it does not follow that a reading of the King James version of the Bible in our public schools is essential to such teaching. Respondents frankly concede that the reading of any version would accomplish the same purpose. The difficulty in reading any version in the public schools seems to be in agreeing upon the version to be read and the person to read it. But it is not necessary, for the teaching of religion to the youth, that it be taught in the public schools. We have many churches whose function it is to teach religion. The teaching of that particular subject in public schools seems to be so fraught with difficulties and dissensions that it is not practical to undertake it.

The King James version is a translation by scholars of the Anglican church bitterly opposed to the Catholics, apparent in the dedication of the translation, where the Pope is referred to as "that man of sin," and in which the translators express themselves as expecting to be "traduced by Popish persons" who will malign them, because such persons desire to keep the people in "ignorance and darkness." We are satisfied that neither the evidence nor reason will justify us in sustaining the trial court's finding that the differences in the two versions of the Bible for a religious purpose are not substantial. History of the conflicts between Catholics and Protestants over those very differences refute such conclusion. It makes no difference what our personal views may be as to the importance of the controversial words. As officers of the state, speaking for the state, neither we nor the teachers of the public schools can say that one side is right and the other wrong. We must leave that to the conscience of those involved.

[20] State ex rel. Finger v. Weedman.

The court pointed out that the reading of the Bible and the offering of prayer "is devotional, a form of religious instruction, and not a part of the secular work of the school." It contended that if one should read the Bible only for moral or patriotic instruction, comment would be necessary. But it is read as an act of devotion and worship. Otherwise such exercises would be useless. Further, it said:

In countries where the dominant sect can control religion through the power of the state, oppression results. This state has by its constitution said the power of the state shall not be so used. It is our duty to uphold that constitution. It is essential to religious liberty that one be free to worship according to the dictates of his own conscience, and not only that, but to live and teach his religion. That right cannot be taken away by the state, and it follows that such teaching must belong exclusively to the individual and voluntary organizations of such individuals. The state as an educator must keep out of this field, and especially is this true in the common schools, where the child is immature, without fixed religious convictions, and the parents' liberty of conscience is the controlling factor, and not that of the pupil.

Iowa. The question of the constitutionality of the Iowa statute was raised in the case of Moore v. Monroe.[21] The teachers of the school concerned were accustomed to occupy a few minutes each morning in reading selections from the Bible, in repeating the Lord's Prayer, and in singing religious songs. Complaint was brought by a taxpayer who had two children in school. Although his children had not been required to be present during the religious exercises, he nevertheless objected to such exercises on the ground that the statute was unconstitutional — a violation of the religious liberty clause of the constitution of Iowa, which reads:

The General Assembly shall make no law respecting an establishment of religion, or prohibiting the free exercise thereof; nor shall any person be compelled to attend any place of worship, pay tithes, taxes, or other rates for building or repairing places of worship, or the maintenance of any minister.[22]

The reading of the Bible was carried on by sanction of the Iowa statute which reads:

The Bible shall not be excluded from any public school or institution in the state, nor shall any child be required to read it contrary to the wishes of his parent or guardian.[23]

[21] Moore v. Monroe, 64 Ia. 367, 20 N.W. 475 (1884).
[22] Constitution of Iowa, Article 1, Section 3.
[23] Code of Iowa, 1931, Section 4258.

The court held that this statute was not in violation of the constitution but that it is optional with the individual school teachers as to whether or not they will use the Bible in the schools, and that such option is restricted only by the provision that no child shall be required to read the Bible contrary to the wishes of his parents or guardians. The court deemed that the object of the constitutional provision stipulating that no person should be compelled to attend a place of worship or to contribute to its maintenance or the maintenance of any minister was not to prevent the casual use of a public building as a place for offering prayer or doing other acts of religious worship, but rather to prevent the enactment of a law whereby any person may be compelled to pay taxes for any building used distinctively as a place of worship.

As viewed by the court, the religious objection on the part of the plaintiff did not pertain to the matter of taxation. Rather the objection was to the practice of making religious exercises a part of the educational system, into which the plaintiff's children must either be drawn or be made conspicuous and inconvenienced by being excused. To this the court answered, "But, so long as the plaintiff's children are not required to be in attendance at the exercises, we cannot regard the objection as one of great weight."

In the cases considered above it will be noted that the statutes in the states involved — Kansas, South Dakota, and Iowa — made Bible reading permissible. The statutes of Kansas and South Dakota specify that if the Bible is read in the public schools such reading must be without comment. Though the statute of Iowa does not contain this provision it does provide that no child shall be "required to read it [the Bible] contrary to the wish of his parent or guardian," which provision is found in neither the Kansas nor the South Dakota statute.

In all three states the religious exercises objected to consisted of Bible reading, religious songs, and prayer. No sectarian comments had been made in connection with the Bible reading, nor were there any charges to that effect. In all these cases it was charged that the schools were made places of worship and in two of the states that public funds had been appropriated contrary to the constitutional and statutory provisions of the respective states. The opinions of the courts agreed in declaring that the exercises complained of did not make the schools places of worship within the meaning of the constitutions, nor did they constitute the appropriation of public funds for sectarian purposes.

In the case before the South Dakota court, however, while the Bible reading took place without sectarian comment, pupils had been required to attend the exercises. Because of failure to attend, the pupils in question had been expelled, and a mandamus was sought to compel the school board to readmit them without apology and thereafter to permit them to absent themselves during the reading of the King James Bible. The court granted the relief sought by plaintiffs. However, the decision was in general adverse to Bible reading in the public schools. The court took the position that the practice complained of constituted religious worship, was necessarily devotional, was sectarian, and hence was contrary to the principles of the constitution.

In a number of states where there are no constitutional or statutory provisions specifically prohibiting or permitting Bible reading, cases have been carried to the state supreme courts for opinions on the subject. Some of the courts have upheld Bible reading. In the majority of the cases the courts have left it to the discretion of the state or local school authorities, although in some cases they have prohibited such reading.

Texas. The question of Bible reading came up in Texas in 1908, in the case of Church v. Bullock.[24] An action was brought by Church, an unbeliever, two Catholics, and two Jews against Bullock and other members of the board of school directors of Corsicana to abolish in the public schools the practice of holding morning exercises consisting of Bible reading, repeating the Lord's Prayer, and singing religious songs. The reading of the Bible was without comment, and the King James version was used. Students were requested to take part. They were asked to stand and bow their heads when the Lord's Prayer was offered, although they were not required to participate in prayer. The exercises were conducted in pursuance of a resolution adopted by the board of school directors of that district. The resolution did not require but stated that they did "view with favor" such opening exercises. The pupils were required to be present during the exercises and to behave in an orderly manner.

The constitution of Texas contains the following provisions:

All men have a natural and indefeasible right to worship Almighty God according to the dictates of their own consciences. No man shall be compelled to attend, erect, or support any place of worship or to main-

[24] 109 S.W. 115.

tain any ministry against his consent. No human authority ought . . . to control or interfere with the rights of conscience in matters of religion, and no preference shall ever be given by law to any religious society or mode of worship.[25]

No money shall be appropriated or drawn from the treasury for the benefit of any sect . . . nor shall property belonging to the state be appropriated for any such purposes.[26]

And no law shall ever be enacted appropriating any part of the permanent or available school fund to any other purpose whatever; nor shall the same, or any part thereof, ever be appropriated to or used for the support of any sectarian school . . .[27]

In addition to these constitutional provisions a Texas statute provides that "no part of the public school fund shall be appropriated to or used for the support of any sectarian school."[28]

The court by unanimous decision held that the practices here complained of did not convert the school into a sectarian or religious society within the meaning of the constitution, that it was not a violation of the religious liberty clause, and that it did not constitute an appropriation of public funds for sectarian or religious purposes. The word *sect*, according to the court's definition, is "a body of persons distinguished by particularities of faith and practice from other bodies and adhering to the same general system," and "a religious society is a voluntary association of individuals or families united for the purpose of having a common place of worship and to provide a proper teacher to instruct them in religious doctrines and duties, and to administer the various ordinances of religion." The school as conducted did not come within the court's definition of either a sect or a religious society, nor did the practice in question make the school "a place of worship" within the meaning of the constitution, for such was declared to be a place where persons meet together for the purpose of worshiping God.

It was admitted that "the right to instruct the young in the morality of the Bible might be carried to such an extent in the public schools as would make it obnoxious to the constitutional inhibition, not because God is worshiped, but because by the character of the services the place would be made 'a place of worship.'"

Colorado. In 1927 a mandamus action was sought by the people

[25] Constitution of Texas, Article 1, Section 6.
[26] *Ibid.*, Section 7.
[27] *Ibid.*, Article 7, Section 5.
[28] Texas Civil Statutes, 1928, Article 2899.

in relation to Charles L. Vollmar against George K. Stanley, president of the board of education, District 118, Weld County.[29] The plaintiffs were Catholic school patrons. The board required the teacher, as a part of the morning exercises in each classroom, to read portions of the King James version without comment. The pupils were not permitted to leave the room during the reading. The court held that the reading of the Bible without comment in the public schools was not a violation of the part of the Fourteenth Amendment which states "nor shall any state deprive any person of life, liberty, or property, without due process of law . . ."[30] nor was it considered a violation of the following provisions of the Colorado constitution:

That the free exercise and enjoyment of religious profession and worship, without discrimination, shall forever hereafter be guaranteed. . . . No person shall be required to attend or support any ministry or place of worship. . . . Nor shall any preference be given by law to any religious denomination or mode of worship.[31]

Neither the general assembly, nor any county . . . shall ever make any appropriation, or pay from any public fund or moneys whatever, anything in aid of any church, or sectarian society or for any sectarian purpose, or to help support or sustain any school . . . any church, or for any sectarian purpose.

No religious test or qualification shall ever be required of any person as a condition of admission into any public educational institution of the state, either as teacher or student; and no teacher or student of any such institution shall ever be required to attend or participate in any religious service whatever. No sectarian tenets or doctrine shall ever be taught in the public schools . . .[32]

The court did hold, however, that attendance of children during the opening exercises must be optional. It reasoned that inasmuch as children have the right to attend either public or private schools, they may be compelled to take the courses that are essential to good citizenship. While it admitted that there is undoubtedly much in the Bible that is essential to good citizenship, it felt that those essentials might be taught from other books than the Bible. Therefore the Bible as such is not so essential to good citizenship that the parents

[29] People v. Stanley, 81 Colo. 276, 255 Pac. 610. The supreme court of Colorado decided the case March 28, 1927. A rehearing was denied May 9, 1927.

[30] Section 1, Paragraph 1.

[31] Article 2, Section 4.

[32] Article 9, Sections 7, 8.

may not exclude it from the instruction of their children; consequently "children cannot be required, against the will of their parents or guardians, to attend its reading." The court concluded that the Bible may be read without comment in the public schools and that children, upon the request of their parents, may be excused from such reading, but whenever comment on the Bible or the reading of a given part of the Bible is claimed to constitute sectarian teaching, the courts will take that phase of the question into consideration.

It should be noted that in these two cases in Texas and Colorado, the constitutional and statutory provisions were very similar. In the Texas school the board of trustees had passed a resolution that they "view with favor" these opening exercises. In the Colorado school the board required such reading in connection with the morning exercises. In both schools the reading was from the King James version, without comment. In the process of reasoning the Texas court arrived at the conclusion that the pupils need not be excused. In other words, they were required to be present and to bow their heads while prayer was offered, though they did not have to participate in the prayer; and in the Colorado case the court decided that the exercises were not contrary to the constitution, but that pupils must be excused during such exercises at the request of parents or guardians.

Michigan. In Michigan certain school patrons sought an order to compel the board of education of Detroit to discontinue the use in the public schools of a book entitled *Readings from the Bible.*[33] This volume was made up almost entirely of extracts from the Bible emphasizing the moral precepts of the Ten Commandments. No comments were made by the teacher upon the matter contained, and she was required to excuse from that part of the session during which it was used any pupil whose parent or guardian should so request. While the court, in a divided opinion, held that no constitutional right of the complainant had been violated, it left the question of Bible reading to the discretion of the state board of education. The case did not involve directly the reading of the Bible or any particular version of the Bible, but rather the reading of a book made up of extracts from the Bible.

The contention by the court that a school board might teach the Christian religion was assailed in the dissenting opinion:

[33] Pfeiffer v. Board of Education of Detroit, 118 Mich. 560 (1898).

If their position is sound, not only should the Bible be taught, but all other forms of Christian religious instruction should be given in the schools. If this reasoning is sound, the constitution left it open to the school authorities to determine what variety of Christian religion they should teach, and the school board of the city of Detroit has the power today to have taught in the public schools of the city of Detroit the theological tenets of any Christian church.

Our constitutional provisions respecting religious liberty mean precisely what they declare.

The Michigan constitution provides:

Every person shall be at liberty to worship God according to the dictates of his own conscience. No person shall be compelled to attend, or, against his consent, to contribute to the erection or support of any place of religious worship, or to pay tithes, taxes, or other rates for the support of any minister of the gospel or teacher of religion. The civil and political rights, privileges and capacities of no individual shall be diminished or enlarged on account of his religious belief.[34]

Authority whereby the legislature may compel "a person to pay taxes for the support of a teacher of religion, or diminishing or enlarging the civil rights of any person on account of his religious belief" is forbidden, said the dissent.

The opinion rendered by the Michigan attorney general is adverse to Bible reading. The question of Bible reading is, however, left optional with the local school board or teacher.

Minnesota. The case of Kaplan v. Independent School District of Virginia involved the school board of Virginia, Minnesota, which had been requested by the ministerial association of the city to place a Bible in every schoolroom and to direct the superintendent to make suitable selections to be read daily without comment by the teacher in each room at the opening of school.[35] The school board had concurred in the request and had placed the King James version in every schoolroom. The superintendent made suitable selections from the Old Testament only. If parent or pupil objected, the pupil might retire from the room during such reading. Action was brought to prohibit the reading of these selections on the grounds that they violated the following constitutional provisions:

The right of every man to worship God according to the dictates of his own conscience shall never be infringed . . . nor shall any control of or interference with the rights of conscience be permitted, or any prefer-

[34] Constitution of Michigan, Article 2, Section 3.
[35] 214 N.W. 18 (1927).

ence be given by law to any religious establishment or mode of worship
. . . nor shall any money be drawn from the treasury for the benefit of
any religious societies . . .

But in no case shall . . . any public moneys or property be appropriated or used for the support of schools wherein the distinctive doctrines,
creed, or tenets of any particular Christian or other religious sect are
promulgated or taught.[36]

The court held by a divided decision that no constitutional provision is infringed by reading the Bible, that the purpose of the
school board in having the Bible read was to implant in the minds
of the pupils higher moral and ethical standards and a knowledge of
the Bible, and that it was not its purpose to teach any religious doctrine. It held that so long as pupils were not compelled to worship
according to the tenets of any creed or taught any sectarian belief or
even required to be present during such reading, there was no violation of the constitutional guarantee of religious liberty.

Mr. Justice Stone in a separate opinion upholding Bible reading
took the position "that there is no legal and particularly no constitutional objection to such compulsion if it should be attempted."
Thus he considered it "simply considerate and tactful, rather than
legally necessary, to permit certain children to absent themselves
during the Scripture reading. . . . It is the difficulty of using the
Bible without giving the instruction a sectarian bend that makes the
wisdom of its use in the public schools questionable."

Since the exercises were not contrary to the constitution, the court
left the question of whether or not the Bible should be read to the
discretion of the school authorities. The position it took is similar
to that taken by the courts of several states — that where the legislatures have vested the administration of public education in school
boards or commissions, the court will not interfere with such regulations unless it is clearly shown that abuses exist. The cases that
have come up in Michigan, Nebraska, and Ohio are examples of
such practice.[37]

Chief Justice Wilson dissented in a very able discussion of the
subject based on the broad general principle that the constitution
guarantees religious freedom in the proper meaning of that term.
He said:

[36] Article 1, Section 16; Article 8, Section 3.
[37] Pfeiffer v. Board of Education of Detroit, 118 Mich. 560 (1898); State v. Scheve, 65
Nebr. 853, 91 N.W. 846 (1902); Board of Education of Cincinnati v. Minor et al., 23 Ohio
St. 211 (1872).

I agree that the reading of the Bible in the schools does not require a taxpayer to "support any place of worship."

The constitution not only says that every man may "worship God according to the dictates of his own conscience" but it says "nor shall any control of or interference with the rights of conscience be permitted."

"Rights of conscience" means what? By conscience we mean that internal conviction or self-knowledge that tells us that a thing is right or wrong. It is the faculty or power within us which decides on the right or wrong of an act and approves or condemns. It is our moral sense which dictates to us right or wrong. Each person is governed by his own views. The "rights of conscience," in religious matters, means the privilege of resting in peace or contentment according to one's own judgment. It is a recognition of a right to religious complacency.

To require the Jewish children to read the New Testament which extols Christ as the Messiah is to tell them that their religious teachings at home are untrue.

The Catholic people do not believe it right to have a Bible read to their children in the absence of the light of construction placed thereon by their church. Are these people to be content to have a Bible read which substantially ignores the doctrine of purgatory, which is one of their vital beliefs? On the contrary, may a Catholic school board have the Catholic version of the Bible read disclosing the theory of purgatory as indicated in the Book of Maccabees and not interfere with the "rights of conscience" of Protestants?

No man must feel that his religion is tolerated. His constitutional "rights of conscience" should be indefeasible and beyond the control or interference of men. The constitution says so.

No decision pro or con has thoroughly considered the construction of the specific language, "nor shall any control of or interference with the rights of conscience be permitted." We have an opportunity here to construe this language. The majority opinion has ignored it. It should be construed in accordance with the best interests of the people. This permits but one conclusion.

Though the majority opinion upheld the reading of the Bible, explicitly stating that they did not wish to express an opinion as to the wisdom of the practice of reading extracts from the Bible, but would leave that to the local school board, there seemed to prevail a feeling that the practice is a needless cause of friction and dissension in the school district.

Ohio. The supreme court of Ohio upheld a resolution passed in 1872 by the board of education prohibiting religious instruction and the reading of religious books, including the Bible, in the public schools of Cincinnati.[38]

[38] Board of Education of Cincinnati v. Minor et al.

Certain taxpayers of the city of Cincinnati brought action against the board of education to enjoin them from carrying into effect two resolutions. One prohibited religious instruction and the reading of religious books, including the Bible, in the common schools of Cincinnati. The other repealed a former regulation requiring that the opening exercises in every department should start with reading of the Bible by or under the direction of the teacher and with appropriate singing by the pupils.

It had been the practice in the Cincinnati schools since 1829 to read, during the opening exercises, portions of the King James version without comment. No sectarian teaching or interference with the rights of conscience had at any time been permitted. The resolutions of the board of education now forbade the reading of the Bible and other books of a religious nature. The action was an effort to prevent the resolutions from being put into effect.

The defense admitted the importance of a knowledge of the Bible but denied that such instruction ought to be imparted in the schools established by the state. By unanimous decision the supreme court of Ohio said that it did not have the right to interfere in the management or control of the schools and that the board's right to pass and enforce the resolutions was sustained.[39]

In this case the court said that reading the Bible and singing constituted a "form of worship," that religious instruction and the reading of religious books, including the Bible, cannot be carried on in schools supported by the taxation of men of all religious opinions without violating the constitution of Ohio, and that "neither Christianity nor any other system of religion is a part of the law of this state." [40]

Justice Welch in speaking for the court said:

Legal Christianity is a solecism, a contradiction of terms. When Christianity asks the aid of government beyond mere impartial protection, it denies itself. Its laws are divine, and not human. Its essential interests lie beyond the reach and range of human governments. United with government, religion never rises above the merest superstition; united with religion, government never rises above the merest despotism; and all history shows us that the more widely and completely they are separated, the better it is for both.[41]

The court left the question of Bible reading to the discretion of the school officials. Twenty-three years later a decision of the court

[39] Ibid.
[40] Constitution of Ohio, Article 1, Section 7; Article 7, Section 2.
[41] Board of Education of Cincinnati v. Minor et al.

of common pleas sustained a rule of the school board requiring Bible reading.[42]

Arizona. The constitution and statutes of Arizona include these provisions:

No tax shall be laid or appropriation of public money made in aid of any church, or private or sectarian school . . .

No sectarian instruction shall be imparted in any school or state educational institution that may be established under this constitution, and no religious or political test or qualification shall ever be required as a condition of admission into any public educational institution of the state, as teacher, student, or pupil . . .[43]

Any teacher who shall use any sectarian or denominational books, or teach any sectarian doctrine, or conduct any religious exercises in his school, or who fails to comply with any provision of this chapter, shall be guilty of unprofessional conduct, and the proper authority shall revoke his certificate.[44]

It will be seen that the statute stipulates not only that the instruction must be nonsectarian and that no sectarian or denominational books may be used, but also that no religious exercises may be conducted. Although no case has come to the courts of Arizona requiring the interpretation of this provision, the wording seems to preclude the reading of the Bible in all the public schools of the state.

California. A California statute states: "No publication of a sectarian, partisan, or denominational character must be used or distributed in any school, or be made a part of any school library; nor must any sectarian or denominational doctrine be taught therein." [45] A further provision declares that any school board which knowingly allows a school to violate this provision forfeits all right to any state or county apportionment of school moneys.[46]

Though no case has been brought before the courts of California directly involving the subject of Bible reading, an effort was made to prevent the purchase of twelve Bibles in the King James version

---

[42] Nessle v. Hum, 1 Ohio N.P. 140 (1895).

[43] Constitution of Arizona, Article 9, Section 10; Article 11, Section 7.

[44] Revised Code of Arizona, 1928, Section 1044 (Struckmeyer).

[45] Constitution of California, Article 4, Section 30; Article 9, Section 8; School Code, Section 3.52 (Code of California, Section 1672).

[46] Statutes and Amendments to the Codes of California, 1931, Section 1672.

for the library of the Selma Union High School.[47] Objections were raised on the ground that the Bible was a sectarian book and that its purchase for the public school library was contrary to the California statute quoted above and to the following constitutional provisions:

The free exercise and enjoyment of religious profession and worship, without discrimination or preference, shall forever be guaranteed in this state . . .

Neither the legislature, nor any county . . . shall ever make an appropriation, or pay from any fund whatever . . . in aid of any religious sect, church, creed, or sectarian purpose . . .

No public money shall ever be appropriated for the support of any sectarian or denominational school . . . nor shall any sectarian or denominational doctrine be taught, or instruction thereon be permitted, directly or indirectly, in any of the common schools of this state.[48]

The court held that the King James version of the Bible is not a sectarian book, the purchase of which would violate these provisions. The mere purchase of such a book does not imply the adoption of the dogma it contains.

The court set up certain standards by which to determine whether or not a book is sectarian:[49] it is the character of the book that determines whether or not it is sectarian, not the authorship nor the approval or disapproval of a sect; to be sectarian a book must teach the peculiar doctrines of a sect as such, and the fact that it is comprehensive enough to include even a number of sects does not make it sectarian; the fact that the author of a religious book belongs to a particular church does not necessarily make his book sectarian, nor is the fact that the King James version of the Bible is commonly used by the Protestant churches and not by the Catholics a test of whether or not the book is sectarian.[50] In view of these standards California, while not permitting the reading of the Bible in the public schools, has declared that the Bible is not a sectarian book

[47] Evans v. Selma Union High School, District of Fresno County, 222 Pac. 801, 31 A.L.R. 1121. The decision was rendered on January 24, 1924, and a rehearing was denied on February 21, 1924. See also the California case, Gordon v. Board of Education of City of Los Angeles, discussed in Chapter V.

[48] Constitution of California, Article 1, Section 4; Article 4, Section 30; Article 9, Section 8.

[49] Evans v. Selma Union High School.

[50] In California a district school board required dancing as a part of the curriculum. Pupils were expelled for refusing to dance. It was held that such a requirement was a violation of the rights of liberty of conscience and religious freedom, that it did not matter whether the children or parents were members of some church or not, and that the children could not be expelled for refusing to dance. Hardwick v. Fruitridge School District, 205 Pac. 49 (1921).

within the meaning of her constitution and permits it to be in her school libraries.

Illinois. In the case of People ex rel. Ring v. Board of Education, certain taxpayers and members of the Roman Catholic church of School District 24 brought action against the board of directors for requiring their children to listen to the reading of the King James Bible.[51] Comments upon the reading were made by the teacher. Pupils were required to stand and assume a devotional attitude as well as to answer questions on Bible passages.

The court was asked to decide, first, whether or not such exercises constituted a violation of freedom of worship as guaranteed by the constitution of Illinois, which says:

> The free exercise and enjoyment of religious profession and worship, without discrimination, shall forever be guaranteed . . . No person shall be required to attend or support any ministry or place of worship against his consent, nor shall any preference be given by law to any religious denomination or mode of worship . . .[52]

and whether or not they were sectarian exercises for which public funds could not be used within the meaning of the following constitutional provision:

> Neither the general assembly nor any county, city, town, township, school district, or other public corporation shall ever make any appropriation or pay from any public fund whatever, anything in aid of any church or sectarian purpose, or to help, support, or sustain any school, academy, seminary, college, university, or other literary or scientific institution controlled by any church or sectarian denomination whatever . . .[53]

The court said:

> The wrong arises, not out of the particular version of the Bible or form of prayer used, whether that found in the Douay or the King James version, or the particular songs sung, but out of the compulsion to join in any form of worship. The free enjoyment of religious worship includes freedom not to worship.[54]

In speaking of discriminations imposed upon Jews, Catholics, and Protestants the court further states:

> The Bible in its entirety is a sectarian book as to the Jew and every believer in any religion other than the Christian religion, and as to those who are heretical or who hold beliefs that are not regarded as orthodox.

[51] 245 Ill. 334 (1910).
[52] Constitution of Illinois, Article 2, Section 3.
[53] *Ibid.,* Article 8, Section 3.
[54] People ex rel. Ring v. Board of Education of District 24, 245 Ill. 334 (1910).

Whether it may be called sectarian or not, its use in the schools necessarily results in sectarian instruction. There are many sects of Christians,
and their differences grow out of their differing constructions of various
parts of the Scriptures — the different conclusions drawn as to the effect
of the same words.

In commenting on the fact that the majority of the people in the
state may be adherents of the Protestant religion, that fact in itself
does not warrant preferences being shown to Protestants or any other
sect, inasmuch as

the law knows no distinction between the Christian and the Pagan, the
Protestant and the Catholic. All are citizens . . . The state is not, and
under our constitution cannot be, a teacher of religion. . . . In our judgment the exercises mentioned in the petition constitute religious worship
and the reading of the Bible in the school constitutes sectarian instruction.

The court held that the reading of the Bible in the public schools,
the singing of hymns, and the repeating of the Lord's Prayer in con-
cert, during which time the pupils were required to rise, bow their
heads, and fold their hands, constitutes worship within the meaning
of the constitution. The court pointed out that under the constitution
of Illinois the state cannot be a teacher of religion. The public school
is supported by taxes which everyone is compelled to pay regardless
of religious or nonreligious affiliations. "The school, like the government, is secular, and not religious, in its purposes. The truths of the
Bible are the truths of religion, which do not come within the province of the public school."

Louisiana. In the case of Herold v. Parish Board of School Directors, the plaintiffs, Herold and others, were Jewish and Catholic
school patrons.[55] The board had passed a resolution requiring the
principals and teachers to open the daily sessions of the public schools
with readings from the Bible, without note or comment, and, when
the teacher was willing, with the Lord's Prayer.

By unanimous vote the court held that the reading of the Bible,
either the Old or New Testament in the King James version, was
not a discrimination against Catholics but was an invasion of the
rights of conscience of the Jews. Hence the court disallowed the enforcement of the resolution.

Here the court recognized the difference between what it termed
the "Rabbinical Bible" and the "Christian Bible." The court did not

[55] 136 La. 1034; 68 So. 116 (1915).

concern itself with the differences, or alleged errors, in the different translations of the Christian Bible, which it termed the "Bibles of the Christians," but concluded that the Jews would have their consciences violated by the reading of such a Bible or the offering of the Lord's Prayer. The practice was held unconstitutional in view of the following constitutional provisions:

Every person has the natural right to worship God according to the dictates of his own conscience . . .

No money shall ever be taken from the public treasury, directly or indirectly, in aid of any church, sect, or denomination of religion . . .[56]

In the Colorado case dealing with the same subject the court said:

It is urged that to absent themselves for a religious reason "subjects the pupils to a religious stigma and places them at a disadvantage." We cannot agree to that. The shoe is on the other foot. We have known many boys to be ridiculed for complying with religious regulations, but never one for neglecting them or absenting himself from them.[57]

This attitude of the Colorado court toward the exemption of certain students from religious exercises is interesting when compared with that of Louisiana. The Louisiana court said:

And excusing such children on religious grounds, although the number excused might be very small, would be a distinct preference in favor of the religious beliefs of the majority, and would work a discrimination against those who were excused. The exclusion of a pupil under such circumstances puts him in a class by himself; it subjects him to a religious stigma . . .

In the Colorado case it is assumed that those who are excused during the readings will ridicule those who remain; in the Louisiana case that those who remain will ridicule those who are excused. These may be taken as examples of the reasoning of different judges in which the conclusions reached are opposite. In this disagreement, however, both conclusions reached are correct. Either one results in discrimination and consequently in oppression.

Nebraska. Miss Edith Beecher, a teacher in the public schools of Beatrice, Gage County, Nebraska, obtained permission from the school board to have religious exercises in her school during school hours, consisting of readings from the Bible, the singing of hymns, and the offering of prayer according to the doctrines and beliefs of

[56] Constitution of Louisiana, Article 1, Section 4; Article 4, Section 8.
[57] People v. Stanley; see above, pp. 53–55.

sectarian churches. An order was sought to prohibit these religious exercises. The court held that the exercises as conducted by the teacher constituted sectarian instruction as well as compulsory attendance at religious exercises contrary to the constitution. No decision was rendered as to whether or not the reading of the Bible without comment would be permissible.[58]

The Nebraska court quoted Judge Taft of the superior court of Ohio in the case of Board of Education v. Minor, in which he said:

The singing of Protestant hymns may be used to communicate dogmatic instruction as effectually as the Bible itself. I cannot doubt, therefore, that the use of the Bible, with the appropriate singing provided for by the old rule, and as practiced under it, was and is sectarian.

The court took the position that the suggestion that it is the duty of the government to teach religion has no basis whatever in the constitution or laws of the state of Nebraska or in the history of her people. The duty of the state with respect to religion is to protect every religious denomination in the peaceable enjoyment of its own mode of public worship.

Nevada. The following constitutional and statutory provisions are found in Nevada and are presumed to exclude the reading of the Bible in the public schools of that state:

No sectarian instruction shall be imparted or tolerated in any school . . .

No public funds of any kind or character whatever . . . shall be used for sectarian purposes.

No books, tracts, or papers of a sectarian or denominational character shall be used or introduced in any schools established under the provisions of this act; nor shall any sectarian or denominational doctrines be taught therein.[59]

New Mexico. In New Mexico are to be found the following constitutional and statutory provisions:

[58] State v. Scheve, 65 Nebr. 853, 91 N.W. 846 (1902). The court very definitely pointed out that it was not passing on the legality or wisdom of Bible reading in the public schools, saying, "Whether it is prudent or politic to permit Bible reading in the public schools is a question for the school authorities to determine; but whether the practice of Bible reading has taken the form of sectarian instruction in a particular case is a question for the courts to determine upon evidence." In the eyes of the court, the practice here complained of constituted sectarian instruction and it was on this basis that the practice was prohibited, but it leaves the matter of Bible reading, presumably if it can be done without sectarian influence, to the school authorities. It is on this basis that the matter of Bible reading is left optional with the school board or teacher. The state department of public instruction for Nebraska has no records of Bible reading in its schools, but it is assumed that very few schools carry on the practice in the state. Reply to questionnaire of November 1, 1932, by the state superintendent of education.
[59] The first two provisions are from Article 11, Sections 9 and 10, of the constitution, the third from Nevada Compiled Laws, 1929, Section 5754.

No religious test shall ever be required as a condition of admission into the public schools or any educational institution of this state, either as a teacher or student, and no teacher or student of such school or institution shall ever be required to attend or participate in any religious service whatsoever.[60]

No teacher shall use any sectarian or denominational books in the schools or teach sectarian doctrines in the schools . . .[61]

The use of any "sectarian or denominational books" or the teaching of "sectarian doctrine" in the schools not only subjects the teacher to immediate dismissal but bars the school from drawing upon the public funds.[62]

New York. In the state of New York the superintendent of schools, by special act of the legislature in 1822, was given power to decide all controversies regarding the administration of the public schools. The superintendents pass upon the cases involving religious and sectarian influences in the public schools. The state attorney general has declared that Bible reading in the public schools[63] is contrary to the following constitutional provision:

Neither the state nor any subdivision thereof shall use its property or credit or any public money . . . in aid or maintenance, other than for examination or inspection, of any school or institution of learning wholly or in part under the control or direction of any religious denomination, or in which any denominational tenet or doctrine is taught.[64]

The report of the committee on education which submitted the above section to the constitutional convention of New York in 1894, contains this significant paragraph:

"There is no demand from the people of the state upon this Convention so unmistakable, widespread, and urgent, none, moreover, so well-grounded in right and reason, as that the public school system of the state shall be forever protected by constitutional safeguards from all sectarian influence or interference, and that public money shall not be used directly or indirectly to propagate denominational tenets or doctrines. . . ." The arguments in favor of such a provision are, in our opinion, conclusive; and the objection that it will result in making the schools "Godless," or that such a constitutional prohibition would imply on the part of the people enacting it hostility, or even indifference, to religion, seem to us to be both groundless and absurd. In adopting this section the Conven-

---

[60] Constitution of New Mexico, Article 12, Section 9.
[61] New Mexico Statutes Annotated, 1929, Chapter 120, Section 1102.
[62] *Ibid.*
[63] University of the State of New York Bulletin, Law Pamphlet 6 (Albany, 1927).
[64] Constitution of New York, Article 9, Section 4.

tion will, in our opinion, most effectively aid all that is highest and best in religion, for, by establishing the principle that state education must necessarily be secular in its character, the field is left open beyond question or misunderstanding for religious teaching in the family, the Sunday school, and the church.[65]

However, in 1936 Joseph Lewis, a taxpayer of the city of New York, sought to restrain the board of education of the city of New York from permitting readings from the Bible in the public schools.[66]

The court held that the reading of portions of the Bible without comment was not in violation of any statutory or constitutional provision of the state of New York.

Utah. Moral education in Utah is permitted,[67] but public aid of church schools is forbidden.[68] The constitution and statutes of the state include the following provisions prohibiting Bible reading in the public schools:

The rights of conscience shall never be infringed. The state shall make no law respecting an establishment of religion or prohibiting the free exercise thereof . . . No public money or property shall be appropriated for or applied to any religious worship, exercise, or instruction, or for the support of any ecclesiastical establishment.

The legislature shall make laws for the establishment and maintenance of a system of public schools, which shall be open to all the children of the state and be free from sectarian control.

The legislature shall provide for the establishment and maintenance of a uniform system of public schools, which shall be open to all children of the state, and be free from sectarian control.

Neither religious nor partisan test or qualification shall be required of any person, as a condition of admission, as teacher or student, into any public educational institution of the state.[69]

It shall be unlawful to teach in any of the district schools of this state while in session, any atheistic, infidel, sectarian, religious, or denominational doctrine and all such schools shall be free from sectarian control.

No partisan, political, or sectarian religious doctrine shall be taught or inculcated in the university, nor any political or religious test shall be required as a qualification of any student, professor, instructor, officer, or employe of the University of Utah.

[65] University of the State of New York Bulletin, Law Pamphlet 6, p. 4.
[66] Lewis v. Board of Education of the City of New York, 157 Misc. 520, 285 N.Y.S. 164 (1935) [modified in other respects in 247 App. Div. 106, 286 N.Y.S. 174 (1936); rehearing denied in 247 App. Div. 873, 288 N.Y.S. 751 (1936); appeal dismissed in 276 N.Y. 490, 12 N.E. (2d) 172 (1937)].
[67] Utah Laws, 1921, Chapter 95, Section 2.
[68] Constitution of Utah, Article 10, Section 13.
[69] *Ibid.,* Article 1, Section 4; Article 3; Article 10, Sections 1 and 12.

Similar provisions apply to the State Agricultural College and the Branch Agricultural College.[70]

Washington. The constitution of the state of Washington stipulates that

All schools maintained or supported wholly or in part by the public funds shall be forever free from sectarian control or influence.

No public money or property shall be appropriated for or applied to any religious worship, exercise, or instruction, or the support of any religious establishment.[71]

These provisions have been interpreted by various attorney generals as prohibiting religious instruction in the public schools, the opening of school with prayer, or the reading of the Bible in the public schools.[72] As a result of these opinions Bible reading is prohibited in the public schools of Washington.[73]

The constitutionality of Bible reading was raised also in the case of Dearle v. Frazier[74] and again in the case of Clithero v. Showalter.[75] Mr. Clithero and thirty-six others presented a petition to the state board of education to make daily Bible reading and twice-a-week instruction in the Bible compulsory in the public schools. The board refused the petition and returned it to the petitioners on the ground "that they had no jurisdiction nor authority to make a decision of any kind upon the petition because it raised a constitutional question." The petitioners thereupon filed a suit in the supreme court of Washington asking a writ of mandamus to compel the superintendent and the board of education to grant the relief sought in the petition. The supreme court held that Article 1, Section 11, of the state constitution which required that "No public money or property shall be appropriated for or applied to any religious worship, exercise, or instruction, or the support of any religious establishment" prohibits the reading or teaching of the Bible in the public schools and that everything demanded in this suit had been denied in Dearle v. Frazier, and that that decision could not be reviewed or overruled. Upon its appeal to the Supreme Court of the United States, the case was dismissed on the grounds that there was not a substantial federal question involved.[76]

[70] Utah Laws, 1921, Chapter 95, Section 1, and Chapter 117; 1925, Chapter 57, Section 1.
[71] Constitution of Washington, Article 9, Section 4; Article 1, Section 11.
[72] Opinions of the Attorney-General, 1915–16, p. 254; 1909–10, p. 135; 1891–92, p. 142.
[73] See above, Chapter III.   [74] 102 Wash. 369 (1918).
[75] Clithero v. Showalter, 159 Wash. 519, 293 Pac. 1000 (1930).
[76] Transcript of Record, Supreme Court of the United States, State of Washington ex rel. George Clithero and Thirty-Six Others v. N. D. Showalter, etc., et al., No. 80, October Term, 1931, pp. 11, 87.

Wisconsin. In a Wisconsin case, Weiss v. District Board, Weiss and others, who were Catholic school patrons, came to the court seeking a writ of mandamus to prevent the reading of the Bible in the public school of District 8 in Edgerton.[77] The Bible appeared on the list of textbooks for the school. The King James version was used. Portions were selected and read by the teacher, though no comments were made on the reading and children were not required to attend such reading.

The Wisconsin statute provides: "But no textbooks shall be permitted in any free public schools which would have a tendency to inculcate sectarian ideas."[78]

The court in a unanimous decision not only held that the Bible was a sectarian book but also that its reading constituted sectarian instruction within the meaning of the state constitution, which reads:

The legislature shall provide by law for the establishment of district schools, which shall be as nearly uniform as practicable; and such schools shall be free and without charge for tuition to all children between the ages of four and twenty years; and no sectarian instruction shall be allowed therein.[79]

It held that Bible reading constituted an interference with the rights of conscience of pupils and that it constituted appropriation of public moneys for the benefit of a religious school, a procedure prohibited by the constitutional provision:

The right of every man to worship Almighty God according to the dictates of his own conscience shall never be infringed; nor shall any man be compelled to attend, erect, or support any place of worship, or to maintain any ministry against his consent; nor shall any control of, or interference with, the rights of conscience be permitted, or any preference be given by law to any religious establishments or modes of worship; nor shall any money be drawn from the treasury for the benefit of religious societies, or religious or theological seminaries.[80]

The order for mandamus prohibiting the reading of the Bible was granted.

The court declared that sectarian instruction as designated in the constitution manifestly refers to instruction in religious doctrines or dogmas which are believed by some religious sects and rejected by

[77] 76 Wis. 177, 44 N.W. 967 (1890).
[78] Wisconsin Laws, 1883, Chapter 251, Section 3.
[79] Constitution of Wisconsin, Article 10, Section 3.
[80] *Ibid.*, Article 1, Section 18.

others; that religion, which the court defined as a system of belief, cannot be taught without offense to those who have their own peculiar views of religion any more than it can be taught without offense to the different sects of religion.

The court said:

When we remember that wise and good men have struggled and agonized through the centuries to find the correct interpretation of the Scriptures, employing to that end all the resources of great intellectual power, profound scholarship, and exalted spiritual attainment, and yet with such widely divergent results; and, further, that the relators conscientiously believe that their church furnishes them means, and the only means, of correct and infallible interpretation — we can scarcely say their conscientious scruples against the reading of any version of the Bible to their children, unaccompanied by such interpretation, are entitled to no consideration.

An important principle was enunciated by the court when it said: "Religion needs no support from the state. It is stronger and much purer without it." This case, said the court, "brings before the courts a case of the plausible, insidious, and apparently innocent entrance of religion into our civil affairs . . ."

The court pointed out that prohibiting the reading of the Bible in the public schools is not a denial of the value of the Holy Scriptures, nor is it a blow to their influence upon the conduct and conscience of men, nor disastrous to the cause of religion. "We most emphatically reject these views. The priceless truths of the Bible are best taught to our youth in the church, the Sabbath and parochial schools, the social religious meetings, and, above all, by parents in the home circle." [81]

It will be noted that in this case the court prohibited the reading of the Bible even though such reading was without comment, students could be excused during such reading, and no other exercise, such as singing of religious hymns or offering of the Lord's Prayer, took place. The court held that reading from the Bible in the schools, although unaccompanied by any comment on the part of the teacher, is "instruction." It did not, however, banish from the district school textbooks which are founded upon the fundamental teachings of the Bible or which contain extracts from it. It pointed out that such teachings and extracts pervade and ornament our secular literature,

[81] It was held that the offering of a nonsectarian prayer by a Catholic priest or a Protestant minister at a public school graduation exercise is not sectarian instruction. State ex rel. Conway v. District Bd. 162 Wis. 482, 156 N.W. 477, L.R.A. 1916D.

that such textbooks are in the schools for secular instruction, and that the constitutional prohibition on sectarian instruction is not intended to include them. The court contended that even though students were permitted to be excused during such reading, the practice tended to destroy the equality of the pupils which the constitution seeks to establish and protect, and put a portion of them to serious disadvantage with respect to the others.

Wyoming. The constitution of Wyoming specifies:

No money of the state shall ever be given or appropriated to any sectarian or religious society or institution.

No sectarian instruction, qualifications, or test shall be imparted, exacted, applied, or in any manner tolerated in the schools of any grade or character controlled by the state, nor shall attendance be required at any religious service therein, nor shall any sectarian tenets or doctrines be taught or favored in any public school or institution that may be established under this constitution.[82]

The above constitutional provisions have been recognized as prohibiting the reading of the Bible in the public schools of Wyoming.

<h3 style="text-align:center">SUMMARY</h3>

It has been seen that in some states the reading of the Bible is required in the public schools. In some it is specifically permitted; in some it is optional; while in others the laws are silent on the subject and no court decisions have been rendered. In still others it is prohibited by statutes, by court decisions, or by both statutes and court decisions. In some states, such as Maine, Minnesota, Nebraska, and Ohio, where the laws are silent on the subject of Bible reading in the public schools, it is a matter to be determined by the discretionary powers resting in the school authorities. In these states the courts will interfere with the exercises of such power only where its abuse is clearly shown.[83]

Such decisions have generally been considered favorable to Bible reading because they leave the power of permitting or rejecting Bible reading with the school authorities.

The validity of Bible reading and religious exercises in the public schools must be considered from the viewpoint of the historical background, the constitutional and statutory provisions, and the

---

[82] Constitution of Wyoming, Article 1, Section 19; Article 7, Section 12.
[83] Donahoe v. Richards, 38 Me. 376 (1854); Kaplan v. Independent School District of Virginia, 214 N.W. 18 (1927); State v. Scheve, 65 Nebr. 853, 91 N.W. 846 (1902); Board of Cincinnati v. Minor et al., 23 Ohio St. 211 (1872).

court decisions of the individual states. Every pupil has the right to enjoy the opportunities offered in the public schools without an infringement of the freedom of worship and liberty of conscience, and the "majority rule" does not apply in matters affecting religion and the rights of conscience as it does in political matters affecting the state.

The constitutional and statutory provisions of the several states generally agree that public money cannot be used for sectarian or religious purposes, that no sectarian books or instruction may be permitted in the public schools, and that the right to worship according to the dictates of conscience shall never be infringed. But whether the reading of the Bible in the public schools constitutes a violation of these provisions is a question on which there is no unanimity of opinion.[84]

The evidence shows clearly that attempts are being made to preserve religious freedom with greater security and to free public school curriculums from religious control and sectarian influence — this in spite of the fact that there has been a strong movement to require Bible reading and other religious exercises in the public schools.

When the public school refuses to teach religion, it invades the rights of no one. It does not reject religion nor does it foster it. It leaves the subject entirely alone and justifies its own existence and support by general taxation on the grounds that its function is to provide secular rather than religious education. Religious instruction in the public schools, whether it consists of reading the Bible, singing hymns, or offering prayer, is, in respect to the taxpayer, a coerced support of religion. Such instruction, especially if it is compulsory, is incompatible with the principles of religious liberty and freedom of conscience.

While the desire to have the Bible read as a part of the morning exercise in the public schools is in many cases a commendable one, it is equally evident that it is a religious motive which prompts the desire.[85] If this were not true, why not read the Talmud, the Koran, or Confucius? They also are rich in moral training.

It is the duty of government to protect but not to favor one re-

[84] See the *Virginia Law Review*, 16:509–10; also Reports of the American Bar Association, 1928, 53:230, 231.
[85] See Frank Swancara, "The Colorado Bible Case," *Lawyer and Banker*, 21:164 (May-June, 1928).

ligion above another.[86] Today the public school has become far reaching in its influence. It is serving a people more divergent in their beliefs and yet a people who in general are more dependent on it for the education of their children than those of any previous time. The public schools are supported by the taxes of Protestants, Catholics, Jews, and infidels alike. All are entitled to equal opportunities and privileges. The injection of Bible reading into the public schools frequently sets up a conflict motivated by religious difference. The Catholic objects to the King James version, the Jew objects to the New Testament, the infidel condemns them all, and even the Protestants wrangle among themselves over religious interpretations.

These facts may seem of themselves insignificant; still to some they warrant the exclusion of Bible reading from the public schools. It is the one course that may be pursued with absolute safety, with the assurance that no one's rights are being trampled upon and with a knowledge that perfect justice has been done. From the cases that have been noted it appears that the courts are looking in that direction, an attitude which accords more perfectly with public opinion at the present time and which more nearly approximates the complete separation of church and state.

[86] This duty is clearly stated by Clarence Manion, professor of law at Notre Dame University, in the South Bend (Indiana) *News-Times* of June 22, 1928.

CHAPTER V

Dismissed and Released Time for Religious Education

I N MANY areas a practice that has been gaining prevalence in recent years and that some people have felt will help solve the problem of religious training in the public schools is that of dismissing pupils during certain periods of the week to obtain religious instruction in the churches or elsewhere.

This plan, frequently referred to as "Dismissed Time for Religious Education," [1] has experienced such favorable approval that either by express statutory provisions, court decisions, rulings of the state attorney generals, or opinions of state boards of education or chief state school officers, approximately forty states now authorize the release of public school pupils for weekly religious education classes. Some states, however, including the District of Columbia, definitely forbid the excusing of pupils for religious instruction. It is claimed that two million pupils are enrolled in dismissed and released time classes in religion in twenty-two hundred communities throughout the United States. This fact naturally raises an important issue, affecting as it does many parents, pupils, and schools.

In the dismissed time program, upon request of their parents or guardians, pupils are permitted to go to the church, or church school, where the kind of religious training they desire will be given them. Such an arrangement not only makes it possible for students to receive religious training from whatever church they wish, but also keeps out of the public schools all the controversial questions of

[1] A distinction is made between "dismissed" time and "released" time for religious instruction. "Dismissed" time is that which schools grant pupils to go to churches, parochial schools, or elsewhere for religious instruction. The public school, by the dismissed time plan, assumes no responsibility after the pupils leave the public school grounds. In more recent years the practice has developed in some instances of permitting the religious instructors, including ministers, priests, rabbis, and various Bible instructors, to come into the public school and take over the religious instruction in certain of the public schoolrooms. The public school officials *release* the pupils certain periods for such religious instruction, hence the term *released time*. It is recognized, however, that a clear distinction between the two terms is not always maintained and the terms are frequently used interchangeably.

Bible reading, comment, sectarian influences, and religious instruction.

Some people, however, view the proposal to give the pupils hours off at stated periods during the week to attend a religious school or church as objectionable in practice even though innocent in appearance. It is maintained that such a practice establishes a precedent which opens wide the door to influences that may nullify the fundamental character of the public school system and that such practice results in taking from the school program time that belongs to regular school work. The great danger, however, in giving time off during school hours for religious instruction is not merely that this plan provides too great a loss of time from secular attendance, but that it constitutes a temptation for ambitious ecclesiastics of every kind to propagate, under the auspices of the public school, their own ideas of religious training. This plan opens the door to conflict among the children themselves in prying into each other's religious affiliations, and to every form of intolerance and bigotry that has plagued mankind under the guise of religion. These are potential dangers that must not threaten our public school system.

This practice, when followed, generally consists in excusing the children early one afternoon a week so that they may go elsewhere for religious instruction. All the pupils may be excused, in which case those who do not go to the churches or church schools for religious instruction may go to their homes. In some cases only those are excused who go for religious instruction, and the others remain in school.

The plan of excusing pupils for certain periods to obtain religious instruction elsewhere has been demonstrated in the industrial city of Gary, Indiana, in what has come to be known as the "Gary Plan." Here the school schedule has been so arranged that all pupils whose parents so request may attend schools conducted by the various churches and synagogues of the city during a part of each school day. The child may be excused during the day to take private lessons at home or to attend one of the churches or church schools. What is taught in these outside classes is not the concern of the public school. The pupils either go directly from home to church school and then to public school, or else directly from public school to church school and then home. Attendance at the church or church school is not compulsory but is entirely a matter between the church school and the home.

The Gary Plan is recommending itself in a number of places as a practical solution to the problem of religious education. The school is in no way concerned in this religious teaching. It merely cooperates to the extent of providing an opportunity for those who desire it, leaving it to the parents to arrange for such teaching and to determine whether or not their children shall receive religious instruction, as well as how they shall get it, and what it shall be. The children receive this instruction under priest, pastor, or teacher in their own church or parish house, or from their parents.

Some states specifically authorize the excusing of children for such religious training. For example, in Minnesota the compulsory attendance statute expressly authorizes school boards to dismiss pupils upon the request of their parents for a period not exceeding three hours a week to obtain religious education elsewhere.[2] More often the period stipulated is not to exceed one hour a week.

In New York State such practice was brought to the attention of the court in the case of Stein v. Brown in 1925.[3] An action was brought by Stein against the school board to enjoin them from allowing pupils of the public schools of the city of Mount Vernon to be excused from school instruction for forty-five minutes once a week for instruction in the churches to which the parents desired them to be sent. The plaintiff also requested that the school board refrain from having printed, in connection with this plan, cards to be filled out by the teacher of the religious instruction in the various churches in order to notify the school authorities that the children had been present. These cards were distributed at the expense of the board of education of Mount Vernon. They were printed at the school as an exercise for the boys in industrial arts. The cost of the cards was paid by a committee on week-day religious education. No use was made of public funds but only of the presses that were property of the city.

The question here was whether the rulings of the board of education were subject to review in any court and whether the use of public property for such printing constituted the use of public funds for sectarian or religious purposes in violation of the following constitutional provision:

Neither the state, nor any subdivision thereof, shall use its property or credit or any public money, or authorize or permit either to be used,

[2] Minnesota General Statutes, 1923, Section 3080.
[3] 211 N.Y.S. 822, 125 Misc. Rep. 692. For a discussion of this case see "Religious Instruction," *Minnesota Law Review*, 11:571, 572 (May 1927).

directly or indirectly, in aid or maintenance, other than for examination or inspection, of any school or institution of learning wholly or in part under the control or direction of any religious denomination, or in which any denominational tenet or doctrine is taught.[4]

The court held that neither the state nor any of its subdivisions could use its property, funds, or credit in aid of a school wholly or in part under the control of any religious denomination. The fact that no particular denomination was favored by such action did not alter the case.

The court held further that to excuse pupils from school for a regular period of religious instruction was unlawful under the New York laws of 1921, which required the attendance of pupils during the school session with the exceptions specified. Religious instruction was not one of those exceptions. It was held unlawful for a board of education to substitute a period of religious instruction away from the school for instruction required at school. To permit the children to leave the school during school hours for religious instruction, said the court, would be, in effect, to substitute religious instruction for the instruction required by law. It was further argued that those who leave the school weekly for religious instruction, being deprived of the instruction given at school during that period, are likely to fall behind those who remain the full time.

The court pointed out that in many school districts there is only one church sufficiently near the school to be reached by children attending that school; that the practice of excusing children for religious instruction would favor that church, whatever its denomination; that religious instruction belongs to the parents of the children, the churches, and the religious organizations of the country, and that hence it should be given outside of the public schools and outside of school hours.

The court held that Section 890 of the educational law, which provides that the rules of the board of education can be reviewed only by the state commissioner of education, does not apply to a taxpayer's suit to enjoin improper use of funds, or to the determination of constitutional questions, or to illegal acts on the part of officers.

However, the part of the decision which prohibited the excusing of pupils for weekly religious instruction was overruled two years later, in 1927, in the case of People ex rel. Lewis v. Graves.[5] Lewis sought

[4] Constitution of New York, Article 9, Section 4.
[5] 245 N.Y. 195.

an order to compel Graves, the commissioner of education, to order the school authorities of White Plains to discontinue the school regulation by which, at the request of their parents, pupils might be excused for half an hour each week just before the end of school to receive religious instruction in church schools. This arrangement of excusing children was made to please people interested in religious instruction in the public schools of the state. The plan had been put into operation in White Plains and, with some varying details, elsewhere. The child so excused would lose no school recitations and would receive no credit for the work taken in the church school. No public money was used to aid the church schools, though the cooperation between the public schools and the church schools required a slight use of the time of the public school teachers in registering and checking excuses. The plan was covered, as we have seen, by suitable regulations of the school authorities in the absence of any legislative enactment.

The court held that the practice of excusing children for thirty minutes a week was not a diversion of public funds sufficient to constitute a violation of the section of the state constitution quoted above, nor was such practice a violation of the educational law providing for compulsory school attendance, which requires that pupils "shall regularly attend upon instruction for the entire time during which the schools . . . are in session." [6]

The court called attention to the need of leaving room for discretion on the part of the school authorities in the practical administration of the public schools; and of giving to the commissioner of education the power to adopt regulations to restrict the local authorities when the administration of week-day instruction in religion, or any plan of outside instruction, in his judgment interferes unduly with the regular school work. On the other hand, the court pointed out that neither the constitution nor the laws of New York discriminate against religion and that denominational religion is merely put in its proper place outside of public aid or support. To maintain a clear distinction between church and state, religion need not be placed at a disadvantage nor given an inferior ranking, but public funds may not be used for its support. In its opinion, which was concurred in by Chief Justice Cardoza, the court said,

Jealous sectaries may view with alarm the introduction in the schools of religious teaching which to the unobservant eye is but faintly tinted

[6] Educational Law of New York State, 1931, Section 621.

with denominationalism. Eternal vigilance is the price of constitutional rights. But it is impossible to say, as a matter of law, that the slightest infringement of constitutional right or abuse of statutory requirement has been shown in this case.

It should be noted that the excused children lost no recitations and received no credit for work done in the church schools. In commenting upon the case, Dr. Frank P. Graves, commissioner of education for the state of New York, said:

In my judgment this plan marks the limits to which public school officials should go in the matter of denominational religious education, and any extension may be regarded as an undue interference with the regular work of the schools. In fact, I believe it would be much better if pupils are to be excused at any time for religious instruction, to dismiss them half an hour early at the end of the week and permit them to go to their respective places for religious instruction, if they wish to go at all. No compulsion should be brought to bear by the school authorities to make them go. Of course the parents might do this, but the machinery of the school should not be used.[7]

In 1941 a rather elaborate experiment in dismissed time for religious education was undertaken in New York City.[8] This program was sponsored by individuals who saw in such an arrangement an opportunity to make the child's religious heritage more nearly an integral part of his education. In the proposal of the plan for New York City, there were those who advocated its inception as a remedy for all of society's ills. On the other hand, there was strong opposition from many who bitterly opposed it as an opening wedge for abuses which would creep into the public school system. They believed that it was an unwarranted and dangerous demand both to church and to school — that the schools were abandoning their public character in order to relieve the churches of what they should regard as their own sacred duty and privilege. It was also charged by some that the churches, in connection with released time, were using the compulsory attendance laws of public education to compel children to study religion, and that in so doing they were contributing to the breakdown of the principles of the separation of church and state.

[7] Opinion rendered to the New York State Sunday School Association by Frank P. Graves, commissioner of education for the state of New York, given in *Religion and Public Schools*, University of the State of New York Bulletin, Law Pamphlet 6 (Albany, 1927), p. 5.

[8] See Walter H. Howlett, "Released Time for Religious Education in New York City," *Religious Education*, March-April 1942; also Imogene M. McPherson and others, "Released Time in New York City," *Religious Education*, January-February 1943.

An interfaith committee was organized consisting of Protestant, Jewish, and Catholic members. An elaborate curriculum was set up, consisting of three cycles, each cycle making provision for four semesters, or two years' work, thus inaugurating a six-year program of religious instruction. Grades three through eight of the public schools in New York City were included in the program. Each pupil was excused for about thirty minutes weekly for thirty to thirty-two weeks each year for six years. The board of education of New York City did not permit any announcement of dismissed time for religious education to be made in the public school. Such announcements were made in the churches, Sunday schools, or through other means of reaching the children and parents interested in the project.

In two years the project grew to the extent that about eight hundred teachers were used in carrying on religious instruction in the released-time program. While there is a difference of opinion as to the degree of success of the program, certain problems have been recognized. There has been some opposition from public school teachers and principals, but a spirit of cooperation has, for the most part, prevailed between the two groups. The Parent-Teacher Association and individual teachers have contributed money to the support of the program. The teachers have participated as individual members of the community, for the board of education prohibits any participation by public school teachers or officers in their professional capacity. Problems that arise are studied by the interfaith committee leaders and a representative of the board of education. Individual teachers from the public schools and principals occasionally meet in conferences held by the ministers and educators in religion to discuss the program.

Adjustments are made in the public school program so that the children are not penalized for their absence from classes, and no special attempts are made to attract the children to remain in the public schools rather than attend their churches or parochial schools for their religious education.

Certain shortcomings of the program have been pointed out by the interfaith leaders. Among these are the difficulties caused by regulation of the board of education that no announcement of dismissed time may be made in the public school. The religion teachers find that the pupils who respond to the program are primarily those who are enrolled in Sunday schools or other church services, that they are failing to reach the great mass of children who do not attend church. Likewise, they have had difficulty in setting up a program that would allow for marked differences in familiarity with the Bible, ranging from those who have considerable knowledge of the Bible to those whose knowledge is fragmentary. Problems of discipline in large groups, of inadequate equipment in some of the churches, and of unqualified and ineffective teachers were also reported. Difficulty was experienced in staggering the program so that religion teachers might pursue their teaching program through a greater number of hours in the day and thus avoid peak-loading of the schedule, a situation which would necessitate a larger number of teachers than would otherwise be necessary. This concentration of the teaching load during certain hours has naturally made it more difficult to secure enough qualified teachers to carry on the religious instruction required by this rather ambitious plan. There are many who still voice misgivings with the New York plan or with any dismissed or released-time program, though it would seem that the only participation involved in this program by the public schools of New York is their willingness to release pupils for the specified time. No phase of the expense appears in any way to be borne by the public schools. Whether the effort put forth by the churches involved will diminish with time, or whether additional demands will be made by interfaith leaders which will result in embarrassment to the public school program, or whether it will be felt that religious prejudices will be developed and embarrassments accrue which will warrant the discontinuance of the program, only time will determine.

Similar programs have been carried on in Syracuse and other cities in New York with varying degrees of success.

In Harrisburg, Pennsylvania, the board of school directors inaugurated a program of dismissed-time for religious education. An action passed by the General Assembly of Pennsylvania empowers the board of school directors to release pupils for not more than one hour per week from school sessions under stipulated rules and regulations. Such a program was adopted by the school board of Harrisburg beginning with the school year 1942–43. After the plan had been in effect for three years — until January 26, 1945, when it was discontinued — the board made the following significant report:

There are a number of factors which should be considered carefully by all concerned in a "released-time" program of religious education. These circumstances contribute to produce results which must be considered also without prejudice to the general problem, motive or value of religious education per se. In this instance these conditions are the result of local experience and the basic principles of public school education and administration:

1. Either by law, by pressure, or by design to meet changing condition, the program of service and activities in the schools has been filled to the present time limits, and any additional encroachment from external sources will more strongly emphasize the need to extend the school day or the school term in order that the schools may have the opportunity to accomplish those things for which public schools were organized.

2. When the privilege of the "released-time" program is granted, the school and not the parent is expected to assume the responsibility for the progressive advancement of the child even in regard to the other extracurricular or elective activities. In order to meet this problem, there must be a curtailment of activities in the school which often are the actual character-building agencies of the school itself.

3. As in Harrisburg, other communities have found that the "released-time" program has neither met the needs of religious education or justified the effect upon the public school program. The public school generally has been our most democratic institution and any program which emphasized the differences of the pupils is harmful. News items from cities where there has been "released-time" for religious education indicate that there is now more intolerance, discrimination, and disunity than previously existed in the public schools of those communities.

4. A recommendation of many persons interested in controlling juvenile delinquency is that there should be more opportunity for utilizing the slack time of "out-of-school" hours for character-building purposes. One of these opportunities could be attendance at classes for religious education. In fact, some such classes are conducted and are better attended than those of the "released-time" program.

Recommendation

WHEREAS the Committee of the Whole sincerely believes that there is a definite need for emphasis upon character building and religious education and is not opposed to religious education in principle but is opposed to the proposed method of "released-time" for religious education, and

WHEREAS the Committee of the Whole has considered carefully the factors as outlined in the above statement which are involved in the adoption of a public school "released-time" program for religious education, and

WHEREAS the "released-time" program in effect in Harrisburg during the schools years 1942 to 1945 inclusive, neither met the needs of religious education nor justified the effect upon the public school program as evidenced by the following tabulation:

Year	Registered	Completed	Senior High School Population
1942–43	970	426	2,867
1943–44	300	128	2,512
1944–45	200	139*	2,524

*Attending as of the date the program was discontinued by the Board on January 26, 1945.

therefore, be it

RESOLVED that the Committee of the Whole recommends that the petition of the Committee for Religious Instruction for the establishment of a "released-time" for religious education program be denied.[9]

As is evident from the above report, in the judgment of the school directors the plan was not satisfactory. The tabulation showing the enrollments for the three years, or until the program was discontinued, reveals a noticeable decline in the number of pupils availing themselves of this service.

Similar disapproval of the dismissed-time program for religious education has been expressed in other places. Recently the board of school commissioners of Baltimore, Maryland, refused a petition for a program of dismissed-time religious education. From the "Report of the Board of Superintendents to the Board of School Commissioners Concerning the Petition for a Program of Released Time Religious Education in the Baltimore Public Schools," we quote:

It is our carefully considered recommendation that the plan proposed in the petition be not approved by the Board of School Commissioners. . . .

Because of deep and continuous concern professionally and personally in the problem of character development among children and youth, we have given much consideration to the various aspects of Character Education. We have examined and evaluated programs carried on in the past, both in Baltimore and elsewhere, programs now being conducted and plans which offer promise for further development in this very important phase of education. The members of this Board are unanimously of the opinion that every child, if his life is to be well based, must come under the effective influence of the church, the home, and the school. We do not believe, however, that it is either necessary or desirable that the child's contact with his church should occur during the time that he is required by law to spend in attendance at public school.

We are opposed to a program of Released Time Religious Education because such a program might have the effect of violating the principle of separation of church and state which is so fundamental a concept in American democracy. Moreover, we have found no indication either in

[9] Report and Recommendations of the Committee of the Whole, Adopted by the Harrisburg, Pennsylvania, Board of School Directors, *Liberty,* Third Quarter, 1946 (Vol. 41, No. 3), p. 32.

the plans presented to us for the local program or in released time programs elsewhere which have been studied through observation and published reports that the purposes of education for character and citizenship would be furthered more effectively by work carried on outside of the schools than by the type of educational activity now being carried on in schools. . . .[10]

In San Diego, California, after nearly a year's trial of dismissed-time for religious education in ten schools of that city, a thorough survey and careful appraisal of the operation and results of the program were made on behalf of the board of education of that city. A public hearing was made available to those who opposed and supported the plan for open discussion of the subject. As a result of the study, on May 13, 1947, the board of education made the following report:

1. The Board of Education represents all the people and is charged with the responsibility of conducting the schools for the best interests of all the people and of all the children.

2. The Board of Education and the individual members thereof, believe wholeheartedly in the necessity for spiritual and religious training in the development of good moral character and citizenship.

3. The development of the spiritual, moral, intellectual and physical faculties of our children is the joint and common responsibility of home, church and school.

4. The schools of San Diego are considered outstanding among school systems for their program of character education.

5. Religious training is the special and particular sphere of the church.

6. Cooperation between home, church and school is necessary to the greatest effectiveness of the work of each and all.

7. In the past 25 or 30 years, the scope and amount of material which the schools are required to teach has been doubled and trebled, but not one minute has been added to the school day.

8. The year's trial of "Released time for religious education" has demonstrated that the program interferes with the progress of school work during the entire day, increases the work of principals and teachers, and results in certain confusion and loss of time to all children in the grade, both those who are released and those who remain. The evidence does not show growth of character or desirable behavior beyond that of the children who did not participate in the released time program. The results do not justify a continuation or extension of the plan.

9. The request for a continuation of the "released time program" falls

[10] "Released School Time for Religious Education," *Liberty,* Third Quarter, 1947, p. 31.

far short of having the support of all the people or even of all the churches or church people.

THEREFORE, RESOLVED that we deny the request for further continuance of "released time for religious education" in the San Diego City Schools;

RESOLVED that we urge the homes and the churches to continue and increase their efforts in spiritual and moral training in their respective spheres;

RESOLVED that we pledge the Board of Education and the schools to continue, in the future as in the past, to stress by every means at our disposal, the teaching of moral and spiritual principles, and character training; and,

RESOLVED, FURTHER, that we pledge earnest cooperation with all worthy plans for religious instruction outside of school time.[11]

A plan for dismissed time for religious education adopted in Wisconsin was ruled to be unconstitutional by the attorney general. Cards asking that children be excused from school one hour each week to receive religious instruction were handed to pupils by the teachers, signed by the parents, returned to the teachers, sorted by them, and passed on to the ministers of the churches designated by such parents. The attorney general [12] decided that public money was being used for religious purposes or for the dissemination of sectarian instruction in public schools, in violation of the provisions of the constitution stating:

nor shall any money be drawn from the treasury for the benefit of religious societies, or religious or theological seminaries.[13]

The legislature shall provide by law for the establishment of district schools, which shall be as nearly uniform as practicable; and such schools shall be free and without charge for tuition to all children between the ages of four and twenty years; and no sectarian instruction shall be allowed therein.[14]

The attorney general ruled that school boards have power to fix hours during which school shall be held and to excuse all pupils or any group of pupils for any reasonable period, provided that neither school boards nor teachers have, as a part of their school work, any direct or indirect connection with the dissemination of religious instruction and that no part of the school machinery is used for that purpose. This may be avoided, of course, by leaving to the parents and the churches the matter of checking on the students after they are dismissed. This ruling in Wisconsin goes a little far-

[11] "Released-Time in San Diego," *Liberty*, Fourth Quarter, 1947, p. 24.
[12] Wisconsin Attorney-General's Opinion 483.
[13] Constitution of Wisconsin, Article 1, Section 18.
[14] *Ibid.*, Article 10, Section 3.

ther than that of New York,[15] which permits the use of a limited amount of school time for registering and checking excuses.[16]

Recently the supreme court of Illinois was called upon to consider the legality of dismissing pupils during school hours to receive religious instruction in the churches of their choice.[17] The practice, which was upheld by the court, consists in excusing pupils for one hour a week to attend classes in religious instruction. It has been in practice in Chicago for a number of years. The board of education of Chicago had adopted a resolution in 1929 authorizing the superintendent to excuse pupils in certain elementary grades, upon written request from their parents for religious instruction.[18]

It appears from the petition presented that out of 249,614 public elementary school pupils, 22,500 are excused for one hour per week, usually the last hour of the day on Wednesday. Pupils receive religious instruction in the Catholic religion at 137 parochial schools and a smaller number of pupils are receiving instruction in the Protestant religions at 57 church buildings of their faith.

In 1943 the state legislature of California made it permissible for pupils with the consent of their parents to be excused from public schools to participate in religious exercises or to receive moral and religious instruction.[19] The law provides that absences in complying with this statute are not counted in computing average daily attendance. However, allocation of state and county school funds are based upon average daily attendance.

The board of education of Los Angeles adopted regulations setting up a plan in compliance with the statute. An interfaith committee was created composed of representatives of various religious denominations, which was to act as a coordinating agent for the denominations participating in the plan. There were a number of denominations, including Catholics, various Protestant groups, and Jews, represented on the committee. At the request of the committee,

[15] People ex rel. Lewis v. Graves; see above, pp. 77–79.

[16] For a description of Bible study as practiced in the Minneapolis schools see the article "Religious Classes Found a Moral Aid" in the *New York Times,* July 5, 1931.

[17] People ex rel. Latimer v. Board of Education of the City of Chicago, 394 Ill. 228, 68 N.E. (2d) 305, 309 (1946).

[18] The board of education of Chicago on August 16, 1929, adopted the following resolution: Proceedings of Board of Education, city of Chicago, August 16, 1929. "The Superintendent of schools recommends that upon the written request of parents, the Superintendent be authorized to excuse pupils in sixth and seventh grade classes one hour a week to attend classes for instruction in religion. Reason: A group of citizens and patrons of the public schools in the Lake View Community have petitioned for the release of their children for religious instruction in nearby churches. This follows the precedent of releasing children to attend Confirmation Classes in accordance with the State Law."

[19] Sec. 8286 of the Education Code of the State of California (1943).

the board of education caused to be sent to parents of pupils in the Los Angeles schools, literature describing the plan, and cards that the parents might return to the board. The cards contained a form for the parents to sign consenting to their children taking part in the plan and designating the faith they were to be taught. The expense involved in the preparation, printing, mimeographing, and mailing of the literature and cards was paid by the public school system. Teachers and superintendents of the schools were directed to keep attendance records and to oversee the working of the plan. Children are segregated according to the preferences expressed by their parents regarding religious instruction and are transported from the school grounds to the places arranged by the interfaith committee and there taught the doctrines of the church to which they have been assigned.

Expenses of transportation are not paid by the public schools nor are the officers and teachers of the school responsible for the children during their absence from school. Children not participating in the program remain in school and such instruction as they may receive is optional with their teacher.

The constitutionality of Section 8286 of the education code making provision for the program was challenged by certain school patrons [20] as being in conflict with various sections of the state constitution. Section 4 of Article 1 provides that "the free exercise and enjoyment of religious profession and worship, without discrimination or preference, shall forever be guaranteed in this state . . ." Section 8 of Article 9 prohibits the appropriation of any public money for the support of any sectarian or denominational school; "nor shall any sectarian or denominational doctrine be taught, or instruction thereon be permitted, directly or indirectly, in any of the common schools of this State." Further, Section 30 of Article 4 prohibits appropriating or granting anything "in aid of any religious sect, church, creed, or sectarian purpose."

It was further alleged that the practice of excusing pupils for religious instruction was developing religious prejudices and ill will among pupils and parents.

The court decision held that neither the California law nor the Los Angeles dismissed time plan is prohibited by the constitution. The court failed to sustain the plaintiff's charge of sectarian antagonism and ill feeling resulting from the conduct of the plan; the

[20] Gordon v. Board of Education of City of Los Angeles et al., 178 Pac. (2d) 488 (District Court of Appeal, Second District, Division I, March 10, 1947).

results of the dismissed time plan, the court held, is a matter of discretion of the board of education with which the courts will not interfere.

Just a few weeks before this California case, Vashti McCollum brought mandamus proceedings in the supreme court of Illinois against the board of education of School District 71 to prohibit released time for religious education in the public school during hours when the public schools are regularly in session and where the teachers of religion came directly into the public school classrooms to do their teaching.[21]

James Terry McCollum, son of Vashti McCollum, around whom the case centers, entered the fourth grade of the district school in the fall of 1943 and along with five others did not participate in the religious education classes during the first semester. He did, however, participate with his mother's consent, during the second semester. Later he transferred from the south-side school, at his mother's request, and enrolled in fifth grade in the Dr. Howard School, and with one other youngster, Elwin Miller, did not attend the religious education classes the first semester. During the second semester, he was the only pupil not participating in the class for religious instruction.

While other members of his class attended the religious education classes, he continued his regular studies in the music room, under the supervision of his regular teacher. On one occasion he was placed at a desk in the hall where it appears he was teased by passing children, who thought he was being punished. On complaint of his mother, this practice was promptly and permanently discontinued, as was that of placing him in the music room when his mother claimed he was a victim of claustrophobia.

The evidence showed that in the fall of 1940 the Champaign Council of Religious Education, a voluntary association of Jewish, Roman Catholic, and Protestant faiths, was formed. They secured permission from the board of education of Champaign School District 71 to offer classes in religious instruction in grades four through nine. Qualified instructors, all materials, and books, as well as incidentals, were to be furnished at the expense of the council. The teachers of the religion classes were not to be teachers in the public schools, but were to be subject to the approval and supervision of the superintendent. Admission to the classes was to be allowed only

[21] People ex rel. McCollum v. Board of Education of School District No. 71, Champaign County, Ill., 396 Ill. 14, 71 N.E. (2d) 161 (January 22, 1947).

upon the express written request of parents and then only to classes designated by the parents. The children were to be excused from attendance in the grade schools for thirty minutes and from the junior high school for forty-five minutes each week to participate in the religious education classes.

Classes were to be scheduled so as not to interfere with the regular school classes, after consultation with the public school teacher. Each faith — Catholic, Jewish, and Protestant — was to have its separate instructional classes, and no expense in connection with the classes was to be borne by the public school. Additional groups were to be freely permitted to participate upon the same terms. Lesson materials and curriculum were to be selected by a committee representing all groups participating and in a manner to avoid any offensive doctrinal, dogmatic, or sectarian teaching. The teaching was to be of Biblical content without interpretation of or attempt to influence belief in the doctrines or creeds of any church.

It should be noted that the classes in religious education were held during school hours and in the regular teaching rooms in the public school buildings which were temporarily turned over to the religious education teachers.

It was charged that the plan constituted the use of public funds for sectarian educational purposes in violation of the constitution of Illinois and the School Code of that state [22] in the additional use of school buildings for independent religious instruction, the additional services of public school teachers, the frequent movement of students from room to room, and in additional expenses in carrying on religious instruction. In answer to these charges, the court held that since the schoolrooms were in use during the current school periods, no doubt the same cost for lights, heat, janitor service and other expenses would exist whether or not the schoolrooms were used at the particular time by these particular classes in religion.

Likewise, any additional wear and tear on the floors and furniture would seem to be inconsequential, and there was no direct appropriation or expenditure of money of any kind for or on behalf of the religious education classes. The court further held that such classes

do not violate the freedom of conscience of any individual or group so long as the classes are conducted upon a purely voluntary basis. Freedom of religion as intended by those who wrote the State and Federal consti-

[22] Section 3 of Article 3 and Section 3 of Article 8 of the constitution; and Section 15–14 of the School Code of Illinois.

tutions means the right of an individual to entertain any desired religious belief without interference from the state. Our government very wisely refuses to recognize a specific religion, but this cannot mean that the government does not recognize or subscribe to religious ideals.

After the supreme court of Illinois had upheld the board of education, the case was appealed to the Supreme Court of the United States.[23] Here the decision of the Illinois court was reversed. Mr. Justice Black in delivering the opinion of the court said:

The foregoing facts, without reference to others that appear in the record, show the use of tax-supported property for religious instruction and the close cooperation between the school authorities and the religious council in promoting religious education. The operation of the state's compulsory education system thus assists and is integrated with the program of religious instruction carried on by separate religious sects. Pupils compelled by law to go to school for secular education are released in part from their legal duty upon the condition that they attend the religious classes. This is beyond all question a utilization of the tax-established and tax-supported public school system to aid religious groups to spread their faith. And it falls squarely under the ban of the First Amendment (made applicable to the States by the Fourteenth) as we interpreted it in *Everson v. Board of Education,* 330 U. S. 1. . . . Here not only are the state's tax-supported public school buildings used for the dissemination of religious doctrines. The State also affords sectarian groups an invaluable aid in that it helps to provide pupils for their religious classes through use of the state's compulsory public school machinery. This is not separation of church and state.

Here for the first time the United States Supreme Court passed upon the constitutionality of a released time program for religious education. In this case the teachers of religion came into the public school buildings and held their classes. It still leaves unsettled other phases of released and dismissed time programs which vary from the Champaign plan. From references which appear in the opinions of the court, there may be some question as to constitutionality where there is undue participation by the public schools. On the other hand, it seems highly probable that the courts are not likely to question the practice of dismissed time for religious education, which in its simplest form consists of shortening one school day to allow all children to go where they please, leaving those who desire to go to the place of their choice for religious instruction or to go to their homes.

[23] People ex rel. McCollum v. Board of Education of School District No. 71, Champaign County, Illinois et al., 16 L.W. 4224 (March 8, 1948).

CHAPTER VI

Allowing Credit for Religious Instruction

ANOTHER question that has arisen in connection with excusing pupils from school to receive religious instruction is whether credit may be given for such work by the public schools and applied toward graduation. It also includes the question of whether or not credit may be given for courses in religion taught in the public schools.

It was decided in the Washington case of State ex rel. Dearle v. Frazier, that credit may not be given in that state for religious instruction received outside the school.[1] Here action was brought by Albert Dearle, a pupil, against Frazier, superintendent of schools, to force Frazier to give him an examination in Bible study, which he had done outside of school, and to allow him credit to be applied toward high school graduation.

In 1915 the state board of education had passed the following resolution:

> Since the board looks with favor upon allowing credits for Bible study done outside of school, it is moved that a committee be appointed to consider a plan for allowing such credits, one-half credit to be given for Old Testament and one-half credit for New Testament on the basis of thirty to thirty-two credits for high school graduation, and that a syllabus of Bible study be issued under the auspices of the state department of education with rules and regulations for the distribution of examination questions at least once a year.[2]

In compliance with this plan a number of schools made provision for outside Bible study. The school was to pay for the syllabus, give the examination, grade the papers, and determine the credit.

The constitution of Washington includes these provisions against the use of public money for any religious exercises or instruction:

> No public money or property shall be appropriated for or applied to

[1] 102 Wash. 369 (1918).
[2] Ibid.

any religious worship, exercise, or instruction, or the support of any religious establishment.

All schools maintained or supported wholly or in part by the public funds shall be forever free from sectarian control or influence.[3]

A Washington statute provides that "It shall be the duty of all teachers to endeavor to impress on the minds of their pupils the principles of morality, truth, justice, temperance, humanity, and patriotism; to teach them to avoid idleness, profanity, and falsehood . . ."[4]

The court by unanimous decision held that the practice provided for in the resolution adopted by the state board of education in 1915 constituted an expenditure of public funds for "religious worship, exercise, or instruction," or for the support of a "religious establishment," which was prohibited by the constitution. The court built up its argument primarily on statements in the constitution: "No public money or property shall be appropriated for or applied to any religious worship, exercise, or instruction . . ."[5] and "All schools maintained or supported wholly or in part by the public funds shall be forever free from sectarian control or influence."[6] These words, the court said, "are sweeping and comprehensive." Not only are "religious exercises" and "instruction" prohibited, "but their natural consequences — religious discussion and controversy." The court pointed out that if the pupil answered in a way that was consistent with the faith of his instructor, he would undoubtedly be counted worthy of a passing grade and receive credit for his work, but that such an arrangement is open to objections on the ground that the examiner may not know the faith and teachings of those of a different sect. Furthermore, to give credit in the public school for such instruction is to give credit for sectarian teaching and influence, which is forbidden by the constitution. The court said:

It is no more than a subterfuge to urge that the public moneys will not be applied for religious instruction because the teaching is done outside the school by a preacher or priest, or in the home of the pupil, or by a religious organization with which the student may be affiliated, for the time of the teachers, as well as their technical skill, will be consumed while under the pay of the state in furnishing the syllabus or outline, the

[3] Constitution of Washington, Article 1, Section 11; Article 9, Section 4.
[4] Washington Laws (Pierce), 1929, Section 5051.
[5] Constitution of Washington, Article 1, Section 11.
[6] Ibid., Article 9, Section 4.

conducting of examinations, the rating of papers, and the determining of proper credits.

The court took the position that a compromise of opinions in these matters would lead to confusion and would result in making the courts the judge in determining what is and what is not religious worship, instruction, or influence. This, it maintained, would be as intolerable to the citizen as it would be to leave the decision to a school board. It is on that basis that some courts have upheld the constitutionality of Bible reading where statutes did not specifically prohibit such reading. Such courts, said the Washington justices,

have inclined to the letter rather than to the spirit of the constitution.

What guarantee has the citizen that the board, having a contrary faith, will not inject those passages upon which its own sect rests its claim to be the true church under the guise of "narrative or literary features"; and if they did so, where would the remedy be found? Surely the courts could not control their discretion, for judges are made of the same stuff as other men . . .

There was no discussion of the policy of excusing the children for religious instruction, the question here involved being whether credit might be given for such instruction. The practice of opening school each morning with prayer as well as reading the Bible is prohibited by opinions rendered by the attorney general.[7]

A number of states allow credit for Bible study. Some of them require this study to be done in conjunction with the state department of education. An example of such practice is found in West Virginia. In 1919 the state board of education adopted a plan of accredited Bible study issued by the West Virginia Council of Religious Education. The Council declares:

This happy consummation is a result of the work of the joint committee representing the State Sunday School Association and the State Education Association . . .

The executive committee of the West Virginia Sunday School Association . . . approved and endorsed the plan as did the West Virginia Education Association. . . . The action of these two bodies was reported to the State Board of Education with the result above reported.

By this action "the West Virginia Commission on Accredited Bible Study" was created, to consist of five members as follows: The general superintendent of the West Virginia Sunday School Association, the state supervisor of high schools, one member elected by the State Board of Edu-

[7] Opinions of the Washington State Attorney-General, 1915–16, p. 254; 1909–10, p. 135; 1891–92, p. 142.

cation, one member elected by the West Virginia Council of Religious Education, one member elected by the West Virginia Education Association.[8]

In the West Virginia plan one high school credit is allowed for Bible study. This credit may be substituted for any elective appearing in the regular high school course. The teacher of the Bible study for which the pupils seek high school credit must meet the academic and professional requirements of the high school in which the credit is sought. Certain equipment is required. Each class must be held in a separate room, which must "be equipped with tables, maps, charts, blackboards, cases for books, and a reference library of at least six (6) volumes, one of which must be a good Bible dictionary." A recitation period of at least forty-five minutes is required. Examinations are to be held twice each year concurrently with the regular semester examinations.

These examinations shall be conducted under the direction of the principal of the high school in which the credit is sought. When the work is done in the high school under arrangement and direction of the principal, papers should be set and examined by the teachers as in all other courses. This applies both when the course is taught by a regular member of the faculty, and by anyone not a member.[9]

Where the Bible course is taken outside school for credit, the commission takes charge of preparing the examinations and grading the papers. The commission has also prepared a syllabus for these Bible courses, which, it states, "are not intended to be made a part of public school teaching, nor are public school funds to be used to provide this Bible teaching." Any version of the Bible may be used — the King James, the American Revised, the Douay, or the Leesser. Whenever a local high school board in West Virginia approves the above plan, it automatically goes into effect in that school, and the Bible syllabus becomes an elective course.

The commission points out that it has found that the state university and all normal schools, as well as the denominational schools and colleges in West Virginia, will accept one unit of credit in Bible study from any of the accredited high schools in the state as one of the units required for college entrance.

The expenses incurred in promotion work are, at the request of the commission, paid by the West Virginia Council of Religious

[8] West Virginia Council of Religious Education Department Leaflet No. 504 (Charleston, 1925).
[9] *Ibid.*

Education. A report issued by this organization on January 1, 1926, showed that thirty-nine classes had been conducted, with an enrollment of 628.[10]

The state of Indiana has adopted a plan for Bible study that is virtually the same as the one West Virginia is following.

In 1916 the state board of education of Virginia authorized certain accredited Bible courses for high school pupils. A commission representing Catholic, Jewish, and Protestant churches was appointed. In the school year 1916-17 one class of 27 pupils prepared for examination in such a course; in the year 1923-24 there were forty classes with an enrollment of 933 pupils.[11] As is the case in most of the states allowing credit for such Bible study, the teaching may be done in Sunday schools, Sabbath schools, vacation schools, YMCA or YWCA classes, or in private schools or classes.

North Dakota has a plan of Bible study for high school students whereby "high school students may take Bible study in the Sunday school, parochial classes, or in separately organized classes, and secure one unit of credit toward graduation." The department of public instruction sets up the standards under which the work must be done, conducts the examinations and issues the credits, and the North Dakota Council of Religious Education "prints the outlines, handles the books, and helps organize the classes." [12] The syllabus for the course consists of a brief outline of the Old and New Testaments, one half unit of credit being allowed for each. The minimum requirement as to text and reference materials is that each student have a copy of the syllabus and a Bible. The instructor should have one map, two reference books for each Testament, and a Bible dictionary for the use of the class. Wherever it is desired to organize a Bible study class, the ministers of the churches consult and arrange with the principal or superintendent of the local high school. No definite amount of time is required to be spent upon the course. The contents of the syllabus may be mastered privately or by class study. No state or public school buildings may be used for religious instruction, nor may such instruction be given by public school teachers during school hours.

---

[10] Report accompanying the West Virginia Council of Religious Education Leaflet No. 504. The figures are obviously for a year's enrollment, but the report is not clear whether they are for the school year 1924-25 or 1925-26.

[11] Official Syllabus of Bible Study for High School Pupils, Virginia State Board of Education Bulletin, Vol. 4, No. 1.

[12] *The North Dakota Plan of Bible Study for High School Students* (Department of Public Instruction, Bismarck).

Maine has an accredited Bible study plan which has been in operation for several years. According to Bertram E. Packard, former state commissioner of education, the plan provides for Bible study conducted by the churches outside the public schools with the aid of outside teachers.[13] The examinations are conducted by the state and credit is given for the work. These credits are accepted by the public high schools, colleges, and universities of the state. According to the commissioner of education, the state department of education desires to encourage religious education but "does not think it wise to enter definitely upon the task of teaching the Bible, for that would tend to break down the principle of the separation of church and state, which, on the whole, has justified itself in American life."

Colorado also has a plan of Bible study, for which credit is allowed toward high school graduation. The plan was worked out with the teachers college at Greeley, Colorado. The experience there led to working out a plan for high school students in other parts of the state.

One of the states that has recently adopted a most elaborate course of study in Bible history is Montana. Elizabeth Ireland, former state superintendent of public instruction, explains its origin thus:

During 1929–30 the Montana State Department of Public Instruction received numerous requests from individual clergymen, from representatives of the ministerial associations in Montana, and from superintendents and principals of high schools for a course of study in Bible history. After a thorough investigation and examination of many courses of study, it was recommended by the Montana clergy and ministerial associations that the Michigan course of study be adopted for use in Montana.[14]

Arrangements were accordingly made and permission was secured to use the Michigan syllabus in the Montana schools. This 172-page syllabus contains outlines of courses and a great number of notes and other discussion. The course outlined includes Great Old Testament Characters, The Bible as Literature, The Life of Christ, The First Century of the Christian Church, The Bible in the Making, The Life of Christ in Picture, Song, and Story, Old Testament History, The Bible as an Interpreter of the Interrelations of Social Institutions and a Guide to Right Living, Biblical Allusions, The Exodus, The Deliverance at the Red Sea, The Waters of Marah, The Quail and the

[13] "Encouraging Religious Education," *United States Daily,* April 25, 1931, p. 10.

[14] Course of Study, State of Montana, Bible History, Syllabi I, II, III (Helena, 1932), published in Montana with the permission of the Michigan Education Association by the state superintendent of public instruction.

Manna, The Smitten Rock, The War with Amalek, The Golden Calf, Moses on Mt. Sinai, and others. Considerable memory work is required. The Ten Commandments are to be memorized, and complete passages of about twenty verses from such selections as the discouragement of Elijah (I Kings 19:1–18), the building of the wall (Nehemiah 4:15–23), the prayer for pardon (Psalms 51:1–19), the transient and the eternal (Psalms 90:1–27), Daniel's being cast into the den of lions (Daniel 6:16–23), and God's rule on earth (Isaiah 2:2–4). The syllabus contains such controversial questions as the creation; the Garden of Eden; the temptation of Eve and sin; Noah, the ark, and the flood; the Ten Commandments; and the divinity of Christ and His miracles.[15] At once the question arises, How are such subjects going to be taught in the public schools? If the answer is that they are taught outside the public schools, then such questions present themselves as, How are the examinations to be given? the papers to be graded? The courses here outlined differ little from courses of Bible study taught in church and denominational schools.[16]

Some years ago there was a controversy between the interfaith committee and the teachers' union of Greater New York over the question of having religion taught to high school students outside of school hours by instructors paid by the churches, and of allowing such students regents' credits for the work taken.[17] The teachers' union protested against allowing such credits as substitutes for secular studies on the ground that it was a violation of the spirit of the principle of the separation of church and state, if not of the letter of the law.

The interfaith committee, which was composed of a certain group of leaders in the Catholic, Jewish, and Protestant faiths, asked for the privilege of instructing high school students of Greater New York in the fundamentals of religion, this instruction to be given outside the school by special instructors paid by the churches. They also requested the school authorities to grant school credits for such religious instruction. When this request was made, the American Association for the Advancement of Atheism likewise petitioned the superintendent of schools in New York to allow their association to have access to these same high school students for the purpose

[15] *Ibid.*

[16] For plans and proposals for allowing credit for outside Bible study in the different states and in various institutions, see Clarence Ashton Wood, *School and College Credit for Outside Bible Study* (New York, 1917).

[17] "Bible Study for New York School Pupils," *Literary Digest*, July 4, 1931, p. 26.

of instructing them in atheism, this instruction likewise to be given outside school hours, by special instructors, and at the expense of the association, and to allow regents' credit for such instruction.

This plan of allowing credit in the public schools for religious instruction has provoked a storm of protest from Catholics, Jews, and Protestants alike. In protesting against the allowance of credit for religious instruction given under the control and direction of religious organizations, the teachers' union seems to have the best of the argument. It declares that such a departure violates the constitution of the state of New York, which reads:

Neither the state, nor any subdivision thereof, shall use its property or credit or any public money, or authorize and permit either to be used, directly or indirectly, in aid or maintenance, other than for examination or inspection, of any school or institution of learning wholly or in part under the control or direction of any religious denomination, or in which any denominational tenet or doctrine is taught.[18]

Aside from the constitutional question involved, there is serious question of the advisability of allowing public school credit toward graduation for religious instruction given by religious teachers under denominational control. The public school system was established for the purpose of giving secular instruction and the church for imparting spiritual instruction, each to work independently in its own sphere. Giving school credit for study and instruction in the church is likely to provoke religious controversy; it may pave the way for still greater encroachments, and may ultimately even open the door to all the evil conditions that attend a union of church and state.

If the state is to grant scholastic credit for religious instruction given under the control of the interfaith committee in the Douay, King James, and Jewish versions, then it is difficult to say on what ground it can refuse similar credit for religious instruction given by leaders of paganism, Mormonism, Christian Science, spiritualism, Swedenborgianism, Buddhism, or Brahmanism. These religions exist in America, and many of them are educating their followers and children in their own religious institutions and at their own expense. It is quite likely that the interfaith committee would object to allowing credit for such teaching, and if it did, it would be guilty of discrimination contrary to the constitution of New York, which provides that "no discrimination or preference" of religion shall be made by law against any citizen on "religious profession."[19]

[18] Constitution of New York, Article 9, Section 4.
[19] *Ibid.*, Bill of Rights.

In the past the movements for a union of church and state, whether they have been Catholic or Protestant, have always been inaugurated with mild measures that appeared innocent enough on the surface. The first step has always been a union of divergent church forces, which have taken the initiative in the preliminary steps. After these divergent church forces have gained the necessary strength and popularity, they have sent out feelers toward the political institutions, in the hope of obtaining cooperation and political aid for the furtherance of church ends. What were first considered voluntary and suggestive measures afterward resolved themselves into ecclesiastical and political coercion.

By some it is feared that any plan of religious instruction for credit will ultimately result in the teaching of religion by the state. That, they say, is virtually what a number of the states are doing today. There is but one way to escape from such a contingency and that is to deny to the state the authority to meddle with religious questions or to form any kind of alliance with church and religion. Only as this demarcation between the functions of the church and those of the state is kept distinct can we protect and safeguard the rights of the citizen and preserve the stability of religion. The fact that a state excludes religion from its educational curriculum and allows credit only for secular studies does not mean that the civil government is hostile to the Bible, to religion, or to religious teaching. It is only evidence of its neutrality toward all sects, which cannot be maintained except by excluding religion from its curriculum. This attitude of neutrality and the exclusion of religion from the curriculum is in fact friendliness toward the Bible and the church, since only by a rigid separation of secular and church affairs can the church have the benefits of religious tranquillity and peace.

CHAPTER VII

Public Aid to Sectarian Schools

THE line between the interest of the state and the interest of the church in the education of children and youth has never been clearly drawn. One group of cases has been concerned with instances where tax money has been voted to aid church-related schools. Another group comprises cases in which the local school boards, because of lack of facilities and of sufficient funds to provide them, have occupied parochial school quarters, and cooperated in certain particulars with the parochial schools in meeting the expense of the combined school. The constitutional question in the first group of cases is whether the state is imparting sectarian and doctrinal instruction. In the second group, the question is whether the state is supporting a religious establishment, in violation of the First Amendment of the federal Constitution, or more precisely, similar provisions in state constitutions.

An early case was decided in Massachusetts in 1869. The schoolhouse of a private school, the Punchard Free School, serving the town of Andover, had burned down, and the state legislature had authorized the town to raise by taxation a sum of money to rebuild it. The court ruled the measure unconstitutional.[1] A Wisconsin case involving the question of public support for the "Jefferson Liberal Institute," a private school at Jefferson, Wisconsin, was decided the same way.[2] A few years later it was ruled in Illinois that the "Hamilton Primary School" might not benefit by the expenditure of public funds.[3]

In agreement with these court decisions was one by the Mississippi court,[4] that an act allowing children to receive the same share of a public fund for attendance at a private school of a certain grade as

---

[1] William Jenkins & Others v. Inhabitants of Andover & Others, 103 Mass. 94.
[2] Curtis's Admin. v. Whipple and Others, 24 Wis. 350 (1869).
[3] The People of the State of Illinois v. William McAdams, 82 Ill. 356 (1876).
[4] Otken v. Lamkin, 56 Miss. 758 (1879). The court held that while the public schools of Mississippi were open to all children within the ages of five to twenty-one years, "this freedom

for attendance in the public schools was a violation of the constitutional provision that

> No religious or other sect . . . shall ever control any part of the school or other educational funds of this state; nor shall any funds be appropriated toward the support of any sectarian school, or to any school that at the time of receiving such appropriation is not conducted as a free school.[5]

A question now arose as to whether a school conducted in a sectarian asylum was a school. It is difficult to understand how a school conducted and maintained in connection with an orphan asylum is different from a grade school conducted in connection with some church or college, or why one should be entitled to appropriations from the public funds any more than the other.

This principle was recognized by the supreme court of Nevada in a case concerning the Nevada Orphan Asylum, a Catholic institution which sought money from state funds.[6] The controller refused to draw the money on the grounds that it constituted an appropriation of public funds for sectarian purposes. The court held that the orphan asylum here in question was a sectarian institution, that the money sought would be used for sectarian purposes, and that consequently the payment of it would be a violation of the constitution, which provides that "no public funds of any kind or character whatever, state, county, or municipal, shall be used for sectarian purposes."[7]

The court declared:

> Under the provisions of our constitution, neither Christianity nor any other system of religion is a part of the law of this state. We have no union of church and state, nor has our government ever been vested with authority to enforce any religious observance simply because it is religion.

The position taken by the Nevada courts is in general agreement with the American principle of complete separation of church and state.[8]

---

of admission to all will not preclude the classification of the schools according to the age, sex, race, or mental acquirements of the pupils — provided, only, that they remain free to all who come within the class to which the particular school is set apart."

[5] Constitution of Mississippi, Article 8, Section 208.

[6] State ex rel. Nevada Orphan Asylum v. Hallock, 16 Nev. 373 (1882).

[7] Constitution of Nevada, Article 11, Section 10.

[8] Congress by statute authorized the incorporation of a hospital in the city of Washington for the care of sick and incapacitated persons. The act set forth the powers and duties of the corporation. Subsequently Congress appropriated money for a building to be erected in connection with this institution at the discretion of an administrative officer of the government. The officer decided that the building should be erected in connection with the hospital. Complaint was brought in an effort to prevent the use of the money appropriated for this purpose

In an Illinois case [9] involving the appropriation of public funds to the Chicago Industrial School for Girls, it was held that the payment by Cook County of the tuition and maintenance of dependent girls committed to this school was prohibited by the constitutional provision which reads:

Neither the general assembly nor any county, city, town, township, school district, or other public corporation shall ever make any appropriation or pay from any public fund whatever, anything in aid of any church or sectarian purpose, or to help support or sustain any school, academy, seminary, college, university, or other literary or scientific institution, controlled by any church or sectarian denomination whatever; nor shall any grant or donation of land, money, or other personal property ever be made by the state or any such corporation, to any church, or for any sectarian purpose. [10]

The Chicago Industrial School for Girls was a corporation. It did not conduct a school, nor did it own nor lease any building, but it placed the girls committed to it in certain institutions under the control of the Roman Catholic church. The payments, though made to the Chicago Industrial School, went in fact to the particular institutions to which the girls were committed. From the appropriations made, the girls received tuition and general maintenance, including board, room, clothing, and medical care.

This same institution was involved also in a later case. [11] In this instance the court sustained a payment made to it. The institution was under the control and management of the Roman Catholic church and in charge of a mother superior. Religious services were held in a chapel on the grounds according to the doctrines of the church, and attendance of all the inmates was required. The sum paid for each person was less than the amount required to maintain and keep a girl in a similar state institution. The payments were made only for girls of Catholic parents who were committed to the institution by the juvenile court.

In New York also a question arose regarding the legality of state

on the ground that the action would be a violation of the constitutional provision relating to the establishment of a religion. Though the hospital had accepted patients without respect to their religious faith, the members of the corporation were of a monastic order of the church. In denying the petition the court held that so long as the hospital is managed in accordance with the statute of its incorporation, the fact that its conduct may be influenced by persons of a particular religious faith does not result in the establishment of any religion in violation of the first amendment to the constitution. Bradfield v. Roberts, 175 U.S. 291 (1899).

[9] Cook County v. Chicago Industrial School, 125 Ill. 540, 18 N.E. 183 (1888).

[10] Constitution of Illinois, Article 8, Section 3.

[11] Dunn v. Chicago Industrial School, 280 Ill. 613, 117 N.E. 735 (1917).

aid to an orphan asylum under sectarian control.[12] The court held that an orphan asylum is neither a school nor an institution of learning; that the constitutional provision that neither the state nor any subdivision should give financial aid to any school or institution of learning wholly or in part under the control of a religious denomination, or in which any denominational tenet or doctrine is taught,[13] had no application to an orphan asylum; and that state aid of a privately owned orphan asylum would be justified by the following constitutional provision:

Nothing in this constitution contained shall prevent the legislature from making such provision for the education and support of the blind, the deaf and dumb, and juvenile delinquents as to it may seem proper; or prevent any county, city, town, or village from providing for the care, support, maintenance, and secular education of inmates of orphan asylums, homes for dependent children, or correctional institutions, whether under public or private control. Payments by counties, cities, towns, and villages to charitable, eleemosynary, correctional, and reformatory institutions, wholly or partly under private control, for care, support, and maintenance, may be authorized, but shall not be required by the legislature. No such payments shall be made for any inmate of such institutions who is not received and retained therein pursuant to rules established by the state board of charities.[14]

The court thus sustained the action of a city in paying the salaries of four teachers in St. Mary's Boys' Orphan Asylum as a contribution toward the secular education of the orphans in the asylum. It was shown that the education corresponded to that furnished to children in the public schools of the city. The asylum might be visited by the state board of charities. No denominational doctrine was taught, nor was any religious instruction imparted during the school hours prescribed by the state board of education.[15]

Another case involving eleemosynary services came before the

[12] Sargent v. Board of Education, 177 N.Y. 317, 69 N.E. 722 (1904), affirming 76 App. Div. 588, 79 N.Y.S. 127 (1902), which affirmed 35 Misc. 321, 71 N.Y.S. 954 (1901).

[13] Constitution of New York, Article 9, Section 4.

[14] Constitution of New York, Article 8, Section 14.

[15] In New York it was held that where waterworks had been leased to a private concern for a term of years with the right to sell or rent water to private concerns or individuals, but with the provision that water should be furnished free to all "school-houses," no mention being made of whether these were private or public schools, the furnishing of such free water was not a violation of Article 9, Section 4, of the constitution, which reads: "Neither the state nor any subdivision thereof, shall use its property or credit or any public money . . . in aid or maintenance, other than for examination or inspection, of any school or institution of learning wholly or in part under the control or direction of any religious denomination, or in which any denominational tenet or doctrine is taught." St. Patrick's Church Society v. Heermans, 124 N.Y.S. 705, 68 Misc. 487 (1910).

supreme court of Georgia in 1922. The court held that when the city of La Grange made a contract with the Salvation Army by which the latter, a sectarian institution, assumed the care of the poor of that city, although at actual cost, that was giving a great advantage and substantial aid to the Salvation Army in the prosecution of its benevolent and religious purposes. The court said:

The giving of loaves and fishes is a powerful instrumentality in the successful prosecution of the work of a sectarian institution. So we are of the opinion that the taking of money from the public treasury of the city of La Grange, in payment to the Salvation Army for its care of the poor of that city, amounts to the taking of money from its treasury, directly and indirectly, in aid of this sectarian institution, in violation of this provision of the Constitution of Georgia.

So we are of the opinion that the court erred in refusing to grant an injunction restraining the execution of the contract between the city and the Salvation Army, and the judgment of the lower court is therefore reversed.

The Georgia court disagreed with the reasoning of the supreme court of Illinois in the case of Dunn v. Chicago Industrial School discussed above, stating:

It is true that the Constitution of Illinois does not declare hostility to religion. So the Constitution of Georgia does not declare hostility to religion. The Constitution of Illinois declares in favor of religious liberty; so does the Constitution of Georgia. The Constitution of Illinois exempts property used for religious purposes from taxation; so does the Constitution of Georgia. But both Constitutions declare against giving aid to sectarian schools and institutions. When the state selects a sectarian institution of learning, and commits to such institution its wards, for whose maintenance and education it pays, it gives the most substantial aid to such an institution. On the same principle the state could undertake to educate all its children in such sectarian institution, and pay them for the education of its children in such institution rather than in public schools and public institutions of learning. Any such course would be giving the most valuable aid to such sectarian schools and institutions.[16]

Sectarian involvements with public funds had in the meantime emerged in a number of school cases. One of these was in Illinois in 1887. A district board had established a public school, paying from public funds a rent of six hundred dollars for ten months, in the basement of a Catholic church, and had employed Catholic teachers. The record does not indicate whether these teachers wore a distinctive

[16] Bennett v. City of La Grange, 153 Ga. 428, 112 S.E. 482.

religious garb, but mass and catechism instruction were conducted before school session began in the morning, and the Angelus prayer was offered after twelve o'clock. When a taxpayer's suit was brought, the court ruled that "as to the first allegation, that the schools have been maintained in the basement of a Catholic church, no importance whatever can be attached to a fact of that character. . . . The school authorities may select a teacher who belongs to any church, or no church, as they may think best." No public funds, the court said, could be used to teach any sectarian doctrine, but the mere maintaining of a public school in a denominational building is not giving aid to religion.[17]

While South Dakota was still a territory it had entered into a contract with Pierre University, a Presbyterian college, to have students sent there by the territorial authorities, to be given teacher training at territorial expense. When the state was organized, the payments were stopped; the college sued and the case reached the supreme court of South Dakota.[18] The constitution of that state specifies that "no money or property of the state shall be given or appropriated for the benefit of any sectarian or religious society or institution"; that no part of the state school fund "shall ever be diverted . . . or used for any other purpose whatever than the maintenance of public schools"; and that "no appropriation of lands, money, or other property or credits to aid any sectarian school shall ever be made by the state . . ."[19]

The court declared that these constitutional provisions forbid the payment by the state of the tuition of a designated class of students in a sectarian university for instruction in the methods of teaching in the public schools.

A ruling in Kansas emphasized that while taxes may be authorized and, under certain conditions, levied for the maintenance of public institutions of learning, such levy must not be for private and sectarian institutions; and officers of a city have no right to impose a tax on the property of citizens in aid of private or sectarian schools.[20]

In a Wisconsin case in 1908, the record shows that school district officers had rented rooms in a Roman Catholic parochial school for twenty years, and had hired nuns in clerical garb as teachers, who had conducted prayers each morning during school hours. All the

[17] Millard v. Board of Education, 10 N.E. 669.
[18] Dakota Synod v. State, 2 S.D. 366, 50 N.W. 632 (1891).
[19] Constitution of South Dakota, Article 6, Section 3; Article 8, Sections 3, 16.
[20] In Atchison, T. & S. F. R. Co. v. Atchison, 47 Kans. 712, 28 Pac. 1000 (1892).

pupils had been Roman Catholic throughout the period concerned, except one or two occasionally. A lower court

found that the school so conducted had at all times been pervaded and characterized by sectarian instruction contrary to law, and granted injunction against continued maintenance thereof, but held that it was within the power of the school district and board to rent rooms as they deemed wise for the maintenance of a distinctively public school, and therefore refused to enjoin the maintenance thereof in the parochial school building.[21]

The state supreme court affirmed the ruling.

The question of whether or not the constitution of Massachusetts prohibited money raised by taxation from being appropriated to maintain or aid any church, religious denomination or society, or any school wholly or in part under sectarian control, was submitted to the justices of the Massachusetts court for an opinion.[22] In the opinion rendered they took the position that all money raised by taxation for the public or common schools must be used exclusively for the support of such schools, that it cannot be diverted to any other school maintained in whole or in part by any religious sect.[23]

In Kentucky the board of trustees of a common school district arranged with Stanton College, a Presbyterian institution, for two rooms in the building of the latter. The public school district board paid the two teachers who taught the sixth, seventh, and eighth grades. The other grades were taught by other Stanton College teachers. County high school pupils attended Stanton College, to which the county board of education paid out of the public school fund a tuition fee of two dollars a month per high school pupil. This arrangement was satisfactory to a large majority of the school patrons. Some, however, objected.[24] Evidence showed that the school was actually being conducted by Mr. Hanley, president of the college, and that bills for repairs and incidental expenses were paid to Stanton College by the public school board. The graded school district owned no school building.

At a rehearing,[25] in which the earlier decision was reversed, the court held that the arrangement described above constituted an

[21] Dorner et al. v. School District No. 5 et al., 118 N.W. 353, 354.

[22] In re Opinion of the Justices, 214 Mass. 599, 102 N.E. 464 (1913).

[23] It was stated that there is no constitutional stipulation prohibiting appropriations for higher educational institutions, societies, or undertakings under sectarian or ecclesiastical control. Such prohibitions are limited to the common schools, which would undoubtedly include the grades and high schools.

[24] Williams v. Board of Trustees of Stanton Graded School District, 172 Ky. 133, 188 S.W. 1058 (1916).

[25] 173 Ky. 708, 191 S.W. 507 (1917).

appropriation of public funds for sectarian purposes and thus was in violation of the constitutional provision that "no portion of any fund or tax now existing, or that may hereafter be raised or levied for educational purposes, shall be appropriated to, or used by, or in aid of, any church, sectarian or denominational school";[26] and that any arrangement whereby a sectarian school was accepted as a public school was unconstitutional. The court took the position that the constitution of Kentucky provided for the complete separation of public and sectarian schools. The fact that the majority of the patrons approved of the arrangement did not make it constitutional.

Not only was it deemed a violation of the constitution to appropriate any part of the common school fund in aid of any "church, sectarian, or denominational school," but it was also declared unlawful for the trustees of any common or graded school to enter into a contract with any educational institution that was directly or indirectly under the influence, supervision, or control of any denominational or sectarian organization.

In holding that payment of tuition fees for high school pupils out of the public school fund was illegal, the court said:

we may with propriety say in passing that the admitted arrangement between the Board of Education of Powell County and Stanton College, under which Stanton College was created a county high school and paid by the Board of Education out of the common school funds tuition fees for county high school pupils, is a flagrant violation of Section 189 of the constitution . . .

About the year 1910 the school board of Maple River in Iowa, with a population predominantly Catholic, sold its public school property and rented space in a Roman Catholic building, where it arranged for classes to be conducted.

The room was on the upper floor of the parochial school building. The teachers were garbed nuns who conducted worship and taught the catechism. Pictures relating to the Catholic faith were on the walls.

It was as thoroughly and completely a religious parochial school as it could well have been . . . under the special charge and supervision of the church. . . . It was a practical elimination of the public school as such and a transfer of its name and its revenues to the upper department of the parochial school.

The nominal rent specified "was never demanded and never paid."

[26] Constitution of Kentucky, Section 189.

A taxpayer's suit brought the case in the year 1918 before the Iowa supreme court. The court ruled for the plaintiff.

The board of directors had no authority to clothe a religious school with the character of a public school. . . . The state shall be watchful to forbid the use or abuse of any of its functions, powers, or privileges in the interest of any church or creed.[27]

The court also stated:

The trial court's finding in favor of the plaintiff should be sustained. We are of the opinion however, that the decree below should, to a certain extent, be modified. As the parochial building is private property, and its owners and patrons have the right to maintain therein a religious school if they are so disposed, the court has neither authority nor desire to deny or interfere with the exercise of such right. It has the authority, however, and it is its duty, to enjoin the defendants and their successors in office from directly or indirectly making any appropriation or use of the public funds for the support or in aid of such parochial school or of any so-called public school maintained or conducted in connection with such parochial school.[28]

In a somewhat similar case in New York in 1929, in which a school board had conducted a public school in church-owned premises, it was ruled that the citizens were not entitled to enjoin the board of education from doing so, when it was not shown that public money was used for denominational support.[29]

Beginning with the year 1933, in the state of Ohio, three efforts were made in succeeding sessions of the state legislature to secure appropriation of state funds for sectarian schools. A proposed amendment to the appropriation bill providing for the expenditure of two million dollars of public funds for the operation of parochial schools in the state was defeated in the lower house by a narrow margin, although it had been passed by the state senate. In a special session called by the governor in 1934, the matter was again brought up by friends of the parochial schools. At that time five million dollars was requested. While a strong church lobby seeking the passage of the bill tried to influence the legislators, an active campaign of opposition was carried on throughout the state, with the result that it was defeated.

The constitution of Ohio provides that

[27] Knowlton v. Baumhover et al., 166 N.W. 202, 206.
[28] *Ibid.*, p. 214.
[29] Ford v. O'Shea, Supt. of Schools et al., 244 N.Y. Sup. 38.

The General Assembly shall make such provisions, by taxation or otherwise, as, with the interest arising from the school trust fund, will secure a thorough and efficient system of common schools throughout the state; but no religious or other sect or sects shall ever have any exclusive right to or control of any part of the school funds of this state.[30]

When the state inaugurated the policy of general taxation for secular educational purposes only, it gave definite promise to its citizens, both religious and nonreligious, that public funds should not be appropriated for other educational purposes than the teaching of secular studies in the public school curriculum, so that all might stand equal before the law. The infidel and the religionist would thus be assured of equal privileges under the law. The benefit the public may receive from the increase of schools and the spread of learning and knowledge does not warrant the appropriation of public funds to private or sectarian schools.

In 1941 the supreme court of Missouri was required to pass upon the constitutionality of taking a parochial school into the public school system of that state.[31]

Several years before, in the town of Meta in Osage County in Missouri, the Catholic parish of St. Cecelia established its own parish or parochial school, which was conducted under the direction of the parish priest. The teachers were members of the Sisters of the Most Precious Blood, a Catholic teaching order. The school building adjoined the parish church and had two schoolrooms on the first floor and a schoolroom and a chapel on the second.

Some years later this parish school was taken into the public school system by the school board of the Meta school district as a public grade school. From then on it was supported by public funds. At the same time, textbooks and courses of study prescribed by the state superintendent of schools were adopted, but apart from this, the school seems to have been conducted as a parochial school in the same manner as before its inclusion in the public system. It was continued under the same name, and in the same building, the three schoolrooms being rented from the parish priest by the school board. The same teachers or other sisters of the same religious order, employed and paid by the school board, constituted the teaching staff of the school. It continued to be referred to as the "Catholic school." No serious question appeared to be raised until about 1939 when the

[30] Article 6, Section 2.
[31] Harfst et al. v. Hoegen et al., Mo., 163 S.W. (2d) 609, 141 A.L.R. 1136 (1941).

consolidation of another school district with the Meta district took place.

Antagonistic feelings developed among the people of the two districts, all of whom appear to have been members of the Roman Catholic church, resulting in a suit by parents of the public school children against members of the school board seeking an injunction against the use of school funds for purposes alleged to be sectarian and religious. The usual school day began with prayer in the morning. After prayer, the pupils were marched, one room at a time, to the nearby Catholic church for mass. After mass the pupils were marched back to their schoolrooms where they received religious instruction. They studied the Catholic catechism and the Children's Catholic Bible. On one or two days of each week, the parish priest gave religious instruction to the pupils in the midmorning, either at the church or in the schoolhouse chapel. On Friday afternoons the pupils were again marched to the church for confession. On the pupils' report cards appeared the subject "Religion" and a grade in this subject was given to each pupil. The teachers wore the garb of their religious order while teaching.

The court found that the statement to the county superintendent of schools that "We put the St. Cecelia parochial school into the public school system," was fully borne out by the facts in the case. The court stated "it was not only put there but it was maintained there with public funds."

The court held that

the inclusion of a Catholic parochial school in the public school and maintenance thereof as a part of and as an adjunct to the parish church in its religious teachings and where children of every faith may be compelled to attend and have attended, constitutes a denial of constitutional guarantee of religious freedom, notwithstanding that attendance at mass was customary before school hours or that religious instruction might be given during recess periods or that participation of non-Catholic children in such services might not be required.

In 1940 the Grace Avenue Parochial School was incorporated into the public school system of North College Hill, a suburb of Cincinnati. The school board rented the school and employed Catholic nuns for its teachers. In 1942 a school board was elected which terminated the arrangements with the parochial school. However, in 1946, a school board with different personnel again rented the school in question for an annual rental of six thousand dollars, to be paid to Archbishop McNicholas of the Roman Catholic diocese of Cincinnati. It not only incorporated the school into the public system, but signed an agreement to pay from public funds the salaries of eight nuns who taught in the school. The matter came into court when Mrs. Frieda Reckman, a resident and taxpayer of North College Hill, brought suit to enjoin the board of education from further payments of tax funds for the operation of the Grace Avenue Parochial School.

A report of the National Education Association contains the following account:

This school enrolled only Catholic pupils and was taught largely by Catholic sisters, wearing the garb of their religious order. It was conducted as a sectarian school, but paid for out of public funds. Sectarian religious instruction was given each day as a regular part of the school program. The symbolic decorations of the building were of a sectarian nature. The sisters were paid from public funds under contract with the local board of education.[32]

A great deal of agitation resulted. Political and religious issues developed. Sectarian groups were formed and religious lines were drawn. On April 28, 1947, the following statement was prepared by the Council of Churches of Greater Cincinnati for distribution in the Cincinnati area and throughout the country:

The principle of the separation of church and state was established on the basis that any state support, however slight, for any church or religious establishment would lead first to bitter wrangling between the adherents of different religions for tax favors and ultimately to that worst of all tyrannies, religious persecution. As President Madison pointed out in his famous "Memorial Against Religious Assessments," the first step towards church support, direct or indirect, from tax funds is the first step towards a return of the Spanish Inquisition. Recent disorders in North College Hill prove the soundness of the prophecy of bitter feelings when tax support for any church becomes a public issue. We dare not wait to see whether the rest of Madison's prophecy is sound. . . . The principle of separation of church and state is not a worn out slogan to be evaded by legal fiction. It is the keynote of our religious freedom. As such, it is worth protecting. For that reason, we shall support wholeheartedly the move to stop tax support for any church school, in North College Hill or any other place.[33]

As a result of the controversy, the North College Hill school board

[32] Harold E. Fey, "They Stand for Free Schools," *Christian Century*, July 2, 1947, p. 824.
[33] *Ibid.*

resigned, making it necessary under Ohio school law for the courts to take jurisdiction.

In some communities where the people are predominantly of a particular sect, appropriations are sometimes made to parochial schools by local officers. That such practices and other forms of aid are fairly prevalent is evident from the following statement that appeared in an editorial in *America* on July 29, 1947: "The NEA was not unaware, when it passed its resolution calling for ex-parte aid from Federal Government, that public funds are actually being allocated, in no less than 350 instances, to American parochial schools today." [34]

The following counsel and warning which appeared as an editorial in the *Pittsburgh Catholic*, official organ of the Pittsburgh diocese, is pertinent:

There are weighty reasons why Catholics should not seek the state contributions for the education furnished by their schools, to which, in all justice, they are entitled. These reasons have been repeatedly set forth by leaders of the church in this country; they have dictated the position taken by Catholics thus far, and their importance is strongly confirmed by recent developments. When state funds are accepted, some measure of state interference and control must also be accepted. State money for Catholic schools means close dealings with public officials; it means political connections; it means dictation regarding the manner in which the schools are to be conducted. . . .

Under favorable conditions, assistance from the public treasury is a handicap and a difficulty; under unfavorable circumstances it can become a catastrophe.

The entire history of the church, emphasized by recent events, shows that public funds come at too dear a price. Mexico had state aid, and so had Spain and Germany and Italy and France. And it proved a weakening, demoralizing connection. Better the sacrifice and the limitations which independence requires than the unsound edifice built on the deceptive, treacherous basis of state aid. [35]

Tremendous pressure is being brought to bear today upon both state legislatures and Congress to secure public funds for the aid of sectarian schools. Many believe that with a "first" and "second breach" in the wall between church and state already made — by empowering the local school authorities to use school funds to pro-

---

[34] "Further Developments at North College Hill," an editorial in *Liberty*, Fourth Quarter, 1947 (Vol. 42, No. 4), p. 19.
[35] *Pittsburgh Catholic*, March 17, 1938.

vide free textbooks and free transportation for parochial schools [36] —
a "third and a fourth breach and still others will be attempted." [37]

For a number of years bills have been introduced at successive
sessions of Congress, proposing to grant federal aid to public schools.
A desire to protect states' rights has prevented the passage of these
bills. There has also been opposition from certain denominations,
because no provision has been made for aid to parochial schools.

The Eightieth Congress saw the introduction of half a dozen bills,
in Senate and House, providing sums ranging up to $550,000,000 a
year for schools. In some cases these bills frankly call for money to
be paid to parochial schools, but two of them, the so-called Taft Bill
in the senate, and the Mc Cowan Bill in the House of Representatives, endeavor to avoid a direct issue of public funds to private and
parochial schools by providing that the federal appropriation may
be distributed by each state in accordance with that state's own
statutes. The passage of an act of this nature would not only threaten
the public school system, but raise a political and religious issue in
many states. It would intensify sectarian intolerance, create a scram-
ble for public funds, and divide American society into political and
sectarian camps which the Constitution was designed to prevent.

Religious denominations, free as they now are to conduct their
own church schools, need to take alarm at any attempt to form
financial alliances or secure financial funds from the state. Such
alliances are costly, dangerous, and the most vicious of all alliances
between the church and the state. Governmental appropriations of
funds of necessity involve government control. As stated by Mr. Justice Jackson in delivering the opinion of the United States Supreme
Court in the case of Wickard, Secretary of Agriculture, v. Filburn, [38]
"it is hardly lack of due process for the Government to regulate
that which it subsidizes."

Wherever there is financial responsibility, there also resides administrative authority. The old saying, "It's the one who pays the
fiddler that calls the tunes" still has meaning.

[36] For the furnishing of free textbooks to private schools see Chapter XII and on free transportation of pupils to other than public schools see Chapter XIII.

[37] Mr. Justice Rutledge in the dissenting opinion in Everson v. Board of Education of the
Township of Ewing declared, "This is not just a little case over bus fares. Distant as it may be
in its present form from a complete establishment of religion, it differs only in degree, and is
the first step in that direction." He declared the free transportation of pupils to parochial
schools the "second breach," whereas the court's decision in Cochran v. Louisiana State Board
of Education, 281 U.S. 370 (1930), in upholding the use of tax funds for the purchase of textbooks for pupils in parochial schools, was the "first breach" in the wall of separation between
church and state.

[38] 317 U.S. 111 (1942).

The North College Hill episode is but a foretaste of the dissension, the neighborhood bitterness, and the educational chaos that will be experienced on a national scale when "tax funds are entangled with religion and used for a church-dominated education." Such practice can only lead to discord and strife and is fundamentally opposed to the basic idea of separation of church and state.

CHAPTER VIII

Religious Garb in the Public Schools

THE rule that "no religious or political test or qualification shall ever be required as a condition of admission into any public educational institution of the state, as teacher, student, or pupil"[1] may now be said to be the general principle accepted by the public school systems of all the states. This principle does not justify teachers in conducting themselves in a way that is inconsistent with good order, peace, morality, or the safety of the state. It prevents a teacher from being refused employment because of his religion, but it does not prevent him from being refused employment or even dismissed because of views and beliefs based on his religion which may hinder him from discharging properly the duties he has assumed as a teacher in the public schools.[2]

The wearing of religious garb peculiar to a particular sect or denomination by teachers in the public schools has provoked considerable discussion at times and has called forth litigation and specific legislation on the subject in some states.

In 1894 the courts of Pennsylvania in the case of Hysong v. Gallitzin School District considered an action brought by resident taxpayers to prevent the employment of Sisters of Charity in the

---

[1] Constitution of Arizona, Article 11, Section 7.

[2] In 1918 in the case of McDowell v. Board of Education (104 Misc. 564, 172 N.Y.S. 590), the courts in New York State sustained the dismissal of a teacher who was a Quakeress. She was opposed to war and to the existing war with the German government. She would not urge or help her pupils to support the United States government in carrying on the war with Germany. She did not participate in Red Cross activities or buy thrift stamps, nor did she believe that a teacher was under obligation to support governmental measures for carrying on the war. She charged that her dismissal was a violation of the federal and state constitutions on the ground that she had been discriminated against on account of her religion, that this was an attempted restraint upon the Quaker faith. The court in sustaining the dismissal said that the petitioner was not discriminated against because she was a Quakeress, but because her views and beliefs, which she claimed were based upon her religion, prevented her from discharging properly the duty she had assumed.

"Where a person agrees with the state to perform a public duty, she will not be excused from performance according to law merely because her religion forbids her doing so. While the petitioner may be entitled to the greatest respect for her adherence to her faith, she cannot

Gallitzin public schools.[3] The public school board had been employing four Sisters of Charity, who wore while teaching the garb, insignia, and emblems of their order. There was no evidence of any religious instruction or exercises during the school hours. After school was out, Catholic children were required to remain and study the catechism.

The questions brought to the court were whether the exclusion of a Sister of Charity from employment as a teacher because she wore a religious garb in the public schools would be a violation of the religious liberty guaranteed in the Bill of Rights of the constitution of Pennsylvania,[4] and whether the wearing of such religious garb and insignia by the teacher constituted sectarian teaching. The court held that the exclusion of such teachers from the public schools would be a violation of the religious liberty guaranteed to them in the constitution, and that the wearing of the religious garb did not constitute sectarian teaching.

Mr. Justice Williams, in a dissenting opinion, said:

This is not a question about taste or fashion in dress, nor about the color or cut of a teacher's clothing. If it was only this I would favor the largest liberty.

They come into the schools not as common school teachers, or as civilians, but as the representatives of a particular order in a particular church whose lives have been dedicated to religious work under the direction of that church.

The next year, on June 27, 1895, the legislature of Pennsylvania passed an act prohibiting the wearing of such garb in any public school and making liable to fine any board of directors who should violate the provision.[5] The statute prohibited the teacher from wearing such garb only "in said school or whilst engaged in the performance of his or her duty" as a teacher. Fifteen years later, the constitutionality of the act was upheld by the court.[6]

The court held that the legislative act prohibiting the wearing of

be permitted because of it to act in a manner inconsistent with the peace and safety of the state." The statute under which she was removed provides that a teacher shall hold her position, "during good behavior and efficient and competent service, and shall not be removable except for cause after a hearing by the affirmative vote of a majority of the board." (Educational Law, Section 872, as amended by Chapter 786, Section 1, Laws of 1917.) The court held that the board of education had jurisdiction to entertain the charges against the petitioner and that it was within the exercise of their discretion to remove her from her position, her only recourse being an appeal to the commissioner of education.

[3] 164 Pa. St. 629, L.R.A. 203.

[4] Constitution of Pennsylvania, Bill of Rights, Article 1.

[5] Purdon's Pennsylvania Statutes, Title 24, Sections 1129, 1130 (Laws of Pennsylvania, 1895).

[6] Commonwealth v. Herr, 229 Pa. St. 132 (1910).

religious garb in the public schools of Pennsylvania does not violate the First and Fourteenth amendments of the United States Constitution, nor does it do violence to sections 3 and 4 of Article 1 of the constitution of Pennsylvania.

The court declared:

We cannot assent to the proposition that the intent or the effect of the legislation is to disqualify any person from employment as a teacher "on account of his religious sentiments." It is directed against acts, not beliefs, and only against acts of the teacher while engaged in the performance of his or her duties as such teacher. . . . The system of common-school education in this commonwealth is the creature of the State, and its perpetuity and freedom from sectarian control are guaranteed by express constitutional provisions. Subject to these, the power to support and maintain an efficient system of public schools, wherein all the children of the commonwealth above the age of six years may be educated, is vested in the legislature. This carries with it the authority to determine what shall be the qualifications of the teacher, but in prescribing them the legislature may not make religious belief or church affiliation a test. Nevertheless, the power of the legislature to make reasonable regulations for the government of their conduct while engaged in the performance of their duties must be conceded. Primarily it is the province of the legislature to determine what regulations will promote the efficiency of the system and tend to the accomplishment of the object for which it was established. It is only where such regulations are clearly shown to be in violation of the fundamental law, that the courts, even though entertaining a different opinion from that of the legislature as to the necessity for or the wisdom or expedience of adopting them, may annul them.

This supports the claim that a state has the right to determine the qualification of the teachers of the state schools, and to insist that its teachers shall remain neutral upon religious questions, not only in their teaching, but in their acts so far as their peculiar sectarian costumes and beliefs are concerned.[7]

In 1906 a case was brought before the court of appeals, the highest court in New York, which affirmed the decision of the appellate division of the supreme court in an action brought by Nora O'Connor and Elizabeth E. Dowd, public school teachers having proper certification but members of the Sisterhood of St. Joseph and wearing religious garb, against Hendrick, trustee of the school district,

[7] Until 1833 the constitution of Massachusetts prescribed that each town, precinct, parish, etc., should have a Protestant teacher of piety, religion, and morality who was elected by some incorporated religious society. The court ruled that a teacher of an unincorporated religious society could not be regarded as a public Protestant religious teacher and therefore was not entitled to any part of the funds raised by a town, parish, precinct, etc., for such a teacher. Barnes v. Falmouth, 6 Mass. 400 (1810).

for unpaid salary.[8] The salary of the sisters had been withheld because they disregarded the state superintendent's order against the wearing of distinctive religious garb in the schoolroom. The school trustee and defendant had permitted the sisters to continue teaching contrary to the order of the superintendent.[9]

It was held that the order of the state superintendent prohibiting the wearing of the religious garb while engaged in teaching was a reasonable and valid exercise of the power conferred upon him, not because of the religious convictions or membership of the wearers of such apparel, but because the influence of such apparel was distinctly sectarian. The court took the position that while no actual doctrine was taught, there was a violation of the following constitutional provision:

Neither the state nor any subdivision thereof, shall use its property or credit or any public money, or authorize or permit either to be used, directly or indirectly, in aid or maintenance, other than for examination or inspection, of any school or institution of learning wholly or in part under the control or direction of any religious denomination, or in which any denominational tenet or doctrine is taught.[10]

Here we have the plainest possible declaration of the public policy of the state as opposed to the prevalence of sectarian influences in the public schools . . . There can be little doubt that the effect of the costume worn by these Sisters of St. Joseph at all times in the presence of their pupils would be to inspire respect if not sympathy for the religious denomination to which they so manifestly belong. To this extent the influence was sectarian, even if it did not amount to the teaching of denominational doctrine.

The court allowed the teachers their salaries until the time when they were notified not to wear the garb any longer.[11]

[8] O'Connor v. Hendrick, 184 N.Y. 421.

[9] In an earlier decision in a case involving this same school (the Ferris-Sylvester decision, 1902) the school board was ordered to discontinue the renting of "Brendan Hall," a building owned by the Catholic church and used by the district as a school building, and to tax the district and build a new building if necessary. The board had contended that the public school building was too small and it was on these grounds that it rented the hall. With some reluctance they moved back into the district school but continued to employ the sisters as teachers. The sisters continued to wear their religious garb. The O'Connor v. Hendrick case was a result of the superintendent's order prohibiting the wearing of such garb.

[10] Constitution of New York, Article 9, Section 4.

[11] The fact that a teacher may have been teaching in a parochial school does not prevent such a person from being employed in the public school. The Kentucky court held that a teacher's resignation from a church school to become a teacher in a state graded school did not constitute a violation of the law, despite the fact that two other church school teachers became teachers in the graded school but were paid by the church school. In this instance, however, the school had burned down and the steps taken were merely a temporary measure. McDonald v. Parker, 130 Ky. 501, 110 S.W. 810 (1908).

In 1919 Nebraska passed a law prohibiting any teacher employed in any public school of the state from wearing in said school "while engaged in the performance of his or her duty any dress, or garb, indicating the fact that such teacher is a member or an adherent of any religious order, sect, or denomination . . ."[12] Any teacher who violated this provision was guilty of a misdemeanor. In 1923 the state of Oregon passed a similar act.[13]

Some years ago the question was raised whether employees in government Indian schools should be permitted to wear religious garb while on duty as public officers and to display in schoolrooms the insignia distinctive of any religious order or society. The persons affected were government employees engaged by the Indian Office as teachers. They were public officers who had taken the usual oath of office. They had been accustomed to wear while on duty the distinctive garb and insignia of religious societies or orders to which they belonged. They had also caused or permitted to be displayed on the walls and elsewhere in government buildings other insignia, pictures, badges, and mottoes peculiar to these societies.

The schools are a concrete expression of the policy adopted by the government in discharging its trust toward its wards, the Indians. They are owned by the United States and under the laws are subject solely to the management and control of the United States and its agencies. In short, they are public schools.

It was in connection with these schools that Robert G. Valentine, commissioner of Indian affairs, issued Circular 601, which reads as follows:

In accordance with that essential principle in our national life — the separation of church and state — as applied by me to the Indian Service, which as to ceremonies and exercises is now being enforced under the existing religious regulations, I find it necessary to issue this order supplementary to those regulations, to cover the use, at those exercises and at other times, of insignia and garb as used by various denominations. At exercises of any particular denomination there is, of course, no restriction in this respect, but at the general assembly exercises and in the public schoolrooms, or on the grounds when on duty, insignia or garb has no justification.

In government schools all insignia of any denomination must be

[12] Compiled Statutes of Nebraska, 1929, Chapter 79, Section 1417.
[13] "After the passage of this act, it shall be unlawful for any teacher in any public school in the state of Oregon to wear in said school, and while engaged in the performance of his or her duty, any dress or garb of any religious order, sect, or denomination." Oregon Code, 1930, Section 35-2406 (Law of 1923).

removed from all public rooms, and members of any denomination wearing distinctive garb should leave such garb off while engaged at lay duties as government employees. If any case exists where such an employee cannot conscientiously do this, he will be given a reasonable time, not to extend, however, beyond the opening of the next school year after the date of this order, to make arrangements for employment elsewhere than in federal Indian schools.

This led to a hearing before Secretary Fisher of the Department of the Interior on April 8, 1912.[14] Valentine appeared before Secretary Fisher in defense of his circular. The order was issued, he declared, simply because it had become clear that to permit a continuance of the practice against which it was directed would be irreconcilable with the complete separation of church and state. Valentine then cited certain statements to show that separation was an essential principle of American policy, which needed neither defense nor proof of its existence. He pointed out that to continue the practice in question would have been inconsistent with the duty that an executive officer must regard as his — the maintenance of the complete separation of church and state.

The wearing of these ecclesiastical robes and insignia in the schoolroom exerts, he said, a sectarian influence. The garb proclaims to the world that the wearer is set apart from it by vows of extraordinary devotion to a particular order in a particular church; that the life, services, and fortune of the individual are dedicated to a particular cause; that it was this signification to which the objection is raised and not to the wearer. Though the one wearing the garb may be careful in making no mention of it and may endeavor to go about in an inconspicuous way, nevertheless the very presence of such a dress in a schoolroom gives to that school a denominational character. The teachers appear as ecclesiastical persons rather than in the capacity of public officers and teachers.

The wearing of the garb itself in the school does not promote the cause of whatever church it represents. This is the effect on the Indian. And to the casual visitor the school must appear as one conducted by a religious order; he would have no reason to think he was in an institution conducted by the United States. Since I am unable to see how this government can countenance such a use of its agencies, the order forbidding the garb and insignia in the schools was to my mind a necessary supplement to existing regulations.

[14] *Religious Garb in Indian Schools* (Government Printing Office, Washington, D.C., 1912).

Valentine pointed out that as early as 1885 it had been declared in the report of the commissioner of Indian affairs:

It will be the policy of the Bureau, while under its present control, to manage by and through its own appointees all schools which occupy buildings erected with funds furnished by the government. The government should manage its own schools, and the different denominations should manage theirs separately. In a word, in the management of schools, the government should be divorced from sectarian influence or control. Any other course would end in heart-burning, confusion, and failure. But the government can, and does, fairly and without invidious discrimination, encourage any religious sects whose philanthropy and liberality prompts them to assist in the great work of redeeming these benighted children of nature from the darkness of their superstition and ignorance.[15]

Thus it was maintained that, while the general policy of the government might at times have been obscured by the administrative contingencies of the movement, it had always been clear that the public policy, as it had been reiterated year after year by the secretary of the interior and the commissioner of Indian affairs, is to have a system of government schools for Indian children in which sectarianism has no place.

What had actually happened was that the government had taken over certain Catholic Indian schools. The teachers who had been employed in the schools before their transfer were brought over along with the schools. These teachers, it appears, were transferred without even the formality of civil service examinations and were permitted to wear their religious dress and display religious insignia in the schoolrooms. The schools were supported by the government instead of by the Roman Catholic church as before.[16]

Valentine's circular created a great deal of agitation, whereupon President Taft revoked the order until a hearing could be given to all parties concerned. Approximately eight months intervened between the time the hearing was held, April 8, 1912, and the time President Taft made public his decision. In the meantime the order remained suspended, and there was considerable agitation over the question. Newspapers carried articles discussing the hearing and the principles involved.[17] Protestants lined up in opposition to the Catholics.

[15] Annual Report of the Commissioner of Indian Affairs, 1885, p. 14.
[16] *Religious Garb in Indian Schools*, pp. 5–7, 18–24.
[17] Some of these articles appeared in the *Outlook* for March 30, 1912, pp. 718, 719, under the title "Indian Government Schools." See also the *United Presbyterian*, February 29, 1912, and the *New York Weekly Witness*, February 21, 1912.

President Taft permanently revoked the order which he had temporarily suspended. His decision was based upon the findings of the Secretary of the Interior, in which the legal and constitutional phases of the question were discussed and in which the secretary arrived at the conclusion that the question involved was one of administrative policy which did not involve the constitutional provision for the separation of church and state. He therefore thought it unnecessary to adopt any rule requiring the teachers then employed by the government to lay aside their religious garb. He did, however, recognize the desirability of eliminating this religious feature from the government schools by not employing any additional members of religious orders as teachers.[18]

Questions pertaining to the wearing of religious garb in the public schools have arisen in several places in North Dakota. In 1936 an action was brought to the state supreme court in the case of Gerhardt v. Heid.[19]

This case, according to the facts of the court, arose in connection with a consolidated school district in the village of Gladstone, Stark County, North Dakota, where instruction was given in the grades and in high school subjects. During the term opening in September 1935, there were six teachers employed in the school. Four of these teachers were nuns, members of the Sisterhood of St. Benedict. They all held proper certificates entitling them to teach in the public schools of Stark County. There was no evidence that any religious instruction was given or that any religious exercises were conducted. They turned over to the mother house the proceeds of any compensation they received for services rendered after deducting living expenses, clothing, and maintenance. In return for this consideration, they had the assurance from the mother house of the order that upon retirement they were privileged to return there and be cared for during the remainder of their lives. The sisters, while employed as teachers, were governed by the rules of the particular school authorities by whom they were employed.

The court held that the fact that the teachers in question contributed to their order a large part of their earnings and wore their particular religious garb during school hours did not constitute a

---

[18] There were on January 19, 1933, five of these employees wearing religious garb and teaching in the government Indian schools "who were in the service prior to the time of the Garb Order [August 24, 1912], all others having been gradually eliminated from our service." Letter to the authors from the commissioner of Indian affairs, January 19, 1933.

[19] 66 N.D. 444, 267 N.W. 127.

violation of the constitution and the laws of North Dakota nor infringe upon the rights of the plaintiffs. It was further held that while the wearing of religious garb denoted membership in a certain denominational order as would the wearing of the emblem of the Christian Endeavor Society or the Epworth League, the court felt that the wearing of such garb did not make the school in question a sectarian school, that it was free from sectarian control, and that it was not affiliated with any particular religious sect or denomination but was one of the public schools of North Dakota operated under the supervision, direction, and control of the public officers of the state, county, and district in which the school is located.

The court pointed out that no teacher in any public school in North Dakota has a right while engaged in teaching to act as a proselyter for any religious organization, sect, creed, or belief. However, it held that in this case there was no evidence and no claim that any of the teachers attempted to give instruction in religious or sectarian subjects or conducted any religious exercises, nor had they endeavored to impress their own religious beliefs upon pupils while acting as teachers. The court did say: "Whether it is wise or unwise to regulate the style of dress to be worn by teachers in our public schools or to inhibit the wearing of dress or insignia indicating religious belief is not a matter for the courts to determine."

It will be observed that the North Dakota decision differs from that of other courts and states. According to state records there were in 1945–46 seventy-five Catholic sisters teaching in seventeen public schools in nine counties in North Dakota.[20]

Charges are made that in some schools religious instruction is being given during school hours which is contrary to state law. In Selfridge, Solon, and other communities in North Dakota unfavorable publicity is being given to the employment of nuns wearing a religious garb on the ground that the wearing of such religious garb is a religious act peculiar to their church.

Similar questions were raised in New Mexico. In 1948 it was reported in the public press that steps were being taken to test the constitutionality of the employment of members of certain Roman Catholic religious orders as teachers in the public schools of New Mexico. It was charged in a suit that 145 members of Catholic orders were employed in the New Mexico public school system.

As taxpayers, the plaintiffs made the following requests:

[20] See "Nuns to Leave N.D. School," *Bulletin, Friends of the Public Schools,* Vol. IX, No. 3 (October 1946).

1. An injunction barring any school board from hiring or paying a member of a Catholic religious order as a public school teacher.

2. An injunction preventing the state school budget director from making or approving any school budget paying school funds to members of religious orders.

3. That 29 schools in the state now operated as public schools be declared to be parochial schools and ineligible to receive public funds.

4. That all members of Catholic religious orders be declared ineligible and forever barred from teaching in public schools and dismissed.

5. That payment of teachers' salaries to religious orders be declared an illegal expenditure of public funds.

The suit charged that the employment of Catholic nuns and brothers in public schools is not an isolated situation existing in a few schools but "is a general situation and part of a plan or scheme of officers of the Roman Catholic church to introduce the teachings of Catholicism in all public and tax supported schools." [21]

It is contended that when teachers in the public schools, paid from the tax funds furnished by people of all faiths or no faith, appear in such a garb, the public school becomes a place for the flaunting of a unique act in religion, that such acts are favorable to a particular church and therefore constitute an invasion of sectarianism in the public schools.

[21] "Suit Opposing Nuns in Public Schools Filed," *Chicago Daily Tribune,* March 11, 1948, p. 22.

CHAPTER IX

School Buildings

USE OF PUBLIC SCHOOL BUILDINGS FOR RELIGIOUS PURPOSES

THE use of public school buildings for religious purposes has long been a moot question. Many state constitutions contain provisions prohibiting the expenditure of public funds in support of places of worship, but the court decisions are not at all clear in determining what use of a public school building will make it a place of worship. The statutory provisions, as well as court decisions, in regard to the use of public school buildings for religious meetings vary in the different states. Some states specify that public school buildings may be used, at the discretion of the school board, for religious services outside regular school hours if such use does not interfere with school programs.

In Illinois, for example, the statutes give to the board of school directors power

to have the control and supervision of all public school houses in their district, and to grant the temporary use of them, when not occupied by schools, for religious meetings and Sunday schools, for evening schools and literary societies, and for such other meetings as the directors may deem proper . . .[1]

This statute was held to be constitutional by the supreme court of Illinois in a case involving a school board that had granted the temporary use of a schoolhouse for religious meetings and Sunday schools.[2] Since these meetings did not interfere with the regular school work, the court held, the authorization of them was not a violation of the Illinois constitutional provision that no person should be required to support a place of worship against his consent, nor preference be given to any religious denomination or mode of worship; nor did it constitute an appropriation in aid of any church

[1] Revised Statutes of the State of Illinois, 1931, Chapter 122, Section 123.
[2] Nichols v. School Directors, 93 Ill. 61, 34 Am. Rep. 160 (1879).

125

or for sectarian purposes, nor the improper use of school property.[3] It was contended that wear and tear on the building would be so little that any expense to the taxpayer as a result of such use would be "inappreciable," and that the constitutional provisions were not intended to prohibit religious organizations from receiving any incidental benefit whatsoever from the public bodies or authorities of the state.

In a Nebraska case it was held that the occasional use of a schoolhouse for Sunday schools and religious meetings over a period of five years and not more than four times in any one year did not make the schoolhouse a place of worship within the meaning of the constitution, nor did it constitute the improper use of public funds.[4] Where, however, the statute has given the school directors authority to permit the use of school buildings for religious and other purposes, a church organization has no right to use the schoolhouse for religious meetings without permission from the school directors, and the directors may refuse such permission at their discretion.[5]

Other states leave the use of school buildings to be determined by a vote of the people in the district at their school meeting. In Iowa it was held that under a statute conferring authority on the electors of a school district to direct the sale or "other disposition" to be made of any schoolhouse, the school district has the power to permit by vote the use of such buildings for religious purposes.[6] In another case it was held that the electors of a district township have power to order by vote that a schoolhouse be opened for Sabbath School, religious worship, and lectures on moral and scientific subjects at such times as will not interfere with the regular progress of the public schools.[7]

In Indiana, where a statute permits the use of a schoolhouse for other than school purposes "when unoccupied for common school purposes," the court defined the period of occupation for school purposes as extending from the beginning of the school term to its end, including school days, Saturdays, Sundays, and nights, and held that therefore a school trustee might not grant the use of the building for religious purposes during this time.[8] If such permission was to be granted at all, it might be granted only for the summer vacation period.

[3] Constitution of Illinois, Article 2, Paragraph 3; Article 8, Paragraphs 2, 3.
[4] State ex rel. Gilbert v. Dilley, 95 Nebr. 527, 50 L.R.A. (N.S.) 1182 (1914).
[5] School Directors v. Toll, 149 Ill. App. 541 (1909).
[6] Townsend v. Hagen, 35 Ia. 194 (1872).
[7] Davis v. Boget, 50 Ia. 11 (1878).
[8] Baggerly v. Lee, 37 Ind. App. 139, 73 N.E. 921 (1905).

A number of states have held that in the absence of express authority a school board cannot permit the use of a school building for religious meetings.[9] Funds to erect such buildings are raised by taxes, and money so raised cannot be used for a private purpose or to build a place for a religious, political, or social society. That which cannot be done directly cannot be done indirectly. If it is not permissible to levy taxes to build a church, it is not permissible to levy taxes to build a schoolhouse and then lease it for a church. Though no immediate perceptible injury may result, the school building has been used for purposes for which it was not designed.[10]

In Massachusetts the court declared void an attempt by the voters of a school district to authorize taxes for building an elaborate school building that might be an ornament in the community and serve as a meeting place for lectures, exhibitions, or religious services.[11]

In Connecticut the court said that it would not consider void the vote of a district directing the erection of a schoolhouse merely because the school district authorized religious meetings to be held in it in the evening, but that it might under certain conditions prohibit the use of the schoolhouse for improper purposes.[12] This decision, however, was reversed by the Connecticut court two years later, when it was held that, in spite of the favorable vote of a certain school district, the school committee did not have the power to grant the use of a schoolhouse of the district for religious meetings, Sunday school, or other religious services, and that upon the objection of a taxpayer, an injunction might be issued against such use, even though the injury to the schoolhouse or other property might be very slight, or even negligible.[13] This practice has come to be known as the "Connecticut rule" for use of schoolhouses.

USE OF SECTARIAN BUILDINGS FOR PUBLIC SCHOOL PURPOSES

With few exceptions the courts have been in general agreement that the use of part of a church or other sectarian building for school purposes and the payment of rent does not constitute an appropriation or aid to the church or sectarian school within the meaning of constitutional prohibitions, especially where the use of the sectarian building is temporary, arising from an emergency.

That the temporary use of a room in a church for public school

[9] Dorton v. Hearn, 69 Mo. 301 (1878).
[10] Spencer v. School District, 15 Kans. 259, 22 Am. Rep. 268 (1875); Hysong v. Gallitzin School District, 164 Pa. 629 (1894); Bender v. Streabich, 17 Pa. Co. Ct. 609 (1896); Spring v. School Directors, 31 Pittsb. L.J.N.S. (Pa.) 194 (1900).
[11] George v. Second School District, 6 Met. (Mass.) 510 (1843).
[12] Sheldon v. Centre School District, 25 Conn. 224 (1856).
[13] Scofield v. Eighth School District, 27 Conn. 499 (1858).

purposes in an emergency does not constitute an interference with the religious rights of children compelled to attend for public school instruction was the decision of the Illinois court in 1887 and of the New York court in 1921.[14]

In Illinois a school district had voted down a proposition to erect a new schoolhouse. The board had rented the basement of a Catholic church for public school purposes, declaring the act to be an emergency measure. The teachers hired were Catholics, and the Catholic pupils were required to attend mass upstairs in the church before the opening of school. The teachers and the Catholic pupils who wished to do so studied the catechism upon returning to the schoolroom half an hour before the opening of school, and at noon teachers and students said the Angelus in the schoolroom. Complaint was brought by a school patron and taxpayer. None of the pupils had objected to the study of the catechism or the prayers. The court held that the board of education was empowered to rent for public school purposes the basement of the church controlled by the Catholic denomination. It did not appear that the complainant had any children who were required against his wishes to attend or receive any religious instruction. No religious exercises were required.[15]

In a New York case the high school building had burned, and the Sunday school room of the Christian Church was used as an emergency measure. A number of Catholic children in the eighth grade were required to attend for instruction, this grade having been assigned to the chapel of the church. There was no visible evidence of sectarian influences other than a report of the Sunday school classes on the wall, nor was it shown that any religious instruction of any kind took place.

In Tennessee the court said that while it is contrary to law and public policy to allow the public school money to be invested in property in which any religious denomination or society has any rights or interest, this does not prevent school directors, when necessary, from using a building of a parochial character if the trustees consent, or from making any suitable arrangement for the renting and occupation of a building for the use of the public schools.[16]

The Iowa court has taken a similar position, as has that of Texas.[17]

[14] Millard v. Board of Education, 121 Ill. 297 (1887); In the Matter of Roche, 26 N.Y. St. Dept. Rep. 217 (1921).
[15] Millard v. Board of Education.
[16] Swadley v. Haynes, 41 S.W. 1066 (1897).
[17] Scripture v. Burns, 59 Ia. 70, 12 N.W. 760 (1882); Nance v. Johnson, 84 Tex. 401, 19 S.W. 559 (1892).

In 1918, however, the supreme court of Iowa considered a case in which the board of directors of the public school had appropriated money for and conducted a school in the upper room of a parochial school building adjoining the Catholic church to save the expense of repairing the public school building, which was in poor condition, and had employed a sister of a religious order who was in charge of the upper room of the parochial school. The Iowa court held that the board had converted the public school into a sectarian or religious school contrary to the laws of the state, and that the appropriation of money for the support of such a school constituted an illegal use of public funds.[18] Here the study of the catechism and religious instruction were a part of the daily program of the school. On the walls were pictures of the Holy Virgin. The teacher was dressed in a religious garb. The same program that had been carried on in the parochial school was continued after the schoolroom had been taken over by the school district. It was, the court said, "as thoroughly and completely a religious parochial school as it could well have been had it continued in name." The court further said:

The law does not prescribe the fashion of dress of man or woman; it demands no religious test for admission into the teacher's profession; it leaves all men to worship God or to refrain from worship according to their own consciences; it prefers no one church or creed to another. This principle of unfettered individual liberty of conscience necessarily implies — what is too often forgotten — that such liberty must be so exercised by him to whom it is given as not to infringe upon the equally sacred right of his neighbor to differ with him. . . . If there is any one thing which is well settled in the policies and purposes of the American people as a whole, it is the fixed and unalterable determination that there shall be an absolute and unequivocal separation of church and state, and that our public school system, supported by the taxation of the property of all alike — Catholic, Protestant, Jew, Gentile, believer, and infidel — shall not be used, directly or indirectly, for religious instruction, and above all, that it shall not be made an instrumentality of proselyting influence in favor of any religious organization, sect, creed, or belief.[19]

The Iowa court, in quoting the Ohio supreme court in the case of Board of Education of Cincinnati v. Minor, said:

[18] Knowlton v. Baumhover, 182 Ia. 691.
[19] The North Dakota case, Pronovost v. Brunette, 36 N.D. 288, 162 N.W. 300 (1917), had to do with the religious question of leasing a room in a Catholic institution by the public school district. The court, however, did not decide the case upon the religious phase of the question but based its decision on the ground that the board had no authority to lease a building from anyone, as prohibited under the educational laws of the state, since there was in existence sufficient school room for all its purposes.

"True Christianity asks no aid from the sword of civil authority. It began without the sword, and wherever it has taken the sword it has perished by the sword. To depend on civil authority for its enforcement is to acknowledge its own weakness, which it can never afford to do. It is able to fight its own battles. Its weapons are moral and spiritual, and not carnal. . . . True Christianity never shields itself behind majorities. . . .

"*Legal* Christianity is a solecism, a contradiction of terms. When Christianity asks the aid of government beyond mere *impartial protection,* it denies itself." [20]

In Wisconsin a school district had for some twenty years rented from the Roman Catholic church certain rooms in its school building adjoining the church building.[21] In these rooms was conducted the public school of the district, for which the school money of the district had been expended. In addition to the rent, small sums had been paid for fuel, cleaning, and the like. The rooms not rented by the district were used for a parochial school. In the rooms used for the public school certain religious exercises were conducted. Prayers were offered at intervals during the day and church hymns were sung. The pupils regularly attended religious services in the adjoining church before school hours. Frequently children were dismissed to attend weddings and funerals in the church. The teachers wore religious garb. With the exception of one or two of the pupils, all were children of Catholic parents.

The court held that the school had been pervaded by sectarian instruction contrary to law and granted an injunction against its continuance. The court took the position that the school district and board had power to rent rooms for the maintenance of a distinctly public school, the selection to be at the discretion of the school board. The money already paid could not be recovered from either the board or the church, because the actions were known of and voted at the annual school district meeting.

In the same state objection was made to the holding of graduation exercises of the public high school in a church, and to the practice of inviting ministers or priests to offer prayer at these exercises.[22] No charges were made for the use of the churches, nor were the clergymen paid for giving the invocations. The prayer was allegedly free from sectarianism, and graduates were not compelled to attend the exercises. While the court held that none of the rights guaran-

[20] 23 Ohio St. 211 (1872).
[21] Dorner v. School District No. 5, 137 Wis. 147, 118 N.W. 353 (1908).
[22] State ex rel. Conway v. District Board of Joint School District, 162 Wis. 482, 156 N.W. 477 (1916).

teed by the constitution had been violated, it deemed that it would be a wise exercise of official discretion to discontinue such practice if there were a sufficient number of complaints. Since no appropriations of school money were involved, the only question here was whether or not this practice forced persons to attend a place of worship against their consent and thus interfered with the rights of conscience. Graduation exercises, being a part of the school curriculum, are under the direction and control of school boards, and since they are, the school boards cannot escape the responsibility for them. Parents and pupils of all denominations have a right to attend such exercises without having their legal rights invaded, but the court considered that it would be farfetched to say that by voluntarily attending such services one is compelled to attend a place of worship. It considered the complaint about prayers offered at graduation exercises by denominational clergymen a somewhat different question in that a prayer might be either sectarian or nonsectarian in character. The prayer complained of was nonsectarian, however, and the court concluded by saying:

Pupils do not congregate on such an occasion for the purpose of worship, and the short nonsectarian invocation that is usually given is a mere incident which occupies but a few moments. . . . A very different question would arise if an attempt were made to introduce the practice of having prayer as part of the daily routine in our public schools.

CHAPTER X

The Extent of Parental Control

THE question of just where the right of the state ends and that of the parents begins has been the crux of several court cases. Significant among them is the case of Meyer v. Nebraska. In 1919 the Nebraska legislature passed the following law:

Section 1. No person, individually or as a teacher, shall, in any private, denominational, or parochial or public school, teach any subject to any person in any language other than the English language.

Section 2. Languages other than the English language may be taught as languages only after a pupil shall have attained and successfully passed the eighth grade . . .[1]

In the same year the legislatures of two other states, Iowa[2] and Ohio,[3] passed similar statutes. In all three states cases were immediately carried to the court, which in every instance upheld the constitutionality of the law.[4]

[1] Nebraska Laws, 1919, Chapter 249.

[2] The Iowa statute reads as follows:

"Section 1. That the medium of instruction in all secular subjects taught in all of the schools, public and private, within the state of Iowa, shall be the English language, and the use of any language other than English in secular subjects in said schools is hereby prohibited, provided, however, that nothing herein shall prohibit the teaching and studying of foreign languages as such as a part of the regular school course in any such school, in all courses above the eighth grade. . . ."

[3] The Ohio statute reads:

"Section 7762-1. That all subjects and branches taught in the elementary schools of the state of Ohio below the eighth grade shall be taught in the English language only. The board of education, trustees, directors, and such other officers as may be in control shall cause to be taught in the elementary schools all the branches named in Section 7648 of the General Code. Provided, that the German language shall not be taught below the eighth grade in any of the elementary schools of this state.

"Section 7762-2. All private and parochial schools maintained in connection with benevolent and correctional institutions within this state which instruct pupils who have not completed a course of study equivalent to that prescribed for the first seven grades of the elementary schools of this state, shall be taught in the English language only, and the person or persons, trustees, or officers in control shall cause to be taught in them such branches of learning as prescribed in Section 7648 of the General Code or such as the advancement of pupils may require, and the persons or officers in control direct; provided that the German language shall not be taught below the eighth grade in any such schools within this state. . . ."

[4] Bartels v. Iowa, 191 Ia. 1060, 181 N.W. 508 (1921); Bohning v. State of Ohio, 102 Ohio St. 474 (1921); Pohl v. State of Ohio, 102 Ohio St. 474, 132 N.E. 20 (1921); and Meyer v. State

In Nebraska the act was applied to a parochial school which had disregarded its provisions by holding an extra session between the regular morning and afternoon classes for instruction in the German language. It was charged that the law interfered with both personal and religious liberty and with the right of parental control. It was maintained that in many localities it was necessary for a child to have a knowledge of the German language in order to understand the church services, and to receive religious instruction from a parent in the home who spoke the German language.

The Nebraska supreme court upheld the constitutionality of the statute as "reasonably within the police power of the state." In so doing, the court ignored the fact that the statute prohibited instruction in a foreign language by the parent as well as by the teacher, either in or out of school hours. The state court held:

> The salutary purpose of the statute is clear. The legislature had seen the baneful effects of permitting foreigners who had taken residence in this country to rear and educate their children in the language of their native land. The result of that condition was found to be inimical to our own safety. To allow the children of foreigners who had emigrated here to be taught from early childhood the language of the country of their parents was to rear them with that language as their mother tongue. It was to educate them so that they must always think in that language, and, as a consequence, naturally inculcate in them the ideas and sentiments foreign to the best interests of this country. The statute, therefore, was intended not only to require that the education of all children be conducted in the English language, but that, until they had grown into that language, and until it had become a part of them, they should not in the schools be taught any other language. The obvious purpose of this statute was that the English language should be and become the mother tongue of all children reared in this state.
>
> It is suggested that the law is an unwarranted restriction, in that it applies to all citizens of the state, and arbitrarily interferes with the rights of citizens who are not of foreign ancestry, and prevents them, without reason, from having their children taught foreign languages in school. That argument is not well taken, for it assumes that every citizen finds himself restrained by the statute. The hours which a child is able to devote to study in the confinement of school are limited. It must have ample time for exercise or play. Its daily capacity for learning is comparatively small. A selection of subjects for its education, therefore, from among the many that might be taught, is obviously necessary. The legislature no doubt had in mind the

of Nebraska, carried to the Supreme Court, 262 U.S. 390, 43 Sup. Ct. Rep. 625, 67 L. ed. 1042 (1923).

practical operation of the law. The law affects few citizens except those of foreign lineage. Other citizens, in their selection of studies, except, perhaps, in rare instances, have never deemed it of importance to teach their children foreign languages before such children have reached the eighth grade. In the legislative mind, the salutary effect of the statute no doubt outweighed the restriction upon the citizens generally, which, it appears, was a restriction of no real consequence.

Mr. Justice Letton in a dissenting opinion, concurred in by Chief Justice Morrisey, conceded the right of the state to control curriculums of the public schools, that is, schools supported by public taxation, and even the right to place private and church schools under state supervision and to require for these schools "the same general standards." He maintained, however, that the state has no right to prevent parents, after they have given their children the branches of education required by the state, from giving to them a "full measure of education" in addition to the state requirements, whether at home or in a private school.

Meyer, being convicted of violating the statute because he unlawfully taught the subject of reading in the German language to a pupil who had not completed the eighth grade, carried the question to the Supreme Court of the United States, charging that the statute, as construed and applied, unreasonably infringed the liberty guaranteed by the Fourteenth Amendment: "nor shall any state deprive any person of life, liberty, or property, without due process of law . . ."[5]

The opinion of the United States Supreme Court, which declared the Nebraska law unconstitutional, pointed out that a state can determine the curriculums of its own schools. It may reasonably regulate all schools to the extent of inspecting, supervising, and examining them, including teachers and pupils. The state may require attendance at some school. It may also require certain studies essential to good citizenship.

While the court did not define the liberty guaranteed by the Fourteenth Amendment, it concluded that the protection given

denotes not merely freedom from bodily restraint, but also the right of the individual to contract, to engage in any of the common occupations of life, to acquire useful knowledge, to marry, establish a home, and bring up children, to worship God according to the dictates of his own conscience, and, generally, to enjoy those privileges long recognized at common law as essential to the orderly pursuit of happiness by free men.

[5] Constitution of the United States, Fourteenth Amendment, Section 1.

A knowledge of the German language was not regarded as harmful, and the Nebraska statute was declared to be unreasonable in that it deprived the parents of the reasonable control of their children. The right of parents to engage a teacher thus to instruct their children was declared to be within the liberty guaranteed by the amendment. Mr. Justice McReynolds, who delivered the opinion of the court, said in part:

The desire of the legislature to foster a homogeneous people with American ideals, prepared readily to understand current discussions of civic matters, is easy to appreciate. Unfortunate experiences during the late war, and aversion toward every characteristic of truculent adversaries, were certainly enough to quicken that aspiration. But the means adopted, we think, exceed the limitations upon the power of the state, and conflict with rights assured to plaintiff in error. The interference is plain enough, and no adequate reason therefor in time of peace and domestic tranquillity has been shown.

The power of the state to compel attendance at some school and to make reasonable regulations for all schools, including a requirement that they shall give instructions in English, is not questioned. Nor has challenge been made of the state's power to prescribe a curriculum for institutions which it supports. . . . No emergency has arisen which renders knowledge by a child of some language other than English so clearly harmful as to justify its inhibition, with the consequent infringement of rights long freely enjoyed. We are constrained to conclude that the statute as applied is arbitrary, and without reasonable relation to any end within the competency of the state.

As the statute undertakes to interfere only with teaching which involves a modern language, leaving complete freedom as to other matters, there seems no adequate foundation for the suggestion that the purpose was to protect the child's health by limiting his mental activities. It is well known that proficiency in a foreign language seldom comes to one not instructed at an early age, and experience shows that this is not injurious to the health, morals, or understanding of the ordinary child.

Thus the case of Meyer v. State of Nebraska is one of the comparatively small number of cases in which, in applying the Fourteenth Amendment, the Supreme Court of the United States has overruled the decision of a state court and of a state legislature, in this instance repudiating a statute because it was an unwarranted interference with parental control.[6]

[6] The decision in the case of Meyer v. Nebraska does not conflict with the opinion rendered in the case of Berea College v. Commonwealth, 29 Ky. L. 284, 94 S.W. 623 (1906), to the effect that a state may apply to both the public and the private schools its general policy of segregation on the ground of public and race welfare, and may prevent intermarriage of white and colored persons and the immorality which such associations frequently engender.

The *Illinois Law Review* points out that the question may still be raised, however, as to whether a state might require so many specific subjects as to leave no room in the curriculum for elected subjects — religious as well as other subjects desired by the private school. In reality it would result in the state filling the entire curriculum with subjects deemed essential to good citizenship, thereby requiring them to be taught in both public and private schools and leaving no room for electives. The Nebraska case does not cover this question, and the decision leaves it open.[7]

It is quite reasonable to assume, however, that the doctrine of "reasonableness" would undoubtedly come into play, for, as Mr. Justice McReynolds suggests,

liberty may not be interfered with, under the guise of protecting the public interest, by legislative action which is arbitrary or without reasonable relation to some purpose within the competency of the state to effect. Determination by the legislature of what constitutes proper exercise of police power is not final or conclusive, but is subject to supervision by the courts.[8]

Another important case relating to the general subject of parental control resulted from a statute enacted by the legislature of Oregon in the autumn of 1922 known as the Compulsory Education Act.[9] This law directed all parents, guardians, and others having charge

[7] "Teaching of English Language in Schools," *Illinois Law Review*, 18:394 (1924). See also Charles J. Turck, "State Control of Public School Curriculum," in *Kentucky Law Journal*, 15:277–98 (May 1927).

[8] An Indiana statute provided for the teaching of a designated foreign language provided the parents of twenty-five or more children should request it. The court said: "With reference to the act under consideration, we are of the opinion that when the requisite demand is made it becomes the duty of the board of school commissioners to introduce the German language as a study into the particular school where it is demanded . . ." The court held that the school board had "no discretion to refuse, but must act." School Commissioners of Indianapolis v. State ex rel. Sander, 129 Ind. 14.

[9] The act reads as follows: "Any parent, guardian, or other person in the state of Oregon, having control or charge or custody of a child under the age of sixteen years and of the age of eight years or over at the commencement of a term of public school of the district in which said child resides, who shall fail or neglect or refuse to send such child to a public school for the period of time a public school shall be held during the current year in said district, shall be guilty of a misdemeanor and each day's failure to send such child to a public school shall constitute a separate offense; provided, that in the following cases, children shall not be required to attend public schools:

        (a) Children Physically Unable.
        (b) Children Who Have Completed the Eighth Grade.
        (c) Distance from School.
        (d) Private Instruction."

(Oregon Laws, 1923, Chapter 1, Section 5259.)

The act was proposed by initiative petition, filed in the office of the secretary of state on July 6, 1922, and approved by a majority of the votes cast thereon at the general election held November 7, 1922. There were 115,506 votes cast for the act and 103,685 against it.

of children between the ages of eight and sixteen to send them, with certain exceptions, for a full term to the public school of the district where the children resided. The purpose of the law was to close all private and church schools. The operation of the law was postponed until September 1, 1926.[10] In the meantime its provisions adversely affected the operation of private and church schools in the state. In many instances guardians of children wished to place their children in private schools for a term of years, but, expecting such schools to be closed, hesitated to do so.

In the case of Pierce v. Society of Sisters[11] the Supreme Court of the United States held the Oregon statute unconstitutional because it interfered unreasonably with the liberty of parents and guardians to direct the education of the children under their control, and because it violated the rights of denominational and private schools. The right to liberty and property guaranteed by the Fourteenth Amendment to the federal Constitution, the court maintained, involves not merely the right of parents to educate their children where they please but also the right of private and denominational schools to solicit students for their schools unhampered by legislative interference. The court pointed out that the private and church schools were "engaged in a kind of undertaking not inherently harmful, but long regarded as useful and meritorious. Certainly there is nothing in the present records to indicate that they have failed to discharge their obligations to patrons, students, or the state." The state does not have the power to standardize its children by forcing them to accept instruction at the hands of public teachers only, for, declared the court, "The child is not the mere creature of the state; those who nurture him and direct his destiny have the right, coupled with the high duty, to recognize and prepare him for additional obligations."

The rights of parenthood are inherent. These rights may be said to supersede all others. To the parent must be given the right to teach his child or send him to a school where he may be taught the principles the father wishes for him. This is not only the privilege of the parents but their responsibility. It stands to reason that no autocratic power — exercised either by a single individual, by men gathered in a legislative body, or by public vote — can ever by lawful means deprive the parent of this right.

Election day, November 4, 1924, witnessed for the second time

[10] *Ibid.*
[11] 268 U.S. 510, 45 Sup. Ct. Rep. 571, 69 L. ed. 1070 (1925).

within four years the defeat of a proposal, similar to the Oregon law, to close private and sectarian schools in the state of Michigan. The backers of the proposal were said to belong to an organization known as "The Public Schools Defense League" with headquarters in Detroit. The proposal took the form of a constitutional amendment which read as follows:

Section 16. From and after August 1, 1925, all children residing in the state of Michigan between the ages of seven years and sixteen years shall attend public school until they have graduated from the eighth grade.

Section 17. The legislature shall enact all necessary legislation to render said Section 16 effective.

At the time the amendment was being considered in Michigan, the Oregon case was pending in the United States Supreme Court.

The advocates of the proposed amendment conducted a strong campaign, exhibiting in some instances considerable bitterness of spirit. They claimed that they were champions of Americanism and that the best interests of the nation depended upon confining the education of all children to the public schools. The real and overshadowing object of the movement was religious, to judge from the literature and platform propaganda of the promoters, who reasoned that the only way by which the progress of the Roman Catholic church could be checked or destroyed was to close its schools.

The interest in the campaign is evident from the results of the election as published by Secretary of State Charles J. Deland. There were 760,571 votes against and 421,472 for the amendment, making a total of 1,182,043 votes. The presidential vote was 1,160,918, and the vote for the governor totaled the same. Thus 21,125 more votes were cast on the amendment than on any other question in the campaign. There was a majority vote of 339,099 against the amendment.

The case of Pierce v. Society of Sisters is an interesting sequel to Meyer v. Nebraska, in which, though it seems to have been conceded that the state can dictate the curriculums of its own tax-supported schools and to some extent that of private schools as well, the Supreme Court of the United States held that it may not exercise the latter power unreasonably, or interfere unreasonably with parental control.[12]

Taken together, the cases seem to advance the doctrine that the state may require its children to be taught morality and loyalty, and

[12] Andrew A. Bruce, "Right of Parental Control," *Illinois Law Review*, 20:378 (1925).

may require a general knowledge of the English language and of our national Constitution and government. It must, however, leave it to the parents to determine where the education is to be had and what the nature of the education shall be. A private or parochial school may complain if its supply of students is cut off by an illegal statute; consequently a statute unreasonable either with regard to parents or to private schools is invalid. Thus voluntary agencies are given the right to dip into the common reservoir for students just as employers may do for laborers.[13]

As precedents these cases open the door for a large measure of judicial control and may be said to repudiate what until recently was believed to be the growing, if not the established, rule—that the reasonableness of and the necessity for a state statute are for the determination of the state legislatures and state courts. The course taken by the Supreme Court would seem to be in harmony not only with former decisions but with our general principles of government.

In the case of the Oregon school law, for instance, it would hardly seem that the promoters realized what such a course would mean to our educational work and what it would mean to thousands of children. There are many such schools and great numbers of children attending them. These schools are conducted and maintained by both Protestants and Catholics. The public treasury is not drawn upon to erect buildings nor to pay the salaries of the teachers. There may be some exceptions, but they are few.

Our public school system has earned the confidence of the people, and consequently they should support it unstintingly with their taxes. But the very essence of our democracy forbids religious instruction in the state schools. Such a thing is impossible without setting up a state religion. Many parents, of course, want to have their children taught religion at the same time that they are being taught the common branches. When such parents have paid their taxes for the support of the public schools, they have a right to maintain at their own expense schools where their children may be taught what they wish to have them taught. To decide where and how the child shall be educated is a parental prerogative so long as the parent provides for the child the standard intellectual instruction necessary for good citizenship.

Former Vice-President Marshall enunciated an important principle when he said:

[13] Truax v. Raich, 239 U.S. 33 (1915); Truax v. Corrigan, 257 U.S. 312 (1921); and Terrace v. Thompson, 263 U.S. 197 (1923).

Unless I develop into such a brute as to be unable to take care of my child and thus warrant society in removing him permanently from my custody, I should be let alone to look after his health, care for his wants, guide his education, and instill into his mind such religious views as I think will enable him to stand against the temptations of a tempestuous world.

One of the great values of private schools lies in their differences. State institutions must necessarily be of a somewhat similar pattern. There is constant pressure to make all things uniform. In order to maintain our present standing and, above all, to develop, we must have both individuals and institutions that have the courage of their convictions and that dare to be different. This has been true of the private schools. From these schools have come many of the leaders in educational reform and many of our greatest statesmen. It can hardly be said that these institutions have been a detriment; rather they have been an asset.

It may well be summed up in the words of P. P. Claxton, former United States commissioner of education:

We believe in the public school system. It is the salvation of our democracy; but the private schools and colleges have been the salvation of the public schools. These private institutions have their place in our educational system. They prevent it from becoming autocratic and arbitrary, and encourage its growth along new lines.

Some have contended that our public educational system must set the standards for the moral, social, and mental development and training of our youth. That, of course, is the Spartan theory of education. That theory has been combated by our American courts. The laws pertaining to education and school rules and regulations must be observed, but the school, whether it be public or private, is not the sole factor in the development of the child's character. It is simply an aid, though a valuable one, to be sure, to the desired end. The parents are the responsible factors and they may delegate this primary responsibility to no one; only when they fail may the state interfere.

The American courts have at all times protected and perpetuated the right which guarantees to everyone the freedom to worship or not to worship God in the manner he desires, so long as he does not imperil the public safety and morals. The Nebraska German language case and the Oregon school case both sustain this position.

CHAPTER XI

Compulsory School Attendance

Since decisions were handed down by the United States Supreme Court in Meyer v. Nebraska[1] and Pierce v. Society of Sisters,[2] the supreme court of New Hampshire in May 1929 gave its opinion in the case of State v. Hoyt,[3] in which an interpretation was sought of the New Hampshire compulsory school attendance statute requiring children of school age to be sent to a public school or to an approved private school.[4] Hoyt and others were charged by the state with failure to send their children to a public school. Hoyt raised the defense that his child was instructed by a private tutor in his home in the studies required in the public schools, and that the statute violated the federal guarantee of liberty contained in the Fourteenth Amendment to the Constitution.

The supreme court of New Hampshire quoted from a previous decision which it had rendered in 1912 in the case of Fogg v. Board of Education, as follows:

Free schooling furnished by the state is not so much a right granted to pupils as a duty imposed upon them for the public good. If they do not voluntarily attend the schools provided for them, they may be compelled to do so. . . . Education in public schools is considered by many to furnish desirable and even essential training for citizenship, apart from that gained by the study of books. . . . The object of our school laws is not only to protect the state from the consequences of ignorance, but also to guard against the dangers of "incompetent citizenship."[5]

The court recognized that since its former decision in 1912 the power of the state over individuals had been greatly limited by recent decisions of the United States Supreme Court in the cases of Meyer v. Nebraska and Pierce v. Society of Sisters,[6] protecting the

[1] 262 U.S. 390, 43 Sup. Ct. Rep. 625, 67 L. ed. 1042 (1923).
[2] 268 U.S. 510, 45 Sup. Ct. Rep. 571, 67 L. ed. 1070 (1925).
[3] 84 N.H. 38, 146 Atl. 170.
[4] New Hampshire Laws, 1926, Chapter 118, Sections 1, 2.
[5] 76 N.H. 296.
[6] 262 U.S. 390 (1923); 268 U.S. 510 (1925).

141

guaranty of liberty found in the Fourteenth Amendment to the Constitution of the United States; but it was also recognized that no question was raised as to

the power of the state reasonably to regulate all schools, to inspect, supervise and examine them, their teachers and pupils; to require that all children of proper age attend some school, that all teachers shall be of good moral character and patriotic disposition, that certain studies plainly essential to good citizenship must be taught, and that nothing be taught which is manifestly inimical to the public welfare.[7]

The court pointed out that it did not think that the federal decisions went so far as to say that the sole obligation that can be imposed upon the parent by the compulsory school attendance statute is to educate his child; the statute provides also that the parent's method must be approved by the state. It held that under the federal guarantee, so far as it had been interpreted, attendance at some school may be required and that the state may supervise the school attendance.

"The power to supervise," said the court, "necessarily involves the power to reject the unfit, and to make it obligatory to submit to supervision." The local statute does not go beyond these requirements. According to the court the federal decisions did not deny that the state has power to insist upon approving the proposed substitute for public school, that such power is not limited to a mere inspection of what is being done and prosecuting for deficiencies.

The matters so enumerated include all that are involved in this litigation. The power "reasonably to regulate," to require attendance, good character of teachers, studies to be taught and those to be prohibited, all look to laying down rules for future conduct. As the statute does not exceed the exercise of these powers, it is held to be constitutional.

In the adjustment of the parent's right to choose the manner of his children's education, and the impinging right of the state to insist that certain education be furnished and supervised, the rule of reasonable conduct upon the part of each towards the other is to be applied. The state must bear the burden of reasonable supervision, and the parent must offer educational facilities which do not require unreasonable supervision.

If the parent undertakes to make use of units of education so small, or facilities of such doubtful quality, that supervision thereof would impose an unreasonable burden upon the state, he offends against the reasonable provisions for schools which can be supervised without unreasonable expense. The state may require not only that educational facilities

[7] Pierce v. Society of Sisters, 268 U.S. 534.

be supplied but also that they be so supplied that the facts in relation thereto can be ascertained, and proper direction thereof maintained, without unreasonable cost to the state. Anything less than this would take from the state all efficient authority to regulate the education of the prospective voting population.

If any substantial supervisory power remains to the states, it is not perceived how it could well be reduced below the minimum required here. This bears no resemblance to the "affirmative direction concerning the intimate and essential details of such schools," which was held to be invalid in Farrington v. Tokushige, 273 U.S. 284.

The interpretations placed upon the federal cases by the New Hampshire court do not appear to do violence to the opinions rendered by the United States Supreme Court nor does it constitute improper invasion of the rights of parental control.

In the state of Washington a somewhat similar question arose in connection with the case of State v. Counort.[8] Here an effort was made to excuse a child from attending school on the basis that he was receiving instruction from his parents, who claimed they were well qualified to teach him. The Washington court did not insist upon the school being approved in the sense of accreditation; it did insist that the pupils must attend an actual school, public or private, unless excused by the superintendent, who was authorized under the law to excuse certain pupils on the basis of physical conditions or if they had advanced to a certain place in their educational development. In this case it was held that any existing school would meet the requirement of the compulsory attendance law so long as it was an established school, but it must be a school in regular operation. Instruction which might be given the child by his parents in their home did not constitute a school within the meaning of the law.[9]

In New York, in the case of Judd et al. v. Board of Education of Union Free School District No. 2, Town of Hempstead, in which free transportation for pupils of parochial schools was held unconstitutional, the New York Court of Appeals said:

While the provisions of Article 9 of the Constitution formally established the public policy of the State, it is seen, therefore, that they merely crystallize into the fundamental law in mandatory form earlier decisions

---

[8] 69 Wash. 361, 124 Pac. 910 (1912).

[9] Under a South Dakota statute concerning the duty of persons having control of children between certain ages to cause such children to attend regularly a school, a superintendent of the Bethesda Children's Home at Beresford was required to have children residing in the home to attend regularly some public or private school. State ex rel. Johnson v. Cotton, 289 N.W. 71 (1940).

made by the people and recognized by the Legislature since the organization of the State and the adoption of the first Constitution.[10]

The court went on to say:

While a close compact had existed between the Church and State in other governments, the Federal government and each State government from their respective beginnings have followed the new concept whereby the State deprived itself of all control over religion and has refused sectaries any participation in or jurisdiction or control over the civil prerogatives of the State. And so it is in all civil affairs there has been a complete separation of Church and State jealously guarded and unflinchingly maintained. In conformity with that concept education in State supported schools must be non-partisan and non-sectarian. This involves no discrimination between individuals or classes. It invades the religious rights of no one. While education is compulsory in this State between certain ages, the State has no desire to and could not if it so wished compel children to attend the free common public schools when their parents desire to send them to parochial schools (Pierce v. Society of the Sisters of the Holy Names of Jesus and Mary, 268 U.S. 510) . . . but their attendance upon the parochial school or private school is a matter of choice and the cost thereof not a matter of public concern.

This opinion rendered in 1938 is in harmony with the prevailing practice in the states that attendance under compulsory education laws may be in public or private schools, though here again no stipulation is made that such schooling must be in an "accredited" or "approved" school.

The supreme court of Oklahoma took the position that parents are not required to send their children to public school if other means of education are furnished.[11]

In 1947 the supreme court of Pennsylvania held that a parent may send his child to a qualified school other than a public school or to a qualified private teacher or tutor. The court indicated that in such instances the school code of New York does not provide for the child's free transportation.[12]

The general rule that would be deduced — varying in different states according to the specific provisions contained in their compulsory attendance law and not nullified by the decisions rendered by the United States Supreme Court in the cases of Meyer v. Ne-

[10] 278 N.Y. 200, 15 N.E. (2d) 576 (1938).

[11] Consolidated School District 12 v. Union Graded School District No. 3, 184 Okl. 485, 94 P. (2d) 549 (1940).

[12] Connell v. Board of School Directors of Kennett Township et al., 356 Pa. 585; 52 A. (2d) 645 (1947).

braska and Pierce v. Society of Sisters — is that the states, apart from setting up reasonable requirements in parochial or private schools, may require attendance at public or approved private schools.

It would seem to be reasonable not only to leave to the legislature of the state the power to delegate proper officials to approve such private or public schools, inspection and requirements to be within reasonable bounds, but also to give to parents the privilege of choosing which school they wish their child to attend.

CHAPTER XII

Free Textbooks for Private Schools

ROVISIONS in state constitutions prohibiting the appropriation of public funds for the support of any sectarian school, or to any school which at the time of receiving such appropriations is not a part of the public school system, and other similar stipulations, have until recently been recognized as precluding the furnishing of free textbooks to other than public schools. In 1922, in the case of Smith v. Donahue, the New York court held that public funds could not be used to furnish textbooks and school supplies to parochial or other private schools.[1] There the board of education was furnishing textbooks and school supplies to certain parochial schools maintained and controlled by the Roman Catholic church. These schools were independent of the public school system. The court declared that it was the principle of the law, both constitutional and statutory, not to join religious instruction with secular education in the public schools, and that accordingly the state or a subdivision could not assist the parochial schools maintained for the purpose of furthering a given religious tenet. A similar position was taken by Maine in the early case of Donahoe v. Richards.[2] This has been the position taken by state legislatures, courts, and school boards in general.

The position, however, was reversed in 1930 in the case of Cochran v. Louisiana State Board of Education.[3] Cochran, a citizen and taxpayer of Louisiana, brought suit[4] to prevent the state board of education and other state officers from appropriating money from the Severance Tax Fund for purchasing schoolbooks to be supplied free of cost to school children under Acts 100 and 143 of 1928. The grounds were that the acts constituted a violation of the constitution of the state, which declares, "No money shall ever be taken from the

---

[1] 202 App. Div. 656, 195 N.Y.S. 715 (1922).
[2] 38 Me. 376 (1854).
[3] 281 U.S. 370 (1930).
[4] 168 La. 1030 (1929).

public treasury . . . in aid of any church, sect, or denomination of religion, or in aid of any priest, preacher, minister, or teacher there-of"[5] and that it also violated Article 4, Section 4,[6] and the Fourteenth Amendment[7] of the federal Constitution.

Act 100 provides that the Severance Tax Fund of the state

shall be devoted after allowing funds and appropriations as provided by the constitution of the state, first, to supplying schoolbooks to the school children of the state of Louisiana, and that thereafter such further sums as remain in the said Severance Tax Fund shall be transferred to the state public school funds.[8]

That the State Board of Education of Louisiana shall provide the said schoolbooks for school children free of cost to such children out of said tax fund, and thereafter apply the remaining sums out of the said Severance Tax Fund to the state public school funds.[9]

Act 143 made the necessary appropriation.[10]

The supreme court of Louisiana held that furnishing free text-books to school children was not a violation of either the state or the federal Constitution. It held further that the case presented no federal question under Article 4, Section 4, of the federal Constitution, which guarantees to every state a republican form of government and under which political rather than judicial questions arise. It was charged that the purpose of the act was to aid private, religious, sectarian, and other schools not within the public school system by furnishing free textbooks to the children attending them. The Louisiana court pointed out that such money was not appropriated for the use of any school, private, or sectarian, or even public, in the following words:

One may scan the acts in vain to ascertain where any money is appropriated for the purchase of schoolbooks for the use of any church, private,

[5] Constitution of Louisiana, Article 53.
[6] "The United States shall guarantee to every state in this Union a republican form of government, and shall protect each of them against invasion; and on application of the legislature, or of the executive (when the legislature cannot be convened) against domestic violence."
[7] "No state shall make or enforce any law which shall . . . deprive any person of life, liberty, or property, without due process of law."
[8] Louisiana Laws, 1928, Act No. 100, Section 1.
[9] *Ibid.*, Section 2. Section 3 of the act exempts from its provisions persons attending colleges or universities.
[10] "Appropriations out of that fund, $750,000 for each of those years, the appropriations to be used for the following purposes, to wit:
"For purchase of free schoolbooks for the use of school children of this state, to be expended by the State Board of Education of Louisiana as provided by House Bill No. 90 of 1928, Act No. 100 of 1928, or so much thereof as may be necessary." Louisiana Laws, 1928, Act No. 143.

sectarian, or even public school. The appropriations were made for the specific purpose of purchasing schoolbooks for the use of the school children of the state, free of cost to them. It was for their benefit and the resulting benefit to the state that the appropriations were made. True, these children attend some school, public or private, the latter sectarian or non-sectarian, and that the books are to be furnished them for their use, free of cost, whichever they attend. The schools, however, are not the beneficiaries of these appropriations. They obtain nothing from them, nor are they relieved of a single obligation because of them. The school children and the state alone are the beneficiaries. It is also true that the sectarian schools, which some of the children attend, instruct their pupils in religion, and books are used for that purpose, but one may search diligently the acts, though without result, in an effort to find anything to the effect that it is the purpose of the state to furnish religious books for the use of such children. . . . What the statutes contemplate is that the same books that are furnished children attending public schools shall be furnished children attending private schools. This is the only practical way of interpreting and executing the statutes, and this is what the State Board of Education is doing. Among these books, naturally, none is to be expected adapted to religious instruction.

The court affirmed the judgment of the trial court, and Cochran appealed to the Supreme Court of the United States. Chief Justice Hughes, who delivered the opinion, affirmed the decision of the state court. He held that tax money might be appropriated by the state to supply free schoolbooks to children in private as well as in public schools without violating the Fourteenth Amendment when the books furnished for private schools were granted not to the schools themselves but only to or for the use of the children, and when the books were the same as those furnished for public schools, not being religious or sectarian in character. He said:

Viewing the statute as having the effect thus attributed to it, we cannot doubt that the taxing power of the state is exerted for a public purpose. The legislation does not segregate private schools, or their pupils, as its beneficiaries or attempt to interfere with any matters of exclusively private concern. Its interest is education, broadly; its method, comprehensive. Individual interests are aided only as the common interest is safeguarded.

The decision in the case of Cochran v. Louisiana State Board of Education concedes greater rights to the state than that in Meyer v. Nebraska[11] and in Pierce v. Society of Sisters.[12] Those cases conceded to the state the right to require of its future citizens and voters

[11] 262 U.S. 390 (1923).
[12] 268 U.S. 510 (1925).

that they be educated, but declared it to be the right of the parent to decide whether that education should be in public schools, in private schools, or in the home through private tutors. As we have seen, they conceded that the state might regulate and superintend such education to the extent of requiring the children to be trained in good morals and good citizenship. In short, they repudiated the Spartan theory of education.

The Louisiana case authorizes general taxation for the purpose of purchasing textbooks for use in both public and private church schools, though the state constitution prohibits the appropriation of public funds for sectarian purposes. This decision, as has been pointed out, was based on the consideration that the money is not appropriated to the schools, but is expended for textbooks which are given to the children, this gift being made to all the children of the state. To use the words of the court, it is "only the use of the books that is granted to the children, or, in other words, the books are lent to them." The school children and the state alone are, consequently, the beneficiaries. No discrimination is made. All the children of the state receive the same benefits and privileges. There is no question but the Louisiana case goes farther than any case of its kind.

Following the case of Louisiana, Mississippi passed a law providing for textbooks to be loaned to the pupils in all qualified elementary schools of that state. The constitution of Mississippi provides that

no religious or other sect or sects shall ever control any part of the school or other educational funds of this state; nor shall any funds be appropriated toward the support of any sectarian school, or to any school that at the time of receiving such appropriations is not conducted as a free school.[13]

In 1941 certain taxpayers brought suit to prevent the Mississippi State Textbook Rating and Purchasing Board from providing textbooks to pupils in private and sectarian schools. The Mississippi supreme court took a similar position to that taken by the United States Supreme Court in the case of Cochran v. Louisiana State Board of Education, maintaining that the books were only a loan to the pupils and that the purchase of such books was in support of the "child benefit" theory. The court said:

The religion to which children of school age adhere is not subject to control by the state; but the children themselves are subject to its control. If the pupil may fulfil its duty to the state by attending a parochial school

[13] Constitution of Mississippi, Section 208.

it is difficult to see why the state may not fulfil its duty to the pupil by encouraging it "by all suitable means." The state is under a duty to ignore the child's creed, but not its need. It cannot control what one child may think, but it can and must do all it can to teach the child how to think. The state which allows the pupil to subscribe to any religious creed should not, because of his exercise of this right, proscribe him from benefits common to all.[14]

The court reasoned that the appropriation for schools is entirely separate; that the use of the textbook fund constitutes no charge against any public school fund properly so called, or against any trust funds available for particular schools or educational purposes. The books, they contended, belong to and are controlled by the state and are merely loaned to the individual pupil; the privilege of requisitioning such books by qualified private or sectarian schools to loan to its pupils does not place in such schools the control of any part of the educational funds of the state.

A number of states now empower local school authorities to distribute textbooks free of charge to the pupils of parochial schools.[15]

In 1941 the attorney general of Indiana gave an opinion that the Indiana law providing free textbooks, though very general in its nature, does not include parochial school children.[16]

In that same year the legislature of Oregon voted to provide public money to purchase textbooks for pupils in private or parochial schools as well as in the public schools. Opposition to this law resulted in the circulation of petitions to secure a referendum on the subject. Sufficient signers were secured to insure placing of the question on the ballot in 1942, but the state supreme court ruled that the title under which the petitions were circulated was not worded properly and the petition was thrown out.

The plan of state aid to all students without regard to whether they attend private or public schools has been in general practice for some time in matters of health. To some the furnishing of free textbooks to children regardless of what school they attend is simply an extension of the law recognized in the field of public health. Others maintain that the furnishing of free textbooks to the children of parochial schools is the "first breach" in the wall between church and state. If it is conceded that textbooks essential to education may be furnished to all children through state appropriations, might it not be granted that athletic supplies or musical instruments are es-

[14] Chance v. Mississippi State Textbook Rating and Purchasing Board, 200 So. 706 (1941).
[15] For example, New Mexico Statutes, 1941, Annotated, Vol. 4, Ch. 55, Secs. 1703, 1711.
[16] Opinions of the Attorney General, Indiana, 1941, p. 284.

sential to an education and that therefore might properly be paid for by the state? And that since teachers are necessary in furnishing children an education, all teachers should be paid by the state; that on whatever basis we justify the purchase of textbooks from public tax funds, on that same basis we may justify the purchase of buildings by public tax funds in which to study these books. May it not be that if government money can be used for church schools it can also be used for the support of our churches, and that we are moving toward a union of church and state in America.

CHAPTER XIII

Free Transportation to Private Schools

THE transportation of school children was no problem in the days when boys and girls tramped a mile or two to the little red schoolhouse at the center of the town, or at the corner of the section line. Sometimes the farmer-father might provide a ride, or a helpful neighbor join in a share and share alike plan, or there might be an incidental "hitch"; otherwise, the children walked.

When the consolidated school plan was put into operation, the money spent for the little town or district schoolhouses was concentrated for more effective buying in the building trades market, and better, though fewer, schools were built. Instructors with more technical training could be employed. But with the consolidated school, the one or two miles were increased for many of the pupils to five, six, or even ten.

Hence came the era of pupil transportation. Concentration of funds, and of course increase in school taxes, provided means for horses and wagons, hired by the boards of consolidated school districts, to bring the children to school. When the automobile supplanted the horse, the school bus supplanted the school wagon.

With the transportation of pupils came laws and rulings and court decisions on the subject. Legislation followed the evolution of the practice and regulated it, and the courts in turn defined what the legislatures had intended by their laws.

The first question was whether provision for hauling the children to school was required of the school boards or whether it was optional. In many districts pupil transportation was arranged for as need arose by the local school boards, without authorization higher than their own discretionary powers. Demands for wider and more complete transportation service were met with the argument that the rendering of such service was optional, not mandatory, and that it would be given only as funds and equipment and necessity dictated.

State legislatures, when they enacted laws dealing with school problems, began to include provisions for the transportation of pupils. The service became more and more general and was looked upon as a concomitant of school operation. When parents found themselves living a considerable distance from the routes of school transportation facilities, and their pleas to have their children accommodated went in some instances unheeded, they brought suit in the courts.

Again and again decisions were handed down that the furnishing of transportation to school pupils was a matter of discretion with the school boards,[1] and was mandatory only when the laws made it so.[2] When specific allotments of funds for pupil transportation had been exhausted, no further service in this category could be demanded.[3]

In order to meet the needs, service has not been limited to buses; contracts have been made with, or regulations have been applied to, street railway companies for the transportation of school pupils at less than regular rates. This has been held to be permissive.[4]

Although the laws require that school boards shall provide proper and sufficient facilities for maintaining an adequate school system, it has been ruled that failure to provide pupil transportation is not a failure to provide these facilities.[5] Pupil transportation has been called a function in maintaining and developing the school system. There has arisen on numerous occasions the important question of whether transportation of pupils is a benefit to the pupil only, or whether it is also a benefit for, and to the interest and progress of, the school as an institution.

In determining such benefits reference has frequently been made

[1] Newcomb et al. v. Inhabitants of Rockford et al., 66 N.E. 587 (1903); Queeny v. Higgins et al., 114 N.W. 51 (1907); Fogg v. Board of Education of Union School District of Littleton et al., 82 Atl. 173 (1912); State ex rel. Brand v. Mostad et al., 148 N.W. 831 (1914); Berry v. School Board of Barrington, 95 Atl. 952 (1915); Jennings, County Judge et al. v. Carson, 184 S.W. 562 (1916); McKenzie et al. v. Board of Education of Floyd County et al., 124 S.E. 721 (1924); Douglas et al. v. Board of Education of Johnson County et al., 138 S.E. 226 (1927); Hein v. Luther, Clerk of District Court No. 2, etc., et al., 221 N.W. 386 (1928); Bruggeman v. Independent School District No. 4, Union Township, Mitchell County, 289 N.W. 5 (1939); Harwood v. Dysart Consolidated School District et al., 21 N.W. (2d) 334 (1946).

[2] Eastgate v. Osago School District of Nelson County, 171 N.W. 96 (1919); State ex rel. Robison v. Desonia et al., 215 Pac. 220 (1923); Bruggeman v. Independent School District No. 4, Union Township, Mitchell County, 289 N.W. 5 (1939); Hines v. Pulaski County Board of Education et al., 166 S.W. (2d) 37 (1942).

[3] Henry C. Mills et al. v. School Directors of Consolidated District No. 537, 154 Ill. App. 119 (1910); Berry v. School of Barrington, 95 Atl. 952 (1915); Douglas et al. v. Board of Education of Johnson County et al., 138 S.E. 226 (1927).

[4] Commonwealth v. Interstate Consolidated Street Railway Co., 73 N.E. 530 (1907), affirmed by the United States Supreme Court, 207 U.S. 79; Public Service Railway Co. v. Board of Public Utilities Commissioners, 80 Atl. 27 (1917).

[5] Board of Education of Frelinghuysen Township v. Atwood, County Superintendent of Public Instruction, 62 Atl. 1130 (1906).

to the case of Pierre University, a denominational college owned and maintained for sectarian purposes. The university sued the state of South Dakota for continuance of support for students sent to the institution by the state while still a territory, for teacher training. The supreme court of South Dakota ruled that it was unconstitutional for public funds to be paid to any sectarian school, in spite of the service rendered. Reference was made in the decision to the definition of aid, as given in Webster's dictionary: "to support, either by furnishing strength or means to help to success." [6]

In view of the repeated claims that aid can be given to pupils without aiding the school, a case which concerned the furnishing of school supplies to pupils in parochial schools is of interest. The court pointed out clearly that

the school is not the building; it is the organization, the union of all the elements in the organization, to furnish education in some branch of learning. . . . It is the institution, and the teachers and scholars together, that make it up. The pupils are a part of the school. . . . It seems to us to be giving a strange and unusual meaning to words if we hold that the books and the ordinary school supplies, when furnished for the use of pupils, is a furnishing to the pupils, and not a furnishing in aid of maintenance of a school of learning. It seems very plain that such furnishing is at least indirectly in aid of the institution, and that, if not in actual violation of the words, it is in violation of the true intent and meaning, of the Constitution, and in consequence equally unconstitutional.[7]

A number of state supreme courts have ruled that to transport pupils to a school—and in each instance the cases involved parochial schools—was to benefit the institution to which the pupils were brought.[8] The service is still to be accounted as aid, even though it must be called "indirect." [9]

Against this contention is the opinion that aid can be given by the state to pupils without being a benefit to be recognized in law as aid to the institution which the pupils attend. In support of this position, reference is frequently made to the Louisiana textbook

[6] Dakota Synod v. State, 50 N.W. 632, 635 (1891).

[7] Smith v. Donahue et al., 195 N.Y.S. 715, 721 (1922).

[8] State ex rel. Traub v. Brown, 172 Atl. 835, 837 (1934); Judd et al. v. Board of Education of Union Free School District No. 2, Town of Hempstead, Nassau County, et al. (Bennett, Attorney General et al., Interveners), 15 N.E. 576, 581 (1938); Gurney et al. v. Ferguson et al., 122 Pac. (2d) 1002, 1004 (1942); Sherrard v. Jefferson County Board of Education et al., 171 S.W. (2d) 963, 968 (1942); Mitchell v. Consolidated School District No. 21 et al., 135 Pac. (2d) 79, 82 (1943).

[9] Judd et al. v. Board of Education of Union Free School District No. 2, Town of Hempstead, Nassau County, et al. (Bennett, Attorney General et al., Interveners), 15 N.E. 576, 582 (1938).

case.[10] This principle has been applied in several cases to the question of whether state funds may be used in transporting pupils to parochial schools. In one decision it was recognized that such transportation is an aid to the school, but not sufficiently to prevent the legislature from providing the pupils the necessary transportation.[11] In another case it was argued that "the fact that in a strained and technical sense the school might derive an indirect benefit from the enactment, is not sufficient to defeat the declared purpose and the practical and wholesome effect of the law."[12] Again, the aid, it was contended, is only incidental, such as is provided by many other public services, like sidewalks, streets, highways, sewers, and police and fire protection.[13]

Whenever the courts have recognized that transportation of pupils to parochial schools at public expense was an aid to a sectarian institution, the service was declared unconstitutional because it resulted in a union of church and state contrary to the state constitutions having jurisdiction. In a Wisconsin case it was shown that public school buses had transported twenty-seven children out of a district where the public school had been closed to another district. Twenty-five of these children went to a parochial school; only four pursued some studies in the public school. The court ruled that

the whole scope and purpose of the statute is to comply with the provisions of the constitutional mandate, and that requires that free, nonsectarian instruction be provided for all persons of school age. The board is not authorized to expend public funds for any other purpose. The contract made by the district board whereby it attempted to provide transportation of pupils to a private school was an act beyond its authority and therefore invalid. . . . The school board is by statute authorized to provide transportation for such children of school age as desire to attend a public school and no other.[14]

It has been recognized that parents who preferred parochial to public schools were permitted by law to follow their choice. But in South Dakota it has been ruled that under prevailing statutes school boards have no authority to transport parochial school pupils, and legal arrangements cannot be made to do so. Constitutional objections were not raised in the case in point.[15] In a Delaware case it

[10] Borden v. Louisiana State Board of Education, 123 So. 655 (1929); Cochran v. Louisiana State Board of Education, 123 So. 664, 281 U.S. 370 (1930). See Chapter XII.
[11] Board of Education of Baltimore County v. Wheat, 199 Atl. 628, 632 (1938).
[12] Nichols et al. v. Henry, 191 S.W. (2d) 930, 935 (1945).
[13] Bowker v. Baker et al., 167 Pac. (2d) 256, 261 (1946).
[14] State ex rel. Van Straten v. Milquet, 192 N.W. 392, 395 (1923).
[15] Hlebanja v. Brewe, 236 N.W. 296, 297 (1931).

was held that controlling statutes made it illegal to use public funds, whether general or school funds, for the transportation of parochial school pupils.[16]

In a New York case, however, the constitutional issue was squarely met. Under an amended state statute, the commissioner of education issued an order that public funds might be used to transport pupils to parochial schools. A taxpayer brought suit, and the court ruled that under the New York constitution

aid or support to the school "directly or indirectly" is proscribed. The two words must have been used with some definite intent and purpose; otherwise why were they used at all? Aid furnished "directly" would be that furnished in a direct line, both literally and figuratively, to the school itself, unmistakably earmarked, and without circumlocution or ambiguity. Aid furnished "indirectly" clearly embraces any contribution, to whomsoever made, circuitously, collaterally disguised, or otherwise not in a straight, open and direct course for the open and avowed aid of the school, that may be to the benefit of the institution or promotional of its interests and purposes. How could the people have expressed their purpose in the fundamental law in more apt, simple and all-embracing language? Free transportation of pupils induced attendance at the school. The purpose of the transportation is to promote the interests of the private school or religious or sectarian institution that controls and directs it. . . . Without pupils there could be no school. It is illogical to say that the furnishing of transportation is not an aid to the institution while the employment of teachers and furnishing of books, accommodations and other facilities are such an aid. In the instant case, $3,350 was appropriated out of public moneys solely for the transportation of the relatively few pupils attending the specific school in question. If the cardinal rule that written constitutions are to receive uniform and unvarying interpretation and practical construction is to be followed, in view of interpretation in analagous cases it cannot successfully be maintained that the furnishing of transportation to the private or parochial school out of public money is not in aid or support of the school.[17]

It must be noted that in 1938 the New York state constitution was amended to legalize bus transportation to any kind of school without distinction.

In harmony with the New York case was an Oklahoma decision in 1942. When a school district attempted to transport pupils through

---

[16] State ex rel. Traub et al. v. Brown et al., 172 Atl. 835, 836 (1934). See dismissal of this case before the supreme court of Delaware in 1938, 197 Atl. 478.

[17] Judd et al. v. Board of Education of Union Free School District No. 2, Town of Hempstead, Nassau County et al. (Bennett, Attorney General et al., Interveners), 15 N.E. (2d) 576, 582, 583 (1938).

the expenditure of public funds to parochial schools, the court ruled that

The appropriation and directed use of public funds in transportation of public school children is openly in direct aid to public schools "as such." When such aid is purported to be extended to a sectarian school there is in our judgment a clear violation of the above-quoted provisions [Section 5, Article 2] of our Constitution.[18]

In Kentucky, the school law included a section requiring that the state furnish transportation to pupils attending private schools. The state supreme court ruled this portion of the law unconstitutional.

The portion of the law requiring that pupils attending private schools be given the same transportation rights as pupils of public schools violates constitutional provision requiring that taxes be levied and collected "for public purposes" only and that no sums shall be collected for education other than in "common schools" until the question of taxation is submitted to legal voters, as against the claim that the statute was for the aid of children, and not for the schools.[19]

In commenting on arguments of the defendants, based upon the Louisiana textbook case, the court said:

It is obvious that the Louisiana case and a few others of similar import relied on for defendants are contrary to the great weight of authority, and are lacking in persuasive reasoning and logic. We are of the opinion, therefore, that the Act here under consideration is unconstitutional and therefore void.[20]

A Washington case in 1943 also ruled against transportation of parochial school pupils as unconstitutional. The court said:

We cannot . . . accept the validity of the argument that transportation of pupils to and from school is not beneficial to, and in aid of, the school. Even legislation providing for transfer of pupils to and from the public school is constitutionally defensible only as the exercise of a governmental function furthering the maintenance and development of the common school system. We think the conclusion is inescapable that free transportation of pupils serves to aid and build up the school itself. That pupils and parents may also derive benefit from it, is beside the question.[21]

In 1945 the state of Washington passed a law providing for trans-

[18] Gurney et al. v. Ferguson et al., 122 Pac. (2d) 1002, 1004.
[19] Synopsis 6 in Sherrard v. Jefferson County Board of Education et al., 171 S.W. (2d) 963 (1942).
[20] Ibid., p. 968.
[21] Mitchell v. Consolidated School District No. 21 et al., 135 Pac. (2d) 79, 82.

portation of parochial school children. In 1947 this enactment was in the process of being challenged in the Washington courts.

In order to remove the question of parochial pupil transportation from the constitutional area, it has been strongly argued that it is a duty of the state to protect and benefit all its citizens, and that it is legal to transport parochial pupils at public expense on eleemosynary grounds or on the grounds of police power. The eleemosynary argument was put forward to support a school resolution that a group of 141 physically handicapped pupils be transported at public expense for instruction in a parochial school where religious tenets were taught. The supreme court of New York County ruled that this service was in the same category as providing pupils with lunch. The case was carried through the New York court of appeals to the state supreme court, where it was dismissed for lack of constitutional grounds for the appeal.[22]

The Kentucky supreme court ruled in 1942 that the portion of the school law which required transportation of parochial school children was unconstitutional.[23] But while reaffirming its decision in connection with a later case, it ruled constitutional an amendment to the law giving county superintendents authority to provide public funds to transport parochial pupils — not, however, by special taxation, but in the general budget. The court stated that the act "constitutes simply what it purports to be — an exercise of police power for the protection of childhood against the inclemency of the weather and from the hazards of present-day traffic."[24]

In a California case the argument of police power was stressed. A state law authorizing transportation of parochial pupils was upheld, and in its decision the court stated:

Raising the standard of intelligence of youth and providing for the safety of children are legitimate objects of government and are authorized under the police powers. It is also true that the transportation of pupils to and from public schools is one of the legitimate methods adopted to help promote education and safeguard children. If the transportation of pupils to and from public schools is authorized, as it certainly is, and if the benefit from that transportation is to the pupils, then an incidental benefit flowing to a denominational school from free transportation of its pupils

[22] Lewis v. Board of Education of the City of New York, 275 N.Y. 480, 544; 11 N.E. (2d) 307, 643 (1937).
[23] Sherrard v. Jefferson County Board of Education.
[24] Nichols et al. v. Henry, 191 S.W. (2d) 930, 932, 933, 934 (1945). Compare with the argument of an earlier Maryland decision that compulsory school attendance justifies furnishing transportation to parochial school pupils: Board of Education of Baltimore County v. Wheat, 199 Atl. 628, 632, 633 (1938).

should not be sufficient to deprive the legislature of the power to authorize a school district to transport such pupils.[25]

Exception is taken to the position based on police power in the case of Gurney et al. v. Ferguson et al., in which the court ruled that transportation for parochial school children was not "furnished in regulating traffic within the police power, or primarily in promoting the health and safety of the children of the state." [26]

Up to 1946 there had been decided in the courts eleven cases, seven opposed to transporting parochial school children, four favoring. The two most recent cases, Nichols v. Henry (Kentucky, 1945) and Bowker v. Baker (California, 1946), both in favor of transporting school children to parochial schools, argued strongly the need of safeguarding the health and welfare of the children.

It was with this emphasis that the United States Supreme Court in a five to four decision upheld the first school bus case to reach it. The case came to the court from New Jersey late in 1946. The New Jersey law called in question stated that all pupils should have the benefit of transportation to school, and that where no school bus routes were available to a pupil, he might ride on the highway buses, and his parents or guardians would be reimbursed by the state. One Everson, a taxpayer, brought suit against the township of Ewing, because the school board had reimbursed parents when their children rode to a parochial school on the highway buses. The law forbade reimbursement when the pupils attended private schools that were operated partly or in whole for profit.

The decision in the case was handed down on February 10, 1947. The findings of the court were that the New Jersey law is constitutional. This decision declared constitutional the transporting of parochial children at public expense when the state law made provision for it. The argument of the court supporting the legislation was presented under two heads, corresponding to the plea of the appellant.

The first was a consideration of the question of whether payments for transportation from public funds, provided by all the taxpayers, to parents who chose to send their children to church schools, was a violation of the "due process" clause of the Fourteenth Amendment. The court decided it was not. The state legislature had passed legislation authorizing such payments, and the highest New Jersey court had approved it. The court said:

The fact that a state law, passed to satisfy a public need, coincides with

[25] Bowker v. Baker et al., 167 Pac. (2d) 256, 261, 262 (1946).
[26] 122 Pac. (2d) 1002, 1004 (1942).

the personal desires of the individuals most directly affected is certainly an inadequate reason for us to say that the legislature has erroneously appraised the public need.[27]

The second classification in the majority decision considered the question of whether the New Jersey statute violated the First Amendment of the federal Constitution because it gave support to a religious establishment by paying the transportation of pupils to parochial schools. The court emphasized that under the First Amendment church and state in the United States must be kept separate.

Neither a state nor the Federal Government can set up a church. Neither can pass laws which aid one religion, aid all religions, or prefer one religion over another. Neither can force or influence a person to go to or remain away from church against his will or force him to profess a belief or disbelief in any religion. No person can be punished for entertaining or professing religious beliefs or disbeliefs, for church attendance or non-attendance. No tax in any amount, large or small, can be levied to support any religious activities or institutions, whatever they may be called, or whatever form they may adopt to teach or practice religion. Neither a state nor the Federal Government can, openly or secretly, participate in the affairs of any religious organizations or groups and vice versa. . . . New Jersey cannot consistently with the "establishment of religion" clause of the First Amendment contribute tax-raised funds to the support of an institution which teaches the tenets and faith of any church. On the other hand, other language of the amendment commands that New Jersey cannot hamper its citizens in the free exercise of their own religion. Consequently, it cannot exclude Catholics, Lutherans, Mohammedans, Baptists, Jews, Methodists, Non-believers, Presbyterians, or the members of any other faith, *because of their faith, or lack of it,* from receiving the benefits of public welfare legislation. . . .[28]

Two dissents were filed in this case. Mr. Justice Jackson's contended that

The court sustains this legislation by assuming two deviations from the facts of this particular case; first, it assumes a state of the facts the record does not support, and secondly, it refuses to consider facts which are inescapable on the record.[29]

He pointed out that the township of Ewing was not transporting any pupils, but paying the fares of pupils who rode to public or parochial schools.

[27] Everson v. Board of Education of Ewing Township et al., 67 S. Ct. 504, 507 (1947).
[28] *Ibid.*, pp. 511, 512.
[29] *Ibid.*, pp. 513, 514.

This expenditure of tax funds has no possible effect on the child's safety or expenditure in transit. As passengers on the public busses they travel as fast and no faster, and are as safe and no safer, since their parents are reimbursed as before.

Mr. Justice Jackson also contended that

under the Act and resolution brought to us by this case children are classified according to the schools they attend and are to be aided if they attend the public schools or private Catholic schools, and they are not allowed to be aided if they attend private secular schools or private religious schools of other faiths. . . . Our question is simply this: Is it constitutional to tax this complainant to pay the cost of carrying pupils to church schools of one specified denomination? . . .

It is of no importance in this situation whether the beneficiary of this expenditure of tax-raised funds is primarily the parochial school and incidentally the pupil, or whether the aid is directly bestowed on the pupil with indirect benefits to the school. The state cannot maintain a Church and it can no more tax its citizens to furnish free carriage to those who attend a Church. The prohibition against establishment of religion cannot be circumvented by a subsidy, bonus or reimbursement of expense to individuals for receiving religious instruction and indoctrination.[30]

In the second dissent by Mr. Justice Rutledge, the emphasis was upon the fact that by the majority opinion the wall separating church and state in this country was breached.

Neither so high nor so impregnable today as yesterday is the wall raised between church and state by Virginia's great statute of religious freedom and the First Amendment, now made applicable to all the states by the Fourteenth. New Jersey's statute sustained is the first, if indeed it is not the second breach to be made by this Court's action. That a third, and a fourth, and still others will be attempted, we may be sure. For just as Cochran v. Louisiana State Board of Education 281 US 370, 50 S.Ct. 335, 74 L.Ed. 913, has opened the way by oblique ruling for this decision, so will the two make wider the breach for the third. Thus with time the most solid freedom steadily gives way before continuing corrosive decision. . . .

Not simply an established church, but any law respecting an establishment of religion is forbidden. The First Amendment was broadly but not loosely phrased. . . . The Amendment's purpose was not to strike merely at the official establishment of a single sect, creed or religion, outlawing only a formal relation such as had prevailed in England and some of the colonies. Necessarily it was to uproot all such relationships. But the object was broader than separating church and state in this narrow sense. It was to create a complete and permanent separation of the spheres of religious

[30] *Ibid.*, pp. 515, 516.

activity and civil authority by comprehensively forbidding every form of public aid or support for religion. . . .

Does New Jersey's action furnish support for religion by use of the taxing power? Certainly it does, if the test remains . . . that money taken by taxation from one is not to be used or given to support another's religious training or belief, or indeed one's own. . . . The prohibition is absolute for whatever measure brings that consequence and whatever amount may be sought or given to that end. The funds used here were raised by taxation. The Court does not dispute nor could it that their use does in fact give aid and encouragement to religious instruction. It only concludes that this aid is not "support" in law. . . . Here parents spend money to send their children to parochial schools and funds raised by taxation are used to reimburse them. This not only helps the children to get to school and the parents to send them. It aids them in a substantial way to get the very thing which they are sent to the parochial school to secure, namely, religious training and teaching. . . .

An appropriation from the public treasury to pay the cost of transportation to Sunday school, to weekday special classes at the church or parish house, or to the meetings of various young people's religious societies, such as the Y.M.C.A., the Y.W.C.A., the Y.M.H.A., the Epworth League, could not withstand the constitutional attack. This would be true, whether or not secular activities were mixed with religious. If such an appropriation could not stand, then it is hard to see how one becomes valid for the same thing upon the more extended scale of daily instruction. Surely constitutionality does not turn on where or how often the mixed teaching occurs. . . .

Of course discrimination in the legal sense does not exist. The child attending the religious school has the same right as any other to attend the public school. But he foregoes exercising it because the same guaranty which assures this freedom forbids the public school or any agency of the state to give or aid him in securing the religious instruction he seeks. . . .

Whatever might be said of some other application of New Jersey's statute, the one made here has no semblance of bearing as a safety measure or, indeed, for securing expeditious conveyance. The transportation supplied is by public conveyance, subject to all the hazards and delays of the highway and the streets incurred by the public generally in going about its multifarious business.

Nor is the case comparable to one of furnishing fire or police protection, or access to public highways. These things are matters of common right, part of the general need for safety. Certainly the fire department must not stand idly by while the church burns. Nor is this reason why the state should pay the expense of transportation or other items of the cost of religious education. . . .

Two great drives are constantly in motion to abridge, in the name of education, the complete division of religion and civil authority which our forefathers made. One is to introduce religious education and observances into the public schools. The other, to obtain public funds for the aid and support of various private religious schools. See Johnson, the Legal Status of Church-State Relationships in the United States (1934); Thayer, Religion in Public Education (1947); Note (1941) 50 Yale L.J. 917. In my opinion both avenues were closed by the Constitution. Neither should be opened by this Court. . . .[31]

In the meantime, a Pennsylvania case was on its way to the Supreme Court. In the town of Kennett Square, Pennsylvania, parochial children had been riding for some years on the public school buses. In the fall of 1946 the county superintendent order the buses to desist from hauling the parochial school children, since the Pennsylvania law made no provision for such extension of service. Suit was brought and carried to the superior court of Pennsylvania. From there it reached the United States Supreme Court in April 1947. Before the case could be heard, the appellant petitioned the court for permission to withdraw, and the privilege was granted.[32]

In Iowa the school bus transportation system is maintained by an annual two-million-dollar budget. The Iowa law does not specify that only children attending public schools may avail themselves of the pupil transportation service provided by the state of Iowa, but a states' attorney general has ruled that it is illegal to transport pupils to parochial or private schools. A consolidated school district sought a declaratory judgment that parochial school children living along the regular school bus routes be transported to the schools of their choice.

When the case reached the state supreme court, the decision supported the lower courts and ruled that only pupils attending public school might be transported.

We believe that the school laws of the state concern only the public schools unless otherwise expressly indicated, and do and can apply only to the schools within the purview of the school statutes, or under the control and jurisdiction of public school officials, and that this would apply to transportation.[33]

By the end of 1947 courts in six states (Wisconsin, South Dakota, Delaware, Oklahoma, Washington, and Iowa) had prohibited the transportation of parochial pupils at public expense. Maryland, Kentucky, and New Jersey have court decisions supporting such trans-

[31] *Ibid.,* pp. 518, 519, 525, 527, 533, 534.
[32] *Religious News Service,* April 17, 1947.
[33] Silver Lake Consolidated School District v. Parker et al., 29 N.W. (2d) 214, 219 (1947).

portation. New York has amended its constitution to permit the hauling of parochial school pupils, thus nullifying the earlier decision in Judd v. Board of Education. The new state constitution of New Jersey, adopted in November 1947 by popular referendum, provides for transportation of all school children. Wisconsin rejected by popular vote in November 1946 an amendment which would have provided for the hauling of all pupils to school.

As reported by the Federal Council of Churches of Christ in America on January 1, 1947, there were nineteen states and one territory in which constitutions or statutes permitted the transportation of parochial school pupils at public expense.[34]

This question, in its various phases, of the transportation of pupils to private or parochial schools at public expense gives promise of much future controversy and litigation.

[34] These included California, Colorado, Connecticut, Hawaii, Illinois, Indiana, Kentucky, Louisiana, Maryland, Massachusetts, Michigan, New Hampshire, New Jersey, New Mexico, New York, Ohio, Oregon, Rhode Island, Washington, and Wyoming. Federal Council of Churches of Christ in America, *Federal Aid to Sectarian Education?* (New York, April 1947), p. 11.

CHAPTER XIV

Anti-Evolution Laws

A QUESTION that has been closely associated with the subject of religion in the public schools is represented by the so-called anti-evolution laws.

On March 5, 1921, the state of Utah passed the following law:

Section 1. It shall be unlawful to teach in any of the district schools of this state while in session, any atheistic, infidel, sectarian, religious, or denominational doctrine and all such schools shall be free from sectarian control.

Section 2. Nothing in this act shall be deemed to prohibit the giving of any moral instruction tending to impress upon the minds of the pupils the importance and necessity of good manners, truthfulness, temperance, purity, patriotism, and industry, but such instruction shall be given in connection with the regular school work.[1]

It will be noted that this statute provides that no "atheistic" or "infidel" doctrines are to be taught in any of the district schools of Utah. These are specifically designated in addition to the usual "sectarian," "religious," or "denominational" prohibitions. Section 2 permits "moral instruction," but such instruction must be given in connection with the regular school work.

In 1923 the house of representatives of Florida passed the following resolution, in which the senate concurred:

That it is the sense of the legislature of the state of Florida that it is improper and subversive to the best interests of the people of this state for any professor, teacher, or instructor in the public schools and colleges of this state, supported in whole or in part by public taxation, to teach or permit to be taught atheism or agnosticism, or to teach as true Darwinism, or any other hypothesis that links man in blood relationship to any other form of life.[2]

In March 1925 the Tennessee anti-evolution law went into effect. It reads:

[1] Utah Laws, 1921, Chapter 95.
[2] House Concurrent Resolution No. 7, House Journal, 1923, pp. 2200, 2201.

It shall be unlawful for any teacher in any of the universities, teachers' colleges, normal schools, or other public schools of the state which are supported, in whole or in part, by the public school funds of the state, to teach any theory that denies the story of the divine creation of man as taught in the Bible, and to teach instead that man descended from a lower order of animals.[3]

Section 2345 provides that any teacher who violates the statute shall be guilty of a misdemeanor and be subject to a fine of not less than one hundred dollars nor more than five hundred dollars for each offense.

It was under this statute that John Thomas Scopes, a teacher in the public schools of Rhea County, Tennessee, was indicted for denying the story of the divine creation of man as taught by the Bible and teaching instead that man descended from a lower order of animals. He was found guilty before the trial judge and fined one hundred dollars. Scopes appealed to the supreme court of Tennessee, which handed down, on January 15, 1927, a majority vote upholding the constitutionality of the statute. Prominent among the attorneys, numbering approximately a dozen on each side of the case, were Clarence Darrow, who defended Scopes, and William Jennings Bryan, who represented the state. Among the issues in the case was the question of whether or not the anti-evolution act as passed by the legislature violated the constitutional provision that "it shall be the duty of the general assembly . . . to cherish literature and science."[4] Did it violate the constitutional provision "that no preference shall ever be given, by law, to any religious establishment or mode of worship"?[5] Was it a violation of the Fourteenth Amendment of the Constitution of the United States[6] or of the Tennessee constitutional provision "that no man shall be taken or imprisoned, or disseized of his freehold, liberties, or privileges, or outlawed, or exiled, or in any manner destroyed, or deprived of his life, liberty, or property, but by the judgment of his peers or the law of the land"?[7]

Although the court held that the anti-evolution act did not violate the constitution, it did hold that the fine of one hundred dollars assessed by the trial judge was unconstitutional, since under the consti-

[3] Code of Tennessee, 1932, Section 2344.
[4] Constitution of Tennessee, Article 11, Section 12.
[5] Ibid., Article 1, Section 3.
[6] "No state shall make or enforce any law which shall abridge the privileges or immunities of citizens of the United States; nor shall any state deprive any person of life, liberty, or property without due process of law; nor deny to any person within its jurisdiction the equal protection of the laws."
[7] Constitution of Tennessee, Article 1, Section 8.

tution of Tennessee a fine exceeding fifty dollars must be assessed by a jury. Inasmuch as the statute in question did not permit a fine smaller than one hundred dollars, there was no power in the supreme court to correct the error, and the judgment of the lower court was therefore reversed. The court suggested to the attorney general that he make an entry of nolle prosequi, stating that "we see nothing to be gained by prolonging the life of this bizarre case. On the contrary we think the peace and dignity of the state . . . will be the better conserved" by dismissing the case.[8] The attorney general acted in accordance with the suggestion of the court and nol-prossed the action.[9]

Chief Justice Green gave the opinion of the court, Justice Cook concurred, and Justice Chambliss concurred with an extended opinion dealing with the theistic and materialistic theories of evolution; Justice McKinney dissented.[10] The court in the majority opinion said in speaking of Scopes:

He was under contract with the state to work in an institution of the state. He had no right or privilege to serve the state except upon such terms as the state prescribed. His liberty, his privilege, his immunity to teach and proclaim the theory of evolution elsewhere than in the service of the state was in no wise touched by this law.

The court pointed out further that the statute under consideration was not an exercise of the police power in an attempt to regulate the conduct and contracts of individuals in their dealings with each other, but an act of the state as a "corporation, a proprietor, an employer . . . a declaration of a master as to the character of work the master's servant shall, or rather shall not, perform." If the legislature thought that by reason of popular prejudice the courses of education in the study of science in general would be promoted by forbidding the teaching of evolution in the schools of the state, the court declared that it could conceive of no ground to justify its interference.

In the charge made that the act contravenes the provision of Section 3, Article 1, of the constitution providing that "no preference shall be given, by law, to any religious establishment or mode of worship," the court said:

We are not able to see how the prohibition of teaching the theory that man has descended from a lower order of animals gives preference to any

[8] Scopes v. State, 154 Tenn. 105, 289 S.W. 363 (1927).
[9] *New York Times*, January 22, 1927.
[10] Justice Swiggert took no part in the decision, since he had come on the bench during the trial, following the death of Justice Hall.

religious establishment or mode of worship. . . . Belief or unbelief in the theory of evolution is no more a characteristic of any religious establishment or mode of worship than is belief or unbelief in the wisdom of the prohibition laws.

Furthermore, Chapter 27 of the acts of 1925 requires the teaching of nothing. It only forbids the teaching of the evolution of man from a lower order of animals.

The law forbids teaching in the public schools of the state the theory of the evolution of man, but it does not require that anything contrary to that theory be taught. The court pointed out that if the school authorities felt that the statute so hampered the teaching of the science of biology, thereby preventing it from being a desirable course, they were at liberty to omit the course of biology entirely from the school curriculum; that if such a procedure was unfortunate, the misfortune must be charged to the legislature, for the validity of a statute must be determined by its moral and legal effect rather than by its proclaimed motives.[11]

Although it is not within the power of the court to compel the legislature to pass any particular kind of law, positive or negative, it must be kept in mind that if the legislature passes an act that is unconstitutional, the court has not only the power but also the duty to declare such a law unconstitutional.

In the majority opinion the court held that the statute was not subject to attack on the ground of uncertainty. It said that the draftsman of the law used what in rhetoric is called "exposition by iteration," the purpose of the statute being to prohibit the teaching of the evolution theory, which teaching could be prevented by forbidding the teaching of any theory that denied the Bible story of creation. To make this purpose clear the law forbids the teaching that man descended from a lower order of animals.

Justice McKinney dissented from this opinion on the ground that the law in question was not sufficiently explicit to determine its actual meaning. It has been insisted that being a criminal statute it should be definite. It is maintained that there is danger that an intelligent man who entertains the view that the story of Genesis and the principles of evolution can be reconciled may interpret the statute too liberally. As it stands the statute is said to be too indefinite as to what it is that actually constitutes the "teaching of evolution." The evolutionist wonders just how suggestive of the evolution of man must be the facts to make the teacher a criminal under the

[11] Lockner v. New York, 198 U.S. 45 (1905).

Tennessee statutes. Will the medical teacher, for example, be barred from exhibiting blood tests from animals, including man, in the various positions in the scheme of classification, where the different species show relationships chemically which suggest to most students evolution from a common ancestry? So in teaching physiology, biology, or geology, just how far can the teacher go? Can he present all or any data supporting the theory of evolution, provided he does not make the inference?

It is urged that it is uncertain what facts, how strong an array of them, or how much useful information the teacher would have to present to make himself guilty of the crime. There is, therefore, a real basis for urging that the statute is void because of its indefiniteness.

There is also considerable evidence that it was a religious motive that prompted the passage of the act. Whether the legislature of a state, upon the theory of the complete separation of church and state, might properly enact such religious legislation and whether it might provide and regulate a curriculum for the schools of a state that might amount to direct mandatory control over the religious opinions and utterances of the teachers became significant questions.

The indictment against the teaching of the doctrine of evolution is that it contradicts the principles of religion and the story of creation as it is given in the Bible and that it ultimately leads to general unbelief. Such men are cited as Charles Darwin, Herbert Spencer, Thomas Henry Huxley, John Stuart Mill, H. G. Wells, and others whose studies in science have shattered their faith in God and in the Bible as a divine revelation of His will. This position is strengthened by the fact that Clarence Darrow, who declared hmself to be an agnostic, was the leading council for Scopes and the one upon whom the modernists chiefly relied in the Tennessee trial. Thus the popular belief or suspicion seems to prevail that the intensive study of this branch of science generally results in agnosticism. However, outstanding scientists and theologians have signed and circulated statements expressing their belief that the theory of evolution is compatible with the facts of religion and a God of the universe, and that discrepancies between religion and science appear only because of positions taken by extreme evolutionists, or result from a lack of sufficient understanding of the subject.

If there is any justification for such a law, it must be on the ground that in the theory of the complete separation of church and state the state has no right to promote or to favor religion, but that it may only guarantee to everyone the free exercise of religion, thus preventing a concerted action against religion. This is best stated in the preamble to the resolution passed by the legislature of the state of Florida:

Whereas, the public schools and colleges of this state, supported in whole or in part by public funds, should be kept free from any teachings designed to set up and promulgate sectarian views, and should also be equally free from teachings designed to attack the religious beliefs of the public . . .[12]

On the contrary, it has been contended that if the doctrine of fundamentalism can be adopted by the state, by the same logic a Protestant legislature, for example, could pass a law compelling the teaching of the history of the Reformation and penalize a teacher who did not agree with and failed to teach the theses of Luther. A Catholic legislature, on the other hand, could pass a law requiring that the doctrine of transubstantiation be taught as a fact in the public schools. Such a procedure obviously would grossly violate the spirit of religious freedom.

The reports of some of the surveys made in the southern states reveal that the sentiment is definitely against the teaching of evolution in the public schools. They allege that many of the teachers of biology in state-supported schools are teaching materialistic or theistic evolution. They deny the right to teach either of these views on the grounds that to teach materialistic evolution in the public schools is to teach infidelity, and that to teach theistic evolution is to teach a new, or sectarian, view of religion. The reports further show that many Southerners believe in the literal meaning and teaching of the Bible, and that they oppose the teaching of any theory or view which weakens or destroys this faith in their children, especially when such teaching is at their own expense.

Justice Chambliss' opinion, which sustained the constitutionality of the act, practically limits the act to the prohibition of the teaching of materialism. As ordinarily taught, evolution is the theory of the gradual development of human and other life upon earth. It does not undertake to determine the original cause, leaving that to religion and philosophy. It does not deny that God is the original cause, nor that the gradual development of life upon the earth is taking place in accordance with a divine plan. Materialism denies the existence of a God, or of a God as a Creator who is concerned

[12] House Concurrent Resolution No. 7, House Journal, 1923, pp. 2200, 2201.

with the universe. Thus those who believe in God, in Christ, and in evolution find in the gradual development of life upon the earth additional evidence of a divine Creator. The position taken by Justice Chambliss permits the teaching of what he termed the scientific theory of evolution, essential to the teaching of biology.

In answering the contention that the statute violates the Fourteenth Amendment to the Constitution of the United States, providing that no state shall "deprive any person of life, liberty, or property, without due process of law," and Article 1, Section 8, of the Tennessee constitution, providing that "no man shall be taken or imprisoned, or disseized of his freehold, liberties, or privileges, or outlawed, or exiled, or in any manner destroyed, or deprived of his life, liberty, or property, but by the judgment of his peers or the law of the land," the court, as we have seen, maintained there was little basis for such a contention. Scopes was a teacher in the public schools. He was an employee of the state of Tennessee or of a municipal agency of that state. He was under contract with the state to work in one of its institutions, and hence had no right to do other than serve under the terms that the state prescribed. His liberties and his privileges to teach the theory of evolution elsewhere than in the service of the state were in no wise affected by the law. Finally, the statute under consideration was not an exercise of the police power of the state.

The police and proprietary powers are two entirely separate and distinct powers of the state. The state has a different and much more complete control over the persons it employs in its own schools than over those employed in private schools. There are many things a state may do in the exercise of its proprietary power which could not be supported if done in the exercise of its police power. It would seem that without violating any constitutional rights the state may impose restrictions upon the liberties of its employees similar to those a private employer may impose.[13]

In the Tennessee case the court did not state whether it would have supported a similar statute, as coming within the police power of the state, if it had extended to all the schools of the state. This question did not fall within its purview, since the statute pertained to public schools only. The police powers, though never precisely defined by the courts, have generally been exercised only for the safety, health, morals, and general welfare of the public. It has been

[13] This principle was clearly set forth in Atkin v. Kansas, 191 U.S. 207 (1903).

accepted that a *reasonable relation* must exist between the character of the legislation and these principles.[14]

That the state in the rightful exercise of its police power may punish those who abuse the freedom of speech guaranteed to them in the federal Constitution, by utterances that are "inimical to the public welfare, tending to corrupt public morals, incite to crime, or disturb the public peace," was decided in Gitlow v. New York [15] and is not open to question. To these decisions we may add those cases arising out of the National Espionage Act, which prohibits utterances made for the purpose of obstructing the recruiting of soldiers and sailors for the defense of the country in time of war.[16]

What position would be taken by our existent federal court with reference to the Tennessee evolution law is of course a question that is still to be determined. As a result of the nolle prosse action of the attorney general as recommended by the court, it is a question whether it is not impossible for the case to be carried to the United States Supreme Court before being heard by the supreme court of Tennessee.

In a discussion of the constitutionality of the Tennessee statute in the *Yale Law Journal* William Waller comments on the position the United States Supreme Court might be expected to take:

If the Tennessee statute were not confined to public institutions this decision [in the case of Meyer v. Nebraska, in which Justice McReynolds said, "His right thus to teach and the right of parents to engage him so to instruct their children, we think, are within the liberty of the amendment."] would doubtless be controlling. In the present day an enlightened and conscientious court would not hold that the teaching of evolution is "manifestly inimical" to the public welfare. As "police power" legislation it would be clearly invalid. But a more difficult question is whether the statute may not be sustained as an exercise of the state's proprietary control over public educational institutions.

The statute could hardly be said to "prescribe a curriculum." It does not abolish the teaching of certain scientific subjects and thus save that expense to the state. On the other hand, it assumes that they are still to be taught. No change whatever is made in any curriculum of any school. What the statute undertakes to do is to set aside a scientific doctrine which would naturally be taught as an integral and vital part of these subjects,

---

[14] Pierce v. Hill Military Academy, 268 U.S. 510 (1925); Meyer v. Nebraska, 262 U.S. 390 (1923).

[15] 268 U.S. 652, 69 L. ed. 1138 (1925); also Fox v. Washington, 236 U.S. 273 (1914); Gilbert v. Minnesota, 254 U.S. 325 (1920).

[16] Debs v. U.S., 249 U.S. 211 (1919).

and to substitute a standard of truth of its own. The public schools, state and normal schools, and state university are thus deprived of their character of purely educational institutions, and are given the role of protectors of a partisan belief or dogma.[17]

On March 11, 1926, Mississippi passed the following act:

It shall be unlawful for any teacher or other instructor in any university, college, normal, public school, or other institution of the state which is supported in whole or in part from public funds derived by state or local taxation to teach that mankind ascended or descended from a lower order of animals, and also it shall be unlawful for any teacher, textbook commission, or other authority exercising the power to select textbooks for above-mentioned educational institutions to adopt or use in any such institution a textbook that teaches the doctrine that mankind ascended or descended from the lower order of animals.[18]

The statute provides that any teacher or textbook commissioner who is found guilty of violating this act is guilty of a misdemeanor and subject to a fine not to exceed five hundred dollars.[19] The person so convicted must vacate the position held at the time of conviction.

In 1927 an anti-evolution bill was passed by the lower house in Arkansas, but was tabled by the senate. The following year the first anti-evolution initiative measure in history was approved, by a majority of forty-five thousand, at the general election in Arkansas. The bill, which became effective on December 6 of that year, provides

that it shall be unlawful for any teacher or other instructor in any university, college, normal, public school, or other institution of the state which is supported in whole or in part from public funds derived by state or local taxation to teach the theory or doctrine that mankind ascended or descended from a lower order of animals, and also it shall be unlawful for any teacher, textbook commission, or other authority exercising the power to select textbooks for above-mentioned institutions to adopt or use in any such institution a textbook that teaches the doctrine or theory that mankind descended or ascended from a lower order of animals.[20]

The statute also carried with it a penalty of five hundred dollars and dismissal from state service for violation. Thus Arkansas joined Utah, Florida, Tennessee, and Mississippi in placing upon her statute books an anti-evolution law.

[17] "The Constitutionality of the Tennessee Anti-Evolution Act," *Yale Law Journal*, December 1925, pp. 191–200.
[18] Hemingway's Annotated Mississippi Code, 1927, Section 9493.
[19] *Ibid.*, Section 9494.
[20] For a discussion of this act see "The Teaching of Evolution in Arkansas," *School and Society*, 28:677, 678 (December 1, 1928).

In 1927 and 1928 it was predicted that anti-evolution bills would be introduced in many state legislatures.[21]

Professor Arthur O. Lovejoy of Johns Hopkins University points out that those who are primarily interested in propaganda for the theory of evolution have no reason to regret the enactment of anti-evolution laws, for "nothing could do so much to advertise the subject and to arouse the intellectual curiosity of youth concerning the theory as such efforts to keep them from a knowledge of it." [22] However, those who opposed teaching the theory of evolution began an extensive warfare on the evolutionary hypothesis by making a concerted effort to ban textbooks teaching evolution from all state-supported schools and to bar instructors who believed and taught such principles.[23]

Since then the friends of evolution have not been idle. There has been successful opposition to the spread of anti-evolution laws, many educators taking the stand that, whether the theory be true or not, legislation barring the discussion of evolution from the schools will not prove its truth or falsity. They hold that if the theory of evolution is true, then it should be studied in order that we may know more about mankind's advent into the world; and that if it is false, the surest way to detect its spuriousness is to allow light to be thrown upon it from as many unprejudiced minds as possible.

The fundamentalists contend that the customary way of teaching the evolutionary theory does not throw "light upon it from as many unprejudiced minds as possible." Whether this accusation by the fundamentalists be rational or not, the school administration can logically choose to do only one of three things: teach all sides of the controversy without prejudice; eliminate evolutionary textbooks and teachers; decide that the fundamentalists are superstitious or intellectually stagnant and proceed to teach the evolutionary hypothesis as truth without apology or restraint.

[21] For other attempts to pass anti-evolution legislation see Maynard Shipley, "Growth of the Anti-Evolution Movement," *Current History*, 32:330–32 (May 1930).

[22] In the year 1926–27 anti-evolution bills were before the state legislatures of Arkansas, Georgia, Minnesota, Missouri, New Hampshire, Oklahoma, and West Virginia, none of which were enacted into law.

[23] "Anti-Evolution Laws and the Principle of Religious Neutrality," *School and Society*, February 2, 1929, pp. 133–38.

CHAPTER XV

Saluting the Flag

THE United States flag symbolizes the nation. If the nation were removed, the flag would have no significance. In honoring the flag we honor the nation, for it represents the government of the nation.

It has been repeatedly held that saluting the flag is not a religious rite. The supreme court of Georgia said that to require pupils to salute the flag of the United States "is by no stretch of the imagination a religious rite,"[1] but a gesture of patriotism signifying respect for the American government, for its institutions and ideals.

The United States Supreme Court declared

the flag is the symbol of the nation's power, the emblem of freedom in its truest, best sense . . . it signifies government resting on the consent of the governed; liberty regulated by law; the protection of the weak against the strong; security against the exercise of arbitrary power; and absolute safety for free institutions against foreign aggression.[2]

Again the same court said "the flag is the symbol of our national unity, transcending all international differences, however large, within the framework of the constitution."[3]

According to a study made by the United States Department of Education,[4] most of the states require the United States flag to be displayed over or within public school buildings. A few states make the same requirement in connection with private schools. In a number of states it is required that flag programs and special instruction concerning the flag be given in the public schools. In about one fourth of the states, pupils are required to salute the flag or provide for a flag exercise in the public schools. In a few states, teachers are required by oath to promote respect for the flag.

[1] 184 Ga. 580, 192 S.E. 218 (1937).
[2] Halter v. Nebraska, 205 U.S. 34, 43, 51 L. ed. 696, 701 (1906).
[3] Minersville School District v. Walter Gobitis et al., 310 U.S. 586 (1940).
[4] See "The Flag in American Education" by Ward W. Keesecker, specialist in school legislation, United States Department of Education, *School Life*, December 1939, pp. 74, 75.

Training for citizenship has been recognized as a legitimate requirement in the schools of the land, and while there is a difference of opinion as to how this objective can be best realized, such training generally recognizes the importance of an acquaintance with the institutions, ideals, and principles of the American government and a study of its origin and methods of operation. Respect for the flag and instruction relating to the principles for which it stands has been thought frequently to require that pupils salute the flag and take the oath of allegiance. The most common form of this practice has been where either state or local boards of education require both teachers and pupils to participate in the ceremony. The right hand is placed on the breast and the following pledge recited in unison: "I pledge allegiance to my flag, and to the Republic for which it stands; one nation, indivisible, with liberty and justice for all." While the words are spoken, teachers and pupils extend their right hands in salute to the flag.

Requiring the pupils to participate in this exercise has called forth some opposition on the basis that it is an act of worship and that to salute the flag is a form of idolatry. Because of religious convictions, parents and their children have therefore refused to participate in the required salute. In the efforts on the part of school officers to enforce the law, such children have in a number of instances been expelled from school. This has resulted in litigation in both state and federal courts which has been carried to the Supreme Court of the United States.

By the great majority of Christians this issue has not been considered a religious one. Christians of various denominations point out that the Apostle Paul, for example, admonished the people to "Render therefore to all their dues: tribute to whom tribute is due; custom to whom custom; fear to whom fear; honor to whom honor." [4] And the Apostle Peter wrote concerning the Christian's attitude toward his fellow men, toward God, and toward kings: "Honour all men. Love the brotherhood. Fear God. Honour the king." [5] The Old Testament records that "every man of the children of Israel shall pitch by his own standard, with the ensign of their father's house: far off about the tabernacle of the congregation shall they pitch." [6]

In contrast to these views is the position taken by one small sect known as Jehovah's Witnesses, which refuses to salute the flag. They hold that in the light of their religious convictions such an act is a

[4] Romans 13:7.
[5] I Peter 2:17.
[6] Numbers 2:2.

form of idolatry and is in violation of the Biblical injunction, "Thou shalt have no other gods before me. Thou shalt not make unto thee any graven image, or any likeness of any thing that is in heaven above, or that is in the earth beneath, or that is in the water under the earth: Thou shalt not bow down thyself to them nor serve them . . ."[7]

There is a reminder in this attitude of the history of the Quakers and their experience, particularly in England, where they were once severely persecuted for their refusal to salute public officials by the removal of the hat in their presence. The Quakers regarded such a salutation as an act of idolatry and worship. As a result some of them were flogged, imprisoned, and even put to death.

A number of cases bearing on this subject and efforts to enforce the flag salute in the public schools have been carried to the courts.

In 1937 the supreme court of Georgia held that the requirement by the board of education of the Atlanta city schools of saluting the flag was not an unreasonable requirement.[8]

The supreme judicial court of Massachusetts held that it was within the power of the school committee to require the salute to the flag and the pledge of allegiance in every school at least once a week.[9]

More recently the Massachusetts court held that a statute requiring the teacher to display the flag and to have pupils salute the flag and give a pledge of allegiance is designed to inculcate patriotism and to instill a recognition of the blessing conferred by orderly government under the constitution of state and nation, and that the study of such instruments is a proper subject for instruction in the public schools.[10] A similar position was also taken by New Jersey.[11]

The supreme court of California was called upon to give consideration to an appeal where the petitioner, Dorothy Knickerbocker, had been expelled from the Sacramento city schools for refusing to salute the flag.[12] A California statute reads: "Boards of school trustees and city boards of education shall have the power, and it shall be their duty to suspend or expel pupils for misconduct when other means of correction have failed to bring about proper conduct."[13] Judge

[7] Exodus 20:3–5.
[8] 184 Ga. 580, 192 S.E. 218.
[9] Nicholls v. Mayor and the School Committee of Lynn, 297 Mass. 65, 7 N.E. (2d) 577 (1937).
[10] Commonwealth v. Johnson, 309 Mass. 476, 35 N.E. (2d) 801 (1942).
[11] Hering v. State Board of Education, 117 N.J.L. 445, 189 A. 629 (1937).
[12] Gabrielli v. Knickerbocker et al., 74 Pac. (2d) 290 (1938).
[13] Section 1.30 of Article 4 of the School Code of California.

Shields of the superior court of Sacramento, from which this case was appealed, pointed out that the petitioner was an exemplary pupil, but that while the pupils gave the salute to the flag and took the pledge of allegiance, she simply stood silent. As a result of her refusal to salute the flag at the daily flag exercises she was denied the right to attend any public school within the jurisdiction of the Sacramento board of education. She made request to the court to be reinstated.

In referring to the First Amendment of the Constitution of the United States as well as the provision guaranteeing religious liberty contained in the California state constitution, Judge Shields pointed out:

This right which we in this country think is a natural right, and which has been so solemnly announced and safeguarded is subject to this well defined qualification, that laws may be passed essential to the public welfare, and that no religious belief can be asserted against things necessary to the maintenance of government or the preservation of the public health, safety, or morals.

He contended that a requirement to salute the flag does not come within any of these exceptions, though the salute is an admirable exercise and one to which our people have long been devoted. The refusal to salute the flag arouses a general protest because it implies disloyalty to the government. But he pointed out that the petitioner asserted her devotion to her country and her loyalty to everything which the flag represents, and that it was only because of her religious beliefs that she could not salute it, for this to her was an act of worship.

The reasoning of Judge Shields was accepted by the California district court of appeals and the state supreme court. The California supreme court held that the evidence failed to reveal that the school officials had made any attempt to secure obedience from the pupil, but that they had deliberately expelled the applicant and as a consequence they had exceeded their jurisdictional powers in the suspension or expulsion of the petitioner. The court said:

The record before us presents no question of morality; no question of peace; no question of health; no question of disobedience or improper conduct on the part of the petitioner; just a simple question of standing mute while other pupils saluted the flag and repeated the pledge of allegiance. This obviates any necessity for a further consideration of the questions involved or a reference to the rather exhaustive and learned briefs submitted by counsel.

In New York the court of appeals held that the parents of a 13-year-old girl who refused to participate in saluting the flag in the school ceremony were subject to disciplinary action if the girl's refusal amounted to insubordination and disobedience.[14] "A religious belief," said the court, "cannot interfere with the laws which the state enacts for its preservation, safety or welfare." The state could not be required to defer adoption of measures for its own safety and peace until revolutionary utterances and acts led to actual disturbance of peace or imminent and immediate danger or destruction; it could in the exercise of its judgment seek to "prevent evil in its incipiency."

The court upheld the education law requiring the commissioner of education to prepare a program requiring pupils to salute the flag and calling for proper instruction in its use as well as other patriotic exercises that were deemed expedient. The court also held that such ceremonies were not contrary to the freedom of religion guaranteed by the Constitution.

Judge Lehman while concurring in the result issued a separate opinion in which he said:

I concur in the decision and in all that is said in the opinion except in so far as it indicates that the defendant's daughter may, on pain of expulsion, be compelled to salute the flag though such salute be contrary to her religious convictions and her conscience.

The American flag is the symbol of our country; the symbol of the ideals which are embodied in our constitution; the symbol of the spirit which should animate our institutions. In the noble words of Charles Sumner, it is "to be cherished by all our hearts, to be upheld by all our hands."

Schools must inculcate principles of liberty and democracy. Teachers should inspire love of country, etc.

The question remains whether the Legislature intended to direct or could, under our Constitution, direct that a child may be *compelled* to join in the exercises in those rare cases where such exercises are contrary to the religious principles and doctrines of the child and its parents.

Episcopalians and Methodists and Presbyterians and Baptists, Catholics and Jews, may all agree that a salute to the flag cannot be disobedience to the will of the Creator; all the judges of the State may agree that no well-intended person could reasonably object to such a salute; but this little child has been taught to believe otherwise. She must choose between obedience to the command of the principal of the school, and obedience to what she has been taught and believes is the command of God. She has chosen to obey what she believes is the command of God. I cannot assent to the dictum of the prevailing opinion that she must obey the

[14] People ex rel. Fish v. Sandstrom, 279 N.Y. 523, 18 N.E. (2d) 840 (1939).

command of the principal, though trembling lest she incur the righteous wrath of her Maker and be slain "when the battle of Armageddon comes." . . .

An act of disrespect to the flag by child or parent may be punished, but there is no disrespect to the flag in refusal to salute the flag by a child who has been taught that it is a moral wrong to show respect in the form of a salute.

The flag salute would lose no dignity or worth if she were permitted to refrain from joining in it. On the contrary, that would be an impressive lesson for her and the other children that the flag stands for absolute freedom of conscience except where freedom of conscience is asserted "to justify practices inconsistent with the peace or safety of this State."

The salute of the flag is a gesture of love and respect — fine when there is real love and respect back of the gesture. The flag is dishonored by a salute by a child in reluctant and terrified obedience to a command of secular authority which clashes with the dictates of conscience. The flag cherished by all our hearts should not be soiled by the tears of a little child. The Constitution does not permit, and the Legislature never intended, that the flag should be so soiled and dishonored.

Perhaps a case which has received more attention than any other on the subject has been that of Minersville School District v. Walter Gobitis et al.[15] Here Lillian Gobitis, sixteen years old, and her brother, William, fifteen, were expelled from the public schools of Minersville, Pennsylvania, for refusing to salute the national flag as part of a daily school exercise. The local board of education required both teachers and pupils to participate in this ceremony. It consisted of the regular flag salute and the oath of allegiance to the flag. The Gobitis family, according to the records of the court, were members of Jehovah's Witnesses. The children had been brought up conscientiously to believe that to salute the flag as a gesture of respect was forbidden by the Bible.

The Gobitis children were within the age limits of compulsory school attendance under the Pennsylvania laws. As a result of their unwillingness to salute the flag they were dismissed from school and thus were denied a free education. Their parents had placed them in a private school but, to be relieved of the financial burden which such attendance entailed, their father, in behalf of the children and himself, brought suit requesting that his children might be excused from participation in the flag salute ceremony as a condition of his children's attendance at the Minersville school.

Judge Maris of the United States district court granted the relief

[15] Minersville School District v. Walter Gobitis et al., 310 U.S. 586 (1940).

sought.[16] In so doing, he referred to the decisions of state supreme courts which had upheld school boards in similar test cases and then commented:

In so holding it appears to us that the courts overlooked the fundamental principle of religious liberty, namely, that no man, even though he be a school director or a judge, is empowered to censor another's religious convictions or set bounds to the areas of human conduct in which those convictions should be permitted to control his actions, unless compelled to do so by an overriding public necessity, which properly requires the exercises of the police powers.

The United States circuit court of appeals [17] in Philadelphia upheld the decision of the district court, indicating that it was in keeping with the opinion expressed by George Washington in 1789 when he said:

I assure you very explicitly that in my opinion the conscientious scruples of all men should be treated with great delicacy and tenderness; and it is my wish and desire that the laws may always be as extensively accommodated to them as a due regard to the protection and essential interests of the nation may justify and permit.

Justice Clark, in writing the opinion of the court, said:

The school board of Minersville has failed to treat the conscientious scruples of all children with that "great delicacy and tenderness." We agree with the father of our country that they (the school board) should, and we concur with the learned district court in saying that they must.

Explaining the court's attitude toward the conflict between religious scruples and patriotic observances, the opinion continued:

Compulsory flag saluting is designed to better secure the state by inculcating in its youthful citizens a love of country that will incline their hearts and minds to its more willing defense. That particular compulsion happens to be abhorrent to the particular love of God of the little girl and boy now seeking our protection. One conception or the other must yield. Which is required by our Constitution? We think the material and not the spiritual.

Compulsion, rather than protection, should be sparingly exercised. Harm usually comes from doing rather than leaving undone, and refraining is generally not sacrilege. We do not find the essential relationship between infant patriotism and the martial spirit.

This case was appealed from the United States circuit court of ap-

[16] 24 Fed. Supp. 271 (1939).
[17] 108 Fed. (2d) 683 (1939).

peals to the United States Supreme Court. Mr. Justice Frankfurter, in delivering the opinion of the Supreme Court, mentioned the responsibility that confronted the court whenever in the course of litigation it must reconcile the conflicting claims of liberty and authority and said that when the liberty invoked is liberty of conscience and the authority is authority to safeguard the nation's fellowship, "judicial conscience is put to its severest test." The court commented as follows:

The manifold character of man's relations may bring his conception of religious duty into conflict with the secular interests of his fellowmen. When does the constitutional guarantee compel exemption from doing what society thinks necessary for the promotion of some great common end, or from a penalty for conduct which appears dangerous to the general good? To state the problem is to recall the truth that no single principle can answer all of life's complexities. The right to freedom of religious belief, however dissident and however obnoxious to the cherished beliefs of others — even of a majority — is itself the denial of an Absolute. But to affirm that the freedom to follow conscience has itself no limits in the life of a society would deny that very plurality of principles which, as a matter of history, underlies protection of religious toleration. . . .

Our present task then, as is so often the case with courts, is to reconcile two rights in order to prevent either from destroying the other. But, because in safeguarding conscience we are dealing with interests so subtle and so dear, every possible leeway should be given to the claims of religious faith.

In the judicial enforcement of religious freedom we are concerned with a historic concept. See Mr. Justice Cardozo in Hamilton v. University of California, 293 U.S. 245, at 265, 79 L ed 343, 354, 55 S.Ct. 197. The religious liberty which the Constitution protects has never excluded legislation of general scope not directed against doctrinal loyalties of particular sects. Judicial nullification of legislation cannot be justified by attributing to the framers of the Bill of Rights views for which there is no historic warrant. Conscientious scruples have not, in the course of the long struggle for religious toleration, relieved the individual from obedience to a general law not aimed at the promotion or restriction of religious beliefs.

The court maintained that the wisdom of training children in patriotic impulses by those compulsions which necessarily pervade so much of the educational process "is not for our independent judgment." It reversed the decision of the lower courts and upheld the board of education in requiring the flag salute.

In this decision Mr. Justice Stone dissented. A considerable portion of the dissent is given because it is indicative of much careful consideration and in the opinion of many is in harmony with the principles for which our flag stands. As a dissenting opinion it takes the liberal position on the subject. As was true in the matter of naturalization and the bearing of arms,[18] here is another case where the dissent became the majority opinion of the court just three years later.

Mr. Justice Stone in dissenting said:

Two youths, now fifteen and sixteen years of age, are by the judgment of this Court held liable to expulsion from the public schools and to denial of all publicly supported educational privileges because of their refusal to yield to the compulsion of a law which commands their participation in a school ceremony contrary to their religious convictions. They and their father are citizens and have not exhibited by any action or statement of opinion, any disloyalty to the Government of the United States. They are ready and willing to obey all its laws which do not conflict with what they sincerely believe to be the higher commandments of God. It is not doubted that these convictions are religious, that they are genuine, or that the refusal to yield to the compulsion of the law is in good faith and with all sincerity. It would be a denial of their faith as well as the teachings of most religions to say that children of their age could not have religious convictions.

The law which is thus sustained is unique in the history of Anglo-American legislation. It does more than suppress freedom of speech and more than prohibit the free exercise of religion, which concededly are forbidden by the First Amendment and are violations of the liberty guaranteed by the Fourteenth. For by this law the state seeks to coerce these children to express a sentiment which, as they interpret it, they do not entertain, and which violates their deepest religious convictions. It is not denied that such compulsion is a prohibited infringement of personal liberty, freedom of speech and religion, guaranteed by the Bill of Rights, except in so far as it may be justified and supported as a proper exercise of the state's power over public education. . . .

The guaranties of civil liberty are but guaranties of freedom of the human mind and spirit and of reasonable freedom and opportunity to express them. They presuppose the right of the individual to hold such opinions as he will and to give them reasonably free expression, and his freedom, and that of the state as well, to teach and persuade others by the communication of ideas. The very essence of the liberty which they guarantee is the freedom of the individual from compulsion as to what

[18] See Chapter XVI, "Citizenship and the Bearing of Arms." Here it will be seen that in the case of U.S. v. Schwimmer, appealed to the Supreme Court in 1929, Chief Justice Holmes dissented. In the cases of U.S. v. Macintosh and U.S. v. Bland in 1931 the view expressed by Mr. Justice Holmes in his dissent in U.S. v. Schwimmer was adopted by four judges and both cases were five to four decisions. In 1946 in the case of Girouard v. U.S. the minority opinion in all the previous cases became the majority opinion of the court.

he shall think and what he shall say, at least where the compulsion is to bear false witness to his religion. If these guaranties are to have any meaning they must, I think, be deemed to withhold from the state any authority to compel belief or the expression of it where that expression violates religious convictions, whatever may be the legislative view of the desirability of such compulsion.

History teaches us that there have been but few infringements of personal liberty by the state which have not been justified, as they are here, in the name of righteousness and the public good, and few which have not been directed, as they are now, at politically helpless minorities. The framers were not unaware that under the system which they created most governmental curtailments of personal liberty would have the support of a legislative judgment that the public interest would be better served by its curtailment than by its constitutional protection. I cannot conceive that in prescribing, as limitations upon the powers of government, the freedom of the mind and spirit secured by the explicit guaranties of freedom of speech and religion, they intended or rightly could have left any latitude for a legislative judgment that the compulsory expression of belief which violates religious convictions would better serve the public interest than their protection. The Constitution may well elicit expressions of loyalty to it and to the government which it created, but it does not command such expressions or otherwise give any indication that compulsory expressions of loyalty play any such part in our scheme of government as to override the constitutional protection of freedom of speech and religion. And while such expressions of loyalty, when voluntarily given, may promote national unity, it is quite another matter to say that their compulsory expression by children in violation of their own and their parents' religious convictions can be regarded as playing so important a part in our national unity as to leave school boards free to exact it despite the constitutional guaranty of freedom of religion. The very terms of the Bill of Rights preclude, it seems to me, any reconciliation of such compulsions with the constitutional guaranties by a legislative declaration that they are more important to public welfare than the Bill of Rights. . . .

The Constitution expresses more than the conviction of the people that democratic processes must be preserved at all costs. It is also an expression of faith and a command that freedom of mind and spirit must be preserved which government must obey, if it is to adhere to that justice and moderation without which no free government can exist. For this reason it would seem that legislation which operates to repress the religious freedom of small minorities, which is admittedly within the scope of the protection of the Bill of Rights, must at least be subject to the same judicial scrutiny as legislation which we have recently held to infringe the constitutional liberty of religious and racial minorities.

With such scrutiny I cannot say that the inconvenience which may attend some sensible adjustment of school discipline in order that the religious convictions of these children may be spared, presents a problem so momentous or pressing as to outweigh the freedom from compulsory violation of religious faith which has been thought worthy of constitutional protection.

The above dissent was a forecast of the later decision which reversed the Gobitis ruling. Children of the Barnette family disobeyed a ruling of a local school board in West Virginia requiring that all pupils must salute the flag. The Barnette children refused to do so and were expelled from school. Suit was brought on their behalf, and the case went through the lower courts, reaching the United States Supreme Court in the spring of 1943. The court decided against the school district's ruling, with Justices Frankfurter, Roberts, and Reed dissenting.[19]

The court, in declaring that the compulsion of conscience for some citizens in the requirement of flag saluting was unconstitutional, stated:

It is also to be noted that the compulsory flag salute and pledge requires affirmation of a belief and an attitude of mind. It is not clear whether the regulation contemplates that pupils forego any contrary convictions of their own and become unwilling converts to the prescribed ceremony or whether it will be acceptable if they simulate assent by words without belief and by a gesture barren of meaning. It is now a commonplace that censorship or suppression of expression of opinion is tolerated by our Constitution only when the expression presents a clear and present danger of action of a kind the State is empowered to prevent and punish. It would seem that involuntary affirmation could be commanded only on even more immediate and urgent grounds than silence. But here the power of compulsion is invoked without any allegation that remaining passive during a flag salute ritual creates a clear and present danger that would justify an effort even to muffle expressions. To sustain the compulsory flag salute we are required to say that a Bill of Rights which guards the individual's right to speak his own mind, left it open to public authorities to compel him to utter what is not in his mind. . . .

The Fourteenth Amendment, as now applied to the States, protects the citizen against the State itself and all of its creatures — Boards of Education not excepted. These have, of course, important, delicate, and highly discretionary functions, but none that they may not perform within the limits of the Bill of Rights. That they are educating the young for citizenship is reason for scrupulous protection of Constitutional freedoms of the individual, if we are not to strangle the free mind at its source and teach youth to discount important principles of our government as mere platitudes. . . .

[19] West Virginia State Board of Education et al. v. Barnette et al., 319 U.S. 624 (1943).

Struggles to coerce uniformity of sentiment in support of some end thought essential to their time and country have been waged by many good as well as by evil men. Nationalism is a relatively recent phenomenon but at other times and places the ends have been racial or territorial security, support of a dynasty or regime, and particular plans for saving souls. As first and moderate methods to attain unity have failed, those bent on its accomplishment must resort to an ever-increasing severity.

As governmental pressure toward unity becomes greater, so strife becomes more bitter as to whose unity it shall be. Probably no deeper division of our people could proceed from any provocation than from finding it necessary to choose what doctrine and whose program public educational officials shall compel youth to unite in embracing. Ultimate futility of such attempts to compel coherence is the lesson of every such effort from the Roman drive to stamp out Christianity as a disturber of its pagan unity, the Inquisition, as a means to religious and dynastic unity, the Siberian exiles as a means to Russian unity, down to the fast failing efforts of our present totalitarian enemies. Those who begin coercive elimination of dissent soon find themselves exterminating dissenters. Compulsory unification of opinion achieves only the unanimity of the graveyard.

It seems trite but necessary to say that the First Amendment to our Constitution was designed to avoid these ends by avoiding these beginnings. There is no mysticism in the American concept of the State or of the nature or origin of its authority. We set up government by consent of the governed, and the Bill of Rights denies those in power any legal opportunity to coerce that consent. Authority here is to be controlled by public opinion, not public opinion by authority.

Immediately after this decision was handed down, the Kansas supreme court ruled on a state statute making it the duty of the superintendent of public instruction to prepare for the public schools a program providing for the flag salute at the opening of each day of school. The court held that the statute did not authorize the expulsion of a child who, because of sincere religious beliefs, refused to salute the flag.[20] Other state courts have made similar rulings.

[20] State v. Smith, 155 Kan. 588, 127 Pac. (2d) 518 (1943).

CHAPTER XVI

Citizenship and the Bearing of Arms

INVOLVING religious implications, and more particularly affecting the dictates of conscience, has been the question of naturalization and the bearing of arms. In 1929 in the case of U.S. v. Rosika Schwimmer[1] the United States Supreme Court heard the request for citizenship of Rosika Schwimmer. She had been denied naturalization by the United States district court, but the request had been granted by the United States circuit court of appeals and the case was then appealed to the United States Supreme Court. Rosika Schwimmer, widely known as a pacifist, was a resident of Illinois. She was born in Hungary in 1877 and was a citizen of that country. She came to the United States in 1921 to visit and lecture. Later in the same year she declared her intentions of becoming a citizen and filed a petition for naturalization in September 1926.

On the preliminary form she stated that she had read, understood, and fully believed in our form of government and that in becoming a citizen she was willing to take the oath of allegiance. Question 22 of the form, while not warranted by law, raises the following question: "If necessary, are you willing to take up arms in defense of this country?" To this she answered, "I would not take up arms personally." She testified that she did not want to remain subject to Hungary, that she had found the United States nearest her ideals of a democratic republic, and that she could wholeheartedly take the oath of allegiance. But she said, "I cannot see that a woman's refusal to take up arms is a contradiction to the oath of allegiance."

The Naturalization Act of June 16, 1906, requires:

He [the applicant for naturalization] shall, before he is admitted to citizenship, declare on Oath in open court . . . that he will support and defend the Constitution and laws of the United States against all enemies, foreign and domestic, and bear true faith and allegiance to the same.[2]

[1] 279 U.S. 644 (1929).
[2] U.S.C., Title 8, Section 381.

187

She indicated her willingness to support and defend the Constitution and laws by other ways than the bearing of arms. She further stated:

I am willing to do everything that an American citizen has to do except fighting. If American women would be compelled to do that, I would not do that. I am an uncompromising pacifist . . . I do not care how many other women fight, because I consider it a question of conscience. I am not willing to bear arms. In every other single way I am ready to follow the law and do everything that the law compels American citizens to do. That is why I can take the oath of allegiance, because, as far as I can find out, there is nothing that I could be compelled to do that I cannot do . . . With reference to spreading propaganda among the women throughout the country about my being an uncompromising pacifist and not willing to fight, I am always ready to tell anyone who wants to hear it that I am an uncompromising pacifist and will not fight. In my writings and in my lectures I take up the question of war and pacifism if I am asked for that.

The United States Supreme Court pointed out that the right of an alien to become a citizen is not a natural but a statutory right; that in the interpretation of such statutes they will be construed with a definite aim to favor and support the government; that in an application for naturalization the burden is upon the applicant to show that he has the special qualifications for citizenship.

The court declared that the duty of citizens to defend the government by force of arms against all enemies whenever necessity arises is a fundamental principle of the Constitution. The court found that Rosika Schwimmer was unable without mental reservation to take the prescribed oath of allegiance and that an application for naturalization is properly denied where the applicant discloses unwillingness because of conscientious considerations to take up arms in defense of the United States and has a disposition to encourage others to do likewise. Mr. Justice Butler delivered the opinion of the court. Mr. Justice Holmes dissented.

Another case that was to receive widespread attention and which was appealed to the United States Supreme Court for final decision involved the request of Douglas Clyde Macintosh for citizenship.[3] Professor Macintosh was a Canadian by birth. He had come to the United States as a graduate student at the University of Chicago and in 1907 he was ordained as a Baptist minister. In 1909 he began to teach at Yale University and later became a member of the faculty

[3] U.S. v. Douglas Clyde Macintosh, 283 U.S. 605 (1931).

of the Divinity School, chaplain of the Yale Graduate School, and Dwight Professor of Theology.

Following the outbreak of World War I, he voluntarily sought appointment as a chaplain with the Canadian army and saw service at the front. Returning to the United States, he made public addresses in 1917 in support of the Allies. In 1918 he again went to France, where he had charge of an American YMCA hut at the front until the armistice was signed. He then resumed his duties as a professor at Yale.

This case differed from the request made by Rosika Schwimmer in the previous case, where she made application for naturalization on the basis that she was an avowed pacifist, did not believe in war, and that her convictions prevented her from bearing arms in defense of any nation. In this case the applicant was unwilling to promise to bear arms in defense of the United States unless he believed the war to be morally justified. Nor would he promise to refrain from propaganda against the prosecution of a war which he did not believe to be morally justified.

On the preliminary form for petition for naturalization, the following questions, among others, appear. Question 20: "Have you read the following oath of allegiance?" The oath is then quoted. "Are you willing to take this oath on becoming a citizen?" Question 22: "If necessary, are you willing to take up arms in defense of this country?" In response to Question 20 Macintosh answered yes. In response to Question 22 he answered, "Yes, but I should want to be free to judge of the necessity." In a written memorandum subsequently filed, he amplified these answers in the following manner:

20 and 22. I am willing to do what I judge to be in the best interests of my country, but only in so far as I can believe that this is not going to be against the best interests of humanity in the long run. I do not undertake to support "my country, right or wrong" in any dispute which may arise, and I am not willing to promise beforehand, and without knowing the cause for which my country may go to war, either that I will or that I will not "take up arms in defense of this country," however "necessary" the war may seem to be to the government of the day.

It is only in a sense consistent with these statements that I am willing to promise to "support and defend" the government of the United States "against all enemies, foreign and domestic." But, just because I am not certain that the language of Questions 20 and 22 will bear the construction I should have to put upon it in order to be able to answer them in the affirmative, I have to say that I do not know that I can say "yes" in answer to these two questions.

In the hearing before the district court on his application, he had made it clear that he was not a pacifist, that if allowed to interpret the oath for himself he would interpret it as not inconsistent with his position and would be willing to take it. On the other hand, he could only answer Question 22 in the affirmative with the understanding that he would have to believe that the war was morally justified before he would be willing to take up arms or could give it his moral support.

He stated his willingness to give to the United States all the allegiance he ever had given or ever could give to any country but that he could not put allegiance to the government of any country before allegiance to the will of God. He further indicated that he did not anticipate engaging in any propaganda against the prosecution of a war which the government had already declared and which it considered to be justified, but in this respect he preferred not to make any absolute promise at the time of the hearing because of his ignorance of all the circumstances which might affect his judgment with reference to such a war.

He did not question that the government under certain conditions could regulate and restrain the conduct of the individual citizen, even to the extent of imprisonment. He recognized the principle of the submission of the individual citizen to the opinion of the majority in a democratic country, but he did not believe in having his own moral problems solved for him by the majority. He felt this to be inconsistent with what he understood to be the principles of Christianity. Recognizing the right of the government to restrain the freedom of the individual for the good of the social whole, he believed that the individual citizen should have the right to refuse government military service involving, as it probably would, the taking of human life, when his best moral judgment should compel him to do so. On the contrary, however, he was willing to support his country even to the extent of bearing arms if asked to do so by the government in any war which he could regard as morally justified.

Mr. Justice Sutherland, in delivering the opinion of the court in a five to four decision, denied the applicant's request for naturalization on the basis of his unwillingness to promise to bear arms in defense of the United States unless he believed the war to be morally justified or to promise to refrain from propaganda against the prosecution of a war which he did not believe to be morally justified. The court pointed out that naturalization is a privilege to be given, qualified, or withheld as Congress may determine, a privilege which the alien may claim as of right only upon the compliance with the terms which Congress imposes.

Criticizing Dr. Macintosh's position, Justice Sutherland wrote:

When he speaks of putting his allegiance to the will of God above his allegiance to the government, it is evident, in the light of his entire statement, that he means to make *his own interpretation* of the will of God the decisive test which shall conclude the government and stay its hand. We are a Christian people (Church of the Holy Trinity v. United States, 143 U.S. 457, 470, 511), according to one another the equal right of religious freedom, and acknowledging with reverence the duty of obedience to the will of God. But, also, we are a nation with the duty to survive; a nation whose Constitution contemplates war as well as peace; whose government must go forward upon the assumption, and safely can proceed upon no other, that unqualified allegiance to the nation and submission and obedience to the laws of the land, as well those made for war as those made for peace, are not inconsistent with the will of God.

The applicant here rejects that view. He is unwilling to rely, as every native-born citizen is obliged to do, upon the probable continuance by Congress of the long established and approved practice of exempting the honest conscientious objector, while at the same time asserting his willingness to conform to whatever the future law constitutionally shall require of him; but discloses a present and fixed purpose to refuse to give his moral or armed support to any future war in which the country may be actually engaged, if, in his opinion, the war is not morally justified, the opinion of the nation as expressed by Congress to the contrary notwithstanding.

If the attitude of this claimant, as shown by his statements and the inferences properly to be deduced from them, be held immaterial to the questions of his fitness for admission to citizenship, where shall the line be drawn? Upon what ground of distinction may we hereafter reject another applicant who shall express his willingness to respect any particular principle of the Constitution or obey any future statute only upon the condition that he shall entertain the opinion that it is morally justified? The applicant's attitude, in effect, is a refusal to take the oath of allegiance except in an altered form. The qualifications upon which he insists, it is true, are made by parol and not by way of written amendment to the oath; but the substance is the same.[4]

With this remarkable statement of the superiority of government over conscience, the dissent by Chief Justice Hughes, concurred in by Justices Brandeis, Holmes, and Stone, disagreed. The dissent stood strongly on the rights of conscience:

Much has been said of the paramount duty to the state, a duty to be

[4] 283 U.S. 626 (1931).

recognized, it is urged, even though it conflicts with convictions of duty to God. Undoubtedly that duty to the state exists within the domain of power, for government may enforce obedience to laws regardless of scruples. When one's belief collides with the power of the state, the latter is supreme within its sphere and submission or punishment follows. But, in the forum of conscience, duty to a moral power higher than the state has always been maintained. The reservation of that supreme obligation, as a matter of principle, would unquestionably be made by many of our conscientious and law-abiding citizens. The essence of religion is belief in a relation to God involving duties superior to those arising from any human relation. As was stated by Mr. Justice Field, in Davis v. Beason, 133 U.S. 333, 342, 33 L. Ed. 637, 639, 10 S. Ct. 299, 8 Am. Crim. Rep. 89: "The term 'religion' has reference to one's views of his relations to his Creator, and to the obligations they impose of reverence for his being and character, and of obedience to his will." One cannot speak of religious liberty, with proper appreciation of its essential and historic significance, without assuming the existence of a belief in supreme allegiance to the will of God. Professor Macintosh, when pressed by the inquiries put to him, stated what is axiomatic in religious doctrine. And, putting aside dogmas with their particular conceptions of deity, freedom of conscience itself implies respect for an innate conviction of paramount duty. The battle for religious liberty has been fought and won with respect to religious beliefs and practices, which are not in conflict with good order, upon the very ground of the supremacy of conscience within its proper field. What that field is, under our system of government, presents in part a question of constitutional law and also, in part, one of legislative policy in avoiding unnecessary clashes with the dictates of conscience. There is abundant room for enforcing the requisite authority of law as it is enacted and requires obedience, and for maintaining the conception of the supremacy of law as essential to orderly government, without demanding that either citizens or applicants for citizenship shall assume by oath an obligation to regard allegiance to God as subordinate to allegiance to civil power. The attempt to exact such a promise, and thus to bind one's conscience by the taking of oaths or the submission to tests, has been the cause of many deplorable conflicts. The Congress has sought to avoid such conflicts in this country by respecting our happy tradition. In no sphere of legislation has the intention to prevent such clashes been more conspicuous than in relation to the bearing of arms. It would require strong evidence that the Congress intended a reversal of its policy in prescribing the general terms of the naturalization oath. I find no such evidence.[5]

The dissent added:

It seems to me that the applicant has shown himself in his behavior and character to be highly desirable as a citizen and, if such a man is to be

[5] 283 U.S. 635.

excluded from naturalization, I think the disqualification should be found in unambiguous terms and not in an implication which shuts him out and gives admission to a host far less worthy.

On the same day that the United States Supreme Court announced the decision in the Macintosh case, it announced its decision in the case of the United States v. Marie Averil Bland.[6] In this case the applicant for citizenship was born in Canada and came to the United States in 1914. As a graduate nurse she spent nine months in the service of our government in France nursing American soldiers and aiding in psychiatric work. She refused to take the oath of allegiance prescribed by the statute to defend the Constitution and laws of the United States against all enemies except with the written interpolation of the words, "as far as my conscience as a Christian will allow." Mr. Justice Sutherland in delivering the opinion of the court stated that the opinion which had just been announced in United States v. Macintosh would rule the decision in this case, that it had no distinguishing features from the Macintosh case, that in substance the oath had been definitely prescribed by Congress, that the "words of the statute do not admit of the qualification upon which the applicant insists," and thereby denied the application.

Mr. Chief Justice Hughes in dissenting said:

What I have said in the case of United States v. Macintosh [283 U.S. 605 Ante, 1302, 51 S. Ct. 570] with respect to the interpretation of the provisions of the Naturalization Act and of the prescribed oath, I think applies also to this case. The petitioner is a nurse who spent nine months in the service of our government in France, nursing United States soldiers and aiding in psychiatric work. She has religious scruples against bearing arms. I think it sufficiently appears that her unwillingness to take the oath was merely because of the interpretation that had been placed upon it as amounting to a promise that she would bear arms despite her religious convictions. It is the opinion of the Circuit Court of Appeals that the appellant may properly take the oath according to its true significance and should be permitted to take it [42 F. (ed) 842, 844, 845]. I think that the judgment below should be affirmed.

Despite the action taken by the United States Supreme Court in the above cases, some lower courts braved the possibilities of having their decisions reversed by granting citizenship in some instances to conscientious objectors. One such case was that of Professor John P. Klassen of Bluffton College, Ohio. Klassen, although he refused to bear arms, was willing to serve as a noncombatant in time of war as

[6] 283 U.S. 636 (1931).

he had done in the Red Cross with the Russian forces during World War I and later in the Russian revolution. As a refugee from Russia along with thousands of other Mennonites, he had escaped to Canada and then moved to Ohio with his wife in 1924. Because of his beliefs as a Mennonite and because he was forty-six years old (beyond the military age limit), he was granted naturalization papers by Judge E. E. Everett of the Allen common pleas bench sitting in Lima, Ohio. Except for opposition from the American Legion and a few other organizations, the action of conferring citizenship on the Mennonite was acclaimed by public approval.

Likewise, on January 12, 1944, a United States district court in Washington, Judge Charles H. Leavy sitting, granted citizenship to William Robert Kinlock and William McKillop, who were conscientious objectors and had been classed as 1-A-O when drafted into military service for noncombatant duty. According to the court, both applicants were British subjects residing in the United States who had registered under the provision of the Selective Training and Service Act of 1940. In the summer of 1942 they were inducted into the army as conscientious objectors and assigned to a medical unit. At Fort Lewis, Washington, they made application for citizenship.

The commanding officer of the unit to which these applicants were attached was present in court and testified that the unit consisted almost entirely of soldiers who qualified for combat service. He further testified that no distinction whatever was made between these two applicants and other members of the unit in their training; as members of a medical unit they took the basic training provided for such a unit and in all respects were soldiers assigned to duty in a medical unit of the army in time of war. It was further disclosed that hazards incident to service in a medical unit were equal to those of the combat units, since their duties required medical men in time of battle to be at the front lines under fire, and that the same high degree of valor and courage was required.

In response to the contention by the immigration service that the applicants were not eligible for naturalization as held by the Supreme Court in the cases of U.S. v. Schwimmer, U.S. v. Macintosh and U.S. v. Bland, the district court judge made the observation that these opinions were by a divided court. In the Schwimmer case the decision had been a six to three vote and both the Macintosh and Bland cases were five to four decisions; all these cases were reversals of the unanimous decisions of the circuit courts from which they came. "This fact," said the court, "is mentioned, not as a basis to hold in the instant cases that the law is other than announced by the court of last resort, but rather to show that the question of what implications and inferences are to be drawn from the wording of the oath of allegiance, is not at all free from doubt."

The court further contended that after these Supreme Court decisions Congress had passed legislation and "with full knowledge thereof, provided that these applicants and all aliens similarly situated, are entitled to citizenship by virtue of becoming members of the armed forces of the United States, performing military duty, wearing the uniform, and taking the soldiers' oath." The opposition to naturalization by the immigration service for the reason that the applicants did not unequivocally state that they were willing to bear arms was overruled, and the applicants were ordered to be admitted as citizens.

It is interesting to note that in 1946 in the case of Girouard v. U.S.[7] the United States Supreme Court reversed, if not in every detail at least for practical purposes, the decisions reached in the Macintosh, Schwimmer, and Bland cases. In this case James Louis Girouard, the petitioner, was a Canadian-born resident of the United States whose application for citizenship had been granted by the United States district court in Boston, reversed by the United States circuit court of appeals, and finally appealed to the United States Supreme Court.

Mr. Justice Douglas wrote the majority opinion of the court with which four justices concurred. Chief Justice Stone wrote the dissent. Mr. Justice Reed and Mr. Justice Frankfurter joined in the dissent. Mr. Justice Jackson was away and took no part in the decision.

Girouard stated in his application for naturalization that he understood the principles of the government of the United States and that he believed in its form of government and was willing to take the oath of allegiance which reads as follows:

I hereby declare, on oath, that I absolutely and entirely renounce and abjure all allegiance and fidelity to any foreign prince, potentate, state, or sovereignty of whom or which I have heretofore been a subject or citizen; that I will support and defend the Constitution and laws of the United States of America against all enemies, foreign and domestic; that I will bear true faith and allegiance to the same; and that I take this obligation freely without any mental reservation or purpose of evasion: So Help Me God.[8]

To the question in the application "If necessary, are you willing

[7] 328 U.S. 61 (1946).
[8] 54 Stat. 1157, U.S.C., Title 8, Section 735b.

to take up arms in defense of this country?" he replied, "No (Non-combatant), Seventh-day Adventist." In explaining his answer before the examiner he stated that his position as a noncombatant was purely a religious matter with him, that he had no political or personal reasons other than that. He did not claim exemption from all military service but only from combat military duty.

At the hearing in district court the petitioner testified that he was a member of the Seventh-day Adventist denomination, of which approximately 10,000 were then serving in the armed forces of the United States as noncombatants, especially in the medical corps, and that he was willing to serve in the army but would not bear arms. As we have seen, the district court admitted him to citizenship but the circuit court of appeals reversed the decision with one judge dissenting. The circuit court reversed the decision on the authority of U.S. v. Schwimmer, U.S. v. Macintosh, and U.S. v. Bland, feeling that the facts of the present case were within the principles of those cases. The case was appealed to the United States Supreme Court upon a petition for a writ of certiorari, which was granted so that the decisions in the former cases might be re-examined.

The Supreme Court recognized that there were some factual distinctions between this case and the Schwimmer and Macintosh cases, but it contended that the Bland case on its facts was indistinguishable and that the principle emerging from the three cases obliterated any factual distinction among them.

The majority opinion swept aside various arguments and warnings that had been used in the previous cases based upon silence or lack of action on the part of Congress. Noting that when Congress revised the Naturalization Act in 1940 it made "no affirmative recognition of the rule" of the three former cases, the court declared that the only affirmative action taken by Congress since 1931 came in 1942 when, for men in the army, "Congress specifically granted naturalization privileges to non-combatants who like petitioner were prevented from bearing arms by their religious scruples."

The court made reference to the dissents of Mr. Justice Holmes in the Schwimmer case, the dissent of Mr. Justice Hughes in the Macintosh case, and quoted extensively from each of them. It is interesting to note that the dissenting opinions of these justices in the former cases became the majority opinion in the present case. The court said:

The oath required of aliens does not in terms require that they promise to bear arms. Nor has Congress expressly made any such finding a prerequisite to citizenship. To hold that it is required is to read it into the Act by implication. But we could not assume that Congress intended to make such an abrupt and radical departure from our traditions unless it spoke in unequivocal terms.

The bearing of arms, important as it is, is not the only way in which our institutions may be supported and defended, even in times of great peril. Total war in its modern form dramatizes as never before the great co-operative effort necessary for victory. The nuclear physicists who developed the atomic bomb, the worker at his lathe, the seaman on cargo vessels, construction battalions, nurses, engineers, litter bearers, doctors, chaplains—these, too, made essential contributions. And many of them made the supreme sacrifice. Mr. Justice Holmes stated in the *Schwimmer* case (279 U.S. p. 655) that "the Quakers have done their share to make the country what it is." And the annals of the recent war show that many whose religious scruples prevented them from bearing arms, nevertheless were unselfish participants in the war effort. Refusal to bear arms is not necessarily a sign of disloyalty or a lack of attachment to our institutions. One may serve his country faithfully and devotedly, though his religious scruples make it impossible for him to shoulder a rifle. Devotion to one's country can be as real and as enduring among non-combatants as among combatants. One may adhere to what he deems to be his obligation to God and yet assume all military risks to secure victory. The effort of war is indivisible; and those whose religious scruples prevent them from killing are no less patriots than those whose special traits or handicaps result in their assignment to duties far behind the fighting front. Each is making the utmost contribution according to his capacity. The fact that his role may be limited by religious convictions rather than by physical characteristics has no necessary bearing on his attachment to his country or on his willingness to support and defend it to his utmost.

The court added the following significant statement:

The struggle for religious liberty has through the centuries been an effort to accommodate the demands of the state to the conscience of the individual. The victories for freedom of thought recorded in our Bill of Rights recognizes that in the domain of conscience there is a moral power higher than the State. Throughout the ages men have suffered death rather than subordinate their allegiance to God to the authority of the State. Freedom of religion guaranteed by the First Amendment is the product of that struggle.

"We conclude," said the court, "that the *Schwimmer, Macintosh* and *Bland* cases do not state the correct rule of law."

The decision was reversed and the petitioner's request granted. In so doing the Supreme Court had again reversed itself in favor of increased liberties of conscience. Former Attorney General Homer Cummings argued Girouard's case before the high court.

In commenting upon the decision the *New Republic* said:

Mr. Justice Holmes added another laurel to his great liberal reputation when he spoke out against the majority. . . . The implications of the decision may be far reaching. It is bound to influence persistent efforts to stigmatize conscientious objectors as degenerate and immoral persons who should be denied rights granted other citizens. It also narrows the idea that citizenship may be denied for various arbitrary reasons. The Supreme Court has acted wisely. Its decision is a victory in the battle for free thought.[9]

In harmony with many of the comments made in the press at the time is the statement which appeared in the *Christian Century*:

At long last the Supreme Court has invoked its judicial power to dispel a shadow which has darkened the American claim to freedom of conscience for almost twenty years. In a decision rendered on April 22 — the last publicly participated in by the late Chief Justice Stone, who dissented — the court ordered that citizenship be granted to James Louis Girouard, a Canadian-born applicant who had refused to bear arms. As a member of the Seventh-day Adventist Church, Mr. Girouard had declared his willingness to serve in a non-combatant capacity in time of war, as more than 10,000 members of that church actually served, most of them in the medical corps, during the recent conflict. The Supreme Court held that there is nothing in the oath to "support and defend the constitution and laws of the United States of America against all enemies, foreign and domestic," which requires the bearing of arms.[10]

The Girouard decision has been hailed with satisfaction among people in general and especially among those who are awake to the peril in which the individual conscience stands in a world of growing state totalitarianism.

[9] *New Republic*, May 6, 1946, pp. 645, 646.
[10] *Christian Century*, May 6, 1946, p. 583.

CHAPTER XVII

Religion and Freedom of Speech

CHRISTIANITY, in common with Mohammedanism and some other forms of religion, has always claimed the necessity of propagating its beliefs. There is recorded a command of Jesus, "Go ye therefore, and make disciples of all the nations, baptizing them into the name of the Father, and of the Son, and of the Holy Spirit: teaching them to observe all things whatsoever I have commanded you" [1] and another in the Acts: "Ye shall be witnesses unto me both in Jerusalem, and in all Judea, and in Samaria, and unto the uttermost part of the earth." [2] The apostle Paul emphasized the necessity of preaching when he wrote: "How shall they call on him in whom they have not believed? and how shall they believe in him of whom they have not heard? and how shall they hear without a preacher? and how shall they preach except they be sent?" [3]

These admonitions the early Christians took very seriously. When commanded to stop preaching, the apostle Peter replied that he must obey God rather than man. [4] By voice and pen the new sect proclaimed its message.

The right to protest was recognized in England in the Magna Carta, and the petitions of request and protest presented to the English kings were the progenitors of modern legislative "bills." One judge has declared that "freedom of speech and freedom of the press have always been supposed to be the very cornerstone of Anglo-Saxon democratic institutions." [5] This was scarcely the case when under Queen Elizabeth the licensing of printing presses was decreed in order to aid Archbishop Whitgift in his campaign against Puritanism. [6] It was in protest to the Printing Ordinance of 1643, provid-

---

[1] Matthew 28:19, 20 (American Revised Version).
[2] Acts 1:8.
[3] Romans 10:14, 15.
[4] Acts 5:28, 29.
[5] State v. Pierce, 158 N.W. 698 (1916).
[6] John Strype, *Life and Acts of John Whitgift, D.D.* (Oxford: Clarendon Press, 1822 edition), Vol. VI, App. 94, pp. 422ff.

ing for the licensing of printing presses, that Milton wrote his famous *Areopagitica,* in which he declared that "truth and understanding are not such wares as to be monopolized and traded in by tickets and statutes, and standards." In this same treatise Milton made his magnificent statement of choice among liberties: "Give me the liberty to know, to utter, and to argue freely according to conscience, above all liberties."

For any discussion in the United States of freedom of the press, the First Amendment of the Constitution must furnish the basis: "Congress shall make no law respecting an establishment of religion, or prohibiting the free exercise thereof, or abridging the freedom of speech, or of the press; or the right of the people peaceably to assemble. . . ." It is these rights which are exercised in dissemination of religious beliefs.

It was long held by the courts in this country that the First Amendment, guaranteeing these inalienable personal rights, was restrictedly federal. The Fourteenth Amendment, adopted in 1868, applied, of course, to the states. But it was held that only as such rights were set forth specifically in the state constitutions themselves were the states required to respect them.[7] The point of departure in making the First Amendment applicable to the states came primarily with the decision of Gitlow v. the People of New York, handed down in 1925. The court declared that "we may and do assume that freedom of speech and of the press — which are protected by the First Amendment from abridgement by Congress — are among the fundamental personal rights and 'liberties' protected by the due process clause of the Fourteenth Amendment from impairment by the States."[8]

This important point of interpretation passed beyond an assumption within a decade. In DeJonge v. State of Oregon, decided in 1937,[9] the court ruled that "freedom of speech and of the press are

[7] See "Constitutional Law" in *Corpus Juris,* para. 163, d(1), Vol. XII, pp. 744, 745 (1917); Weems v. U.S., 217 U.S. 349, 30 S. Ct. 544, 54 L. ed. 793, 19 Ann. Cas. 705; Keller v. U.S., 213 U.S. 138, 29 S. Ct. 470, 56 L. ed. 737, 16 Ann. Cas. 1066; Twining v. New Jersey, 211 U.S. 78, 29 S. Ct. 14, 53 L. ed. 97; Ughbanks v. Armstrong, 208 U.S. 481, 28 S. Ct. 372, 52 L. ed. 582; Hunter v. Pittsburgh, 207 U.S. 161, 28 S. Ct. 40, 52 L. ed. 151; Barrington v. Missouri, 205 U.S. 483, 27 S. Ct. 582, 51 L. ed. 890; Howard v. Kentucky, 200 U.S. 164, 26 S. Ct. 189, 50 L. ed. 421; Jack v. Kansas, 199 U.S. 372, 26 S. Ct. 73, 50 L. ed. 234; U.S. v. Steffens, 100 U.S. 82, 25 L. ed. 550; Le Master v. Spencer, 203 Fed. 210, 121 CCA 416; In re Mohawk Overall Co., 210 N.Y. 474, 104 N.E. 925; Ex parte Simmons, 5 Okl. Cr. 399, 115 Pac. 380; State v. Norvell, 191 S.W. 536.

[8] 268 U.S. 662, 666. The court stated, "We do not regard the incidental statement in Prudential Ins. Co. v. Cheek, 259 U.S. 530, 543, that the Fourteenth Amendment imposes no restrictions on the States concerning freedom of speech, as determinative of this question."

[9] 299 U.S. 353.

fundamental rights which are safeguarded by the due process clause of the Fourteenth Amendment of the Federal Constitution." [10]

A long succession of cases since 1937 has made it a fixed point of law that the First Amendment applies through the Fourteenth to the individual states and their citizens.[11] This is important because of the highly diversified character of religious life in the United States.

In the realm of religious faith, and in that of political belief, sharp differences arise. In both fields the tenets of one man may seem the rankest error to his neighbor. To persuade others to his own point of view, the pleader, as we know, at times, resorts to exaggeration, to villification of men who have been, or are, prominent in church and state, and even to false statement. But the people of this nation have ordained in the light of history, that in spite of the probability of excesses and abuses, these liberties are in the long view, essential to enlightened opinion and right conduct on the part of the citizens of a democracy. The essential characteristic of these liberties is, that under their shield many types of life, character, opinion and belief can develop unmolested and unobstructed. Nowhere is this shield more necessary than in our own country for a people composed of many races and of many creeds.[12]

It has been well said that "In this country the full and free right to entertain any religious belief, to practice any religious principle, and to teach any religious doctrine which does not violate the laws of morality and property, and which does not infringe personal rights, is conceded to all." [13]

In this atmosphere of freedom the citizen of the United States finds himself at liberty to worship or not to worship, and to propagate, as he may wish, whatever faith he professes. His means of doing so are not limited by law. The right of preaching a religious message is an exercise of freedom of speech. The dissemination of religious ideas through the printed page is an expression of the free-

[10] Cases cited were Gitlow v. New York, 268 U.S. 562 (1925); Stromberg v. California, 283 U.S. 359; Near v. Minnesota, 283 U.S. 697, 707; Grosjean v. American Press Co., 297 U.S. 233, 243, 244; Hebert v. Louisiana, 272 U.S. 312, 316; Powell v. Alabama, 287 U.S. 45, 67.
[11] Among these are Lovell v. City of Griffin, 303 U.S. 444 (1938); Hague, Mayor, et al. v. Committee for Industrial Organization et al., 307 U.S. 486 (1939); Schneider v. State of New Jersey and three other cases, 308 U.S. 147 (1939); Cantwell et al. v. State of Connecticut, 310 U.S. 396 (1940); Chaplinsky v. State of New Hampshire, 315 U.S. 568 (1942); Jones v. City of Opelika and two other cases, 316 U.S. 584 (1942); Murdock v. Commonwealth of Pennsylvania and seven other cases, 319 U.S. 105 (1943); Douglas et al. v. City of Jeanette, 319 U.S. 157 (1943); Martin v. City of Struthers, 319 U.S. 141 (1943); West Virginia State Board of Education et al. v. Barnette et al., 319 U.S. 624 (1943); U.S. v. Ballard, 322 U.S. 78 (1944); Marsh v. State of Alabama, 326 U.S. 501 (1945).
[12] Cantwell et al. v. State of Connecticut, 310 U.S. 310; 60 S. Ct. 900 (1940).
[13] Watson et al. v. Jones et al., 13 Wall. (U.S.) 728 (1872).

dom of the press. These two means of religious propagation are similar as inherent rights.

There are no laws or ordinances granting the right of free speech.
It is a right, constitutionally recognized. The only questions that
arise are how the method, content, and results concern the peace and
liberty of others. This the state must discover and supervise. Religious liberty is absolute,[14] but this is in regard to belief; the exercise
of religious belief is relative.[15] But it has long been held a fundamental right to teach religion.[16]

Early decisions of the courts in the fields of politics and labor have
prepared the way for freedom of speech in religion. When Pierce
appealed from a conviction in Wisconsin, under a corrupt practices
act, for giving out facts he had accumulated concerning political
situations in his community, his appeal was sustained. The Wisconsin supreme court declared that "all of our state courts, as well as
the Federal Court, expressly preserve these rights [of free speech]."[17]
When DeJonge was convicted in Oregon under suspicion of advocating violence because he addressed a meeting under Communist
auspices, his appeal was sustained by the United States Supreme
Court. The opinion stated:

Consistently with the Federal Constitution, peaceable assembly for lawful discussion cannot be made a crime. The holding of meetings for peaceable political action cannot be proscribed. Those who assist in the conduct
of such meetings cannot be branded as criminals on that score. The question, if the rights of free speech and peaceable assembly are to be preserved, is not as to the auspices under which the meeting is held but as to
its purpose; not as to the relations of the speakers, but whether their utterances transcend the bounds of the freedom of speech which the Constitution protects.[18]

A New Jersey ordinance prohibiting statements engendering hate
and racial and religious animosity was enforced against Klapprott,
who was arrested after addressing a meeting of the German-Ameri-
can Bund in the year 1941, when the war atmosphere made for
tenseness of feeling. The New Jersey court of appeals held that the
charges against the accused could not be sustained. It stated:

We do not think such phases of human reaction or emotion can be

[14] Cline et al. v. State, 130 Pac. 512 (1913).
[15] Cantwell et al. v. State of Connecticut.
[16] Watson et al. v. Jones et al. The constitutional right to believe, and to teach one's
beliefs, was clearly stated in the case involving Mrs. Eddy's estate, Glover v. Baker et al.,
83 Atl. 916 (1912).
[17] State v. Pierce, 158 N.W. 696, 698 (1916).
[18] DeJonge v. Oregon, 299 U.S. 353, 365 (1937).

made a legitimate standard for a penal statute. . . . To make the speaker amenable to the criminal law his utterances must be such as to create a "clear and present danger that they will bring about substantive evils" to society (Schenck v. U.S., 249 U.S. 47; 39 S. Ct. 247, 249; 63 L. ed. 4760) that the state has the right to prevent. The utterances must be such as constitute a danger to the State. We cannot say that the statements made by the plaintiffs in error were of this character.[19]

When Gitlow advocated the overthrow of government as constituted, the United States Supreme Court ruled that an act to prevent utterances which could reasonably be expected to result in danger to the state must be sustained, but that the mere teaching of an abstract argument or "academic anarchy" could not be made a basis for conviction.[20]

The curtailment of freedom of speech when it constitutes a danger to the state has been upheld. The federal courts have ruled that

Though one is not punished in these United States for his views and beliefs, yet one may be punished when through his external conduct these views are put into practice, if such practice is fraught with clear and present danger to the safety, morals, health or general welfare of the community, and is violative of laws enacted for their protection.[21]

When certain Japanese, excluded during World War II from California, used what was deemed extreme language in expressing unwillingness to register under the Selective Service Act, they were apprehended, and their conviction was sustained. The decision stated:

Freedom of speech, freedom of the press, and freedom of assembly guaranteed by the First Amendment are fundamental rights. But, though fundamental, they are not in their nature absolute. These rights are not unbridled license to speak, publish or assemble without any responsibility whatever. Their exercise is subject to reasonable restriction required in order to protect the government from destruction or serious injury.[22]

Several labor cases have illustrated the right of free speech as recognized by the courts. Representatives of the Committee of Industrial Organization spoke in Jersey City at open air meetings without a police permit. Their appeal from conviction in the lower courts was sustained by the United States Supreme Court. It was held that the streets and parks of the city were, under proper regula-

---

[19] State v. Klapprott, 22 Atl. (2d), 877, 882.
[20] Gitlow v. People of New York, 268 U.S. 562 (1925).
[21] Baxley v. United States, 134 Fed. (2d) 937, 938 (1943). Compare the ruling in Lawton v. Commonwealth, 164 S.W. (2d) 972 (1942), in which it was ruled that the use of reptiles in a religious meeting was unconstitutional because of its menace to public safety.
[22] Kiyoshi Okamoto et al. v. U.S. and six other cases, 152 Fed. (2d) 905, 907 (1945).

tion, for the use of the citizenry and that discretion on the part of police officials to withhold a permit, because of mere opinion that riots might result, could not be allowed.[23]

When R. J. Thomas, president of the United Automobile Workers spoke in Houston in 1945 in defiance of a court injunction to restrain him from so doing, he was arrested and convicted in the lower courts. The United States Supreme Court, however, reversed the judgment. It stated concerning freedom of speech:

Only the gravest abuses, endangering paramount interests, give occasion for permissible limitation. It is therefore in our tradition to allow the widest room for discussion, the narrowest range for its restriction, particularly when this right is exercised in conjunction with peaceable assembly. . . . If the restraint were smaller than it is, it is from petty tyrannies in that large ones take root and grow. This fact can be no more plain when they are imposed on the most basic rights of all. Seedlings planted in that soil grow great and, growing, break down the foundations of liberty.[24]

In federal court, however, an employer was restrained from using freedom of speech to coerce the will of employees in respect to labor union connections.[25]

In view of the attitude of the courts, restraints in connection with religion are carefully applied. Religious assemblies have always been protected from interference.[26] An expression of religious opinion rarely presents a threat to public safety, but it can be annoying, offensive in sentiment, or a cause of obstruction to public passageways.

In 1940 three members of a family named Cantwell were arrested while soliciting funds for religious purposes, because what they taught gave offense to certain adherents of a different religious group and threatened to cause a disturbance of the peace. They were convicted in the lower courts. When the case reached the United States Supreme Court, the previous decisions were reversed, with a warning against the danger of censorship of speech. Concerning the phonograph records containing the disturbing expressions which the plaintiffs had played the court said,

Although the contents of the records not unnaturally aroused animosity, we think that, in the absence of a statute narrowly drawn to define and punish specific conduct as constituting a clear and present danger, to a substantial interest of the State, the petitioner's communication, con-

[23] Hague, Mayor, et al. v. Committee for Industrial Organization et al., 307 U.S. 496 (1939).
[24] Thomas v. Collins, Sheriff, 65 S. Ct. 315, 323, 328 (1945).
[25] National Labor Relations Board v. American Pearl Button Co., et al., 149 Fed. (2d) 311 (1945).
[26] Cline et al. v. State, 130 Pac. 512 (1913).

sidered in the light of the constitutional guarantees, raised no such clear and present menace to public peace and order as to render him liable to conviction of the common law offence in question.[27]

Three years later the conviction of religionists who had expressed views "respecting governmental policies" and "prophecies concerning the future of state and national government" in this country as well as in other nations was declared unconstitutional.[28]

Religious expression has met restraints. When Chaplinsky was accosted by a police officer while distributing religious literature, he answered with abusive and profane language. The United States Supreme Court ruled that such expressions were not defensible as coming under religious freedom.[29] Police were ruled justified in stopping the use of a loud-speaker in the streets which gave expression to religious teachings by one professing to be a minister of the gospel, because the people had a right to protection from "concentrated and continuous cacophony."[30] When a group of religionists went through the corridors of a hotel, insisting upon talking religion to unwilling listeners, they were arrested for disturbing the peace, and their convictions were sustained.[31]

It has been argued that parades are religious assemblies in motion and are therefore not subject to restraint. A number of cases bear on this point. In the city of Grand Rapids, Michigan, an ordinance was adopted in 1886 which gave the mayor discretion in issuing permits for parades. Shortly after the passage of this ordinance, a charitable and religious organization which throughout its history has made extensive use of the streets for religious meetings, engaged in a parade with the use of drums and singing. They had no permit. Arrest and conviction followed. When the case reached the Michigan supreme court, the court ruled that the plaintiffs must be dismissed because the ordinance gave too much discretion to the mayor. But it stated that

We cannot accede to the suggestion that religious liberty includes the right to introduce and carry out every scheme or purpose which persons see fit to claim as part of their religious system. There is no legal authority to constrain belief, but no one can lawfully stretch his own liberty of action so as to interfere with that of his neighbors, or violate peace and

[27] Cantwell et al. v. State of Connecticut, 310 U.S. 296, 311. See also the quotation from this case on page 201 above.
[28] Taylor v. State of Mississippi and two other cases, 319 U.S. 583 (1943).
[29] Chaplinsky v. State of New Hampshire, 315 U.S. 568 (1942).
[30] Hamilton v. City of Montrose, 124 Pac. (2d) 757, 762 (1942).
[31] People v. Vaughan et al., 150 Pac. (2d) 964 (1944).

good order. The whole criminal law might be practically superseded if, under pretext of liberty of conscience, the commission of crime is made a religious dogma. It is a fundamental condition of all liberty, and necessary to civil society, that all men must exercise their rights in harmony, and must yield to such restrictions as are necessary to produce that result.[32]

In general, however, ordinances regulating the use of the streets for parades and religious activities have been supported. An Indianapolis ordinance was sustained in the case of a man who appeared upon the streets wearing a shirt with lettering upon it, charging a barbershop with unfair labor practices. The threats to public peace stressed in the charges were the danger of stirring up class hatred and of causing traffic congestion by the drawing of crowds.[33]

Licensing of religious parades was supported in three cases in 1940. In a case where a number of religionists, strung out in single file, engaged without a permit in an "information march," and were arrested and convicted, a town ordinance requiring a permit ranging in possible cost up to three hundred dollars was declared constitutional. It was declared that the right to conduct a parade, even if a parade is considered a "religious assembly in motion," is relative, and the religious right involved must be exercised "in subordination to the general comfort and convenience, and in consonance with peace and good order."[34]

Palms led a crowd of more than a hundred religionists into Kutztown, Pennsylvania, and staged a parade with religious placards and sandwich signs. He and his followers played phonographs, operated a sound truck, and insisted on talking to the inhabitants. In consequence of these actions he and a number of his associates were arrested for disorderly conduct. The Pennsylvania superior court affirmed the conviction and declared that the guarantee of religious liberty

does not mean that . . . a sectarian may escape punishment for acts or conduct declared by the legislature to be inimical to the peace, good order and morals of society. A crime is none the less so, nor less odious, because sanctioned by what some particular sect may designate as religion.[35]

A similar case arising in Homestead, Pennsylvania, was decided in favor of the state on the ground that the streets must be kept

---

[32] In re Frazee, 30 N.E. 72, 75.
[33] Watters v. City of Indianapolis, 134 N.E. 482 (1922).
[34] State v. Cox, 16 Atl. (2d) 508; affirmed as Cox v. State of New Hampshire, 61 S. Ct. 726.
[35] Commonwealth v. Palms, 15 Atl. (2d) 481, 483 (1940).

open.[36] But the right of citizens to use the streets for dissemination of religious or political opinion is maintained.[37]

Radio speeches are clearly subject to regulation by federal law. This was stated in a United States Supreme Court decision handed down in 1943 in the case of the National Broadcasting Company, Inc., et al. v. United States et al.[38] There has not as yet been handed down by a high court a decision concerning religious broadcasts.

Thus the right of free speech has been ably defended in the courts. For free assembly in normal places of assembly, and for free speech, there can be required no permit. There is the greatest latitude possible in the content of free speech. There must be immediate danger to society in what is said, and it must be danger which can be defined in clear and unmistakable language, for a speaker to be culpable before the law. Political opinions, and even "academic anarchy," may be topics of free discussion.

However, when the right of free speech is indulged on the streets, the state may take cognizance when the gathering of a crowd interferes with traffic. If the "assembly" takes the form of a procession, the police have a duty to approve the line of march and to see to it that the public convenience and safety are not interfered with. The carrying of banners may be prohibited.

When free speech entails loud and unpleasant noises, as the continuous loud playing of a phonograph over a loud-speaker, it can be stopped. Language that is merely irritating to certain people cannot be challenged, but action can be taken against language which is abusive of certain people and directed abusively at them.

The rights of free speech and of a free press are so closely allied that what applies to one frequently applies to the other.

[36] Commonwealth v. Hessler, *ibid.*, p. 486.
[37] Hannan et al. v. City of Haverhill et al., 120 Fed. (2d) 87, 89 (1941).
[38] 63 S. Ct. 997.

CHAPTER XVIII

Religion and Freedom of the Press

IT IS recognized that preaching through the distribution of religious literature "is an age-old form of missionary evangelism — as old as the history of printing presses. It has been a potent force in various religious movements down through the years."[1] The religious press is not limited as to type of literature. It is not only the printing and sale of books, or the publication and transmission of periodicals which is embraced in the constitutional right. All types of printed matter, it has been pointed out, are protected under the First Amendment as vehicles of the dissemination of opinion.[2]

Freedom of distribution is completely functional, whether it be by sale or gratis. It would be a *reductio ad absurdum* to contend for freedom to print and then prevent distribution.[3] It has been ruled in a state court that an ordinance forbidding the distribution of handbills was constitutional,[4] but such restriction is dependent upon circumstances. It is recognized that each case in which regulation of a right is attempted must be adjudged in view of conditions.[5] In the case of printed matter of a political nature, statements made in favor of a change of government by peaceful means may be published, but an ordinance forbidding advocacy of such changes by force has been ruled constitutional. The expression of opinion cannot be separated from responsibility for results.[6] Printed matter may not incite to violence or slaughter.[7]

The necessity of regulating the use of the streets for the good of the public places a limitation upon the exercise of freedom of the press. Vendors of newspapers have the same guarantees as other per-

[1] Murdock v. Commonwealth of Pennsylvania and seven other cases, 319 U.S. 105, 108 (1943).
[2] Lovell v. City of Griffin, 303 U.S. 444 (1938); Kennedy et al. v. City of Moscow et al., 39 Fed. Sup. 26, 28 (1941).
[3] Lovell v. City of Griffin.
[4] Almassi v. City of Newark, 150 Atl. 217 (1930).
[5] Schneider v. State of New Jersey and three other cases, 308 U.S. 147, 161 (1939).
[6] Barton v. City of Bessemer, 173 So. 626, 628 (1937); Cf. Near v. Minnesota, 283 U.S. 697 (1930).
[7] People v. Most, 64 N.E. 175 (1902).

sons, but also the same responsibilities toward the rights and welfare of the public.[8] In the case of Schneider v. State of New Jersey it was ruled that the right to regulate the use of the streets must be maintained, but that such regulation may not abridge constitutional liberties.[9]

A federal court has ruled that "the streets are natural and proper places for purposes of assembly, of interchange of thought and opinion in religious, political or other matters, either by word of mouth or by the distribution of literature." [10] An ordinance of a Texas city forbidding the passing out of handbills and enforced in 1942 against distribution of religious literature was declared unconstitutional.[11]

City authorities have used the littering of streets as a cause for limiting the distribution of printed matter. In an early case an ordinance against distribution of leaflets or circulars when it caused a littering of the streets, with possible obstruction of the sewers, thus menacing public health, was upheld, but it was specified that such an ordinance must not interfere with the casual passing of leaflets to one or more individuals.[12] In two Milwaukee cases, separated in time by nearly a decade, it was ruled that circularizing the public could be stopped under police power if the streets were littered, provided that isolated acts of distribution were not outlawed and that there was no discrimination in enforcement.[13] A New York City ordinance against littering the streets was declared inapplicable to a case of Negroes passing out tracts against a motion picture film favoring the Ku Klux Klan.[14]

A shift of emphasis regarding responsibility for littering the streets, from giver to receiver of the literature, was indicated on the part of the United States Supreme Court in the Schneider case in 1939. The need for keeping streets clean was ruled not sufficient justification for prohibiting handling literature on the streets.[15] In Martin v. City of Struthers it was ruled that the constitutional right to pass out printed matter may not be abridged even if the minor nuisance of littering the streets might result.[16]

[8] Ex parte Neill, 22 S.W. 923; In re Hayes, 73 So. 362; Riley v. Lee, 11 S.W. 713; Crow v. Shepherd, 76 S.W. 79, 99; United States v. Toledo Newspaper Co., 220 Fed. 458 and 237 Fed. 986; Near v. Minnesota.
[9] 308 U.S. 147.
[10] Hannan et al. v. City of Haverhill et al., 120 Fed. (2d) 87, 89 (1941).
[11] Jamison v. State of Texas, 318 U.S. 413 (1943).
[12] Anderson et al. v. State, 96 N.W. 149 (1903).
[13] City of Milwaukee v. Kassen et al., 234 N.W. 352 (1931); City of Milwaukee v. Snyder, 283 N.W. 301 (1939). Cf. Walters v. City of Indianapolis, 134 N.E. 482 (1922).
[14] People v. Johnson et al., 191 N.Y. Sup. 750 (1921).
[15] Schneider v. State of New Jersey.
[16] 319 U.S. 141 (1943).

A further question involves the matter of literature distributed on the streets by minors. An "infant," a girl nine years old, accompanied by her guardian, was stopped from passing out religious circulars and accepting cash donations, under the operation of the Massachusetts child labor law. The Supreme Court of the United States recognized the right of the parents to give the child religious training, but held that

neither the rights of religion or rights of parenthood are beyond limitation. Acting to guard the general interests in youth's well-being the state as *parens patriae* may restrict the parent's control. . . . Its authority is not nullified merely because the parent grounds his claim to control the child's course of conduct on religion or conscience. . . . The state's authority over children's activities is broader than over like actions of adults. This is particularly true of public activities and in matters of employment. A democratic society rests, for its continuance, upon the healthy, well-rounded growth of young people into full maturity as citizens, with all that implies. It may secure this against impeding restraints and dangers, within a broad range of selection.

It upheld the decision of the state courts, forbidding such occupation by children.[17]

The livest question in relation to the putting of printed matter in circulation by personal distribution has been raised through numerous local ordinances adopted to keep certain aggressive religious sects from passing out freely their circulars, tracts, and leaflets. In the first of these cases to reach the United States Supreme Court, an ordinance of the city of Griffin, Georgia, gave the city manager complete discretion in permitting the distribution of religious tracts in the city. When Alma Lovell attempted to do this work without the required permission, she was arrested, and her case finally reached the highest court. Here it was ruled that such an ordinance as was being enforced in Griffin was unconstitutional, because it denied the rights belonging to citizens on the basis of the First Amendment, through the Fourteenth.[18]

The next year the court ruled that a city ordinance giving police discretion as to what ideas might be disseminated was unconstitutional.[19] Three years later the federal court of appeals for the District of Columbia ruled in the case of Busey that no discriminatory restraints could be brought to bear against constitutional freedoms. "Opportunity to convey ideas in public places may not be made to

---

[17] Prince v. Massachusetts, 321 U.S. 158, 64 S. Ct. 438, 447, 443 (1944).
[18] 303 U.S. 444 (1938).
[19] Schneider v. State of New Jersey.

depend upon a public officer's approval of the ideas, or upon his whim." [20] Florida ruled in 1941 against ordinances restraining the right to distribute literature.[21]

Another series of cases involved not the matter of a permit resting upon the discretion of a city manager, but a license fee for selling, which was enforced upon those selling religious literature. State courts had supported such license fees. In 1939 the superior court of Pennsylvania was without doubt that such license fees were not a trespass upon freedom of religion or of the press.[22] In a Massachusetts case in 1941 it was stated that "No automatic exemption from the requirements of the statute arise on constitutional grounds from the fact that the merchandise sold consisted of pamphlets of a religious nature." [23] In the spring of 1942 the federal courts decided two cases concerning sale of literature in the same terms.[24] But the supreme court of Illinois ruled that it was unconstitutional to exact a license fee from a religionist who was selling religious literature as a form of worship without personal gain and not as a means of livelihood. It was pointed out at that time that a privilege cannot be taxed.[25]

When a case of charging a license tax for the distribution of religious literature reached the United States Supreme Court, its decision was in keeping with previous decisions of lower courts. It ruled that where ordinary commercial methods were used to raise funds for propaganda purposes, it was not a trespass of constitutional rights to charge a license fee, if its enforcement was not discriminatory.[26]

Thus were laid down the lines of a legal struggle concerning the taxing of the right to distribute religious literature. In 1942 there came before the United States Supreme Court a case from Texas involving Largent, who had sold religious literature without securing from the mayor a permit to do so, as required by a municipal ordinance. The Supreme Court ruled that such an ordinance was unconstitutional, because it made discretionary at the hands of the mayor the exercise of rights of religious liberty and freedom of speech and of the press, guaranteed by the First Amendment through the Fourteenth.[27] There was also decided at that time the case of

[20] Busey et al. v. District of Columbia, 129 Fed. (2d) 24, 27 (1942).

[21] 1 So. (2d) 569, 570.

[22] City of Pittsburgh v. Ruffner, 5 Atl. (2d) 224, 228.

[23] Commonwealth v. Pascone, 33 N.E. (2d) 522.

[24] Whistler v. City of West Plains, Mo., et al., 43 Fed. 654; Busey et al. v. District of Columbia.

[25] City of Blue Island v. Kozul, 41 N.E. (2d) 515, 520 (1942).

[26] Jones v. City of Opelika and two other cases, 316 U.S. 584 (1942).

[27] 318 U.S. 418 (1943).

Jamison v. State of Texas. Mrs. Jamison was arrested under a city ordinance which forbade passing out handbills on the streets. She distributed religious leaflets in defiance of the ordinance, and the court ruled that she was within her constitutional rights in so doing.[28]

There followed almost immediately a decision in the case of Thelma Martin, who had passed out religious circulars in spite of an ordinance of the city of Struthers, Ohio, forbidding the distribution of printed matter by the ringing of doorbells or in such a way as to litter the streets. The Supreme Court ruled such an ordinance unconstitutional.[29]

The Supreme Court also faced the issue of license fees for selling literature on the streets and at the doors of residents. It had supported such license fees in the case of Jones v. Opelika. But on May 3, 1943, it decided a group of eight cases under the title of Murdock v. Pennsylvania, declaring unconstitutional license fees for selling religious literature. Murdock and others had defied an ordinance of the city of Jeannette, Pennsylvania, requiring a merchandising license and the payment of license taxes, and upon their arrest and conviction in a lower court, had appealed. The decision of the court was inclusive and definite.

Spreading one's religious beliefs or preaching the Gospel through distribution of religious literature and through personal visitations is an age-old type of evangelism with as high a claim to constitutional protection as the more orthodox types. . . . The cases present a single issue — the constitutionality of an ordinance which as construed and applied requires religious colporteurs to pay a license tax as a condition to the pursuit of their activities. . . .

The mere fact that religious literature is "sold" by itinerant preachers rather than "donated" does not transform evangelism into a commercial enterprise. If it did, then the passing of the collection plate in church would make the church service a commercial enterprise. . . . Freedom of speech, freedom of the press, freedom of religion are available to all, not merely to those who can pay their own way. . . . It is one thing to impose a tax on the income or property of a preacher. It is quite another thing to exact a tax from him for the privilege of delivering a sermon. . . . The power to tax the exercise of a privilege is the power to control or suppress its enjoyment. . . . Those who can tax the exercise of this religious practice can make its exercise so costly as to deprive it of the resources necessary for its maintenance. . . .

A license tax applied to activities guaranteed by the First Amendment

[28] 318 U.S. 413.
[29] 319 U.S. 141 (1943).

would have . . . destructive effect. . . . The power to impose a license tax on the exercise of these freedoms is indeed as potent as the power of censorship which this Court has repeatedly struck down. . . . The judgment in Jones v. Opelika has this day been vacated. Freed from that controlling precedent, we can restore to their high, constitutional position the liberties of itinerant evangelists who disseminate their religious beliefs and the tenets of their faith through distribution of literature. The Judgments are reversed and the causes are remanded to the Pennsylvania Superior Court for proceedings not inconsistent with this opinion.[30]

This decision stands as a Magna Carta for the right of religious evangelism through the printing press.

The following year a case from South Carolina was decided consistently with the case of Murdock v. Pennsylvania. A city ordinance providing for a flat license tax for selling religious literature was declared unconstitutional.[31] The Supreme Court's decision in the next case in this category, Marsh v. State of Alabama, not only ruled that it was not a trespass for a distributor of religious literature to pursue her activities on the streets and at the doorways of a company-owned town, but repeated the dictum that the imposition of a flat license tax or a permit issued by an official at his discretion is unconstitutional.

The result of these decisions was to liberate the distribution of religious literature from censorship and the exaction of license taxes. But while there could be required no permit which left to city officials discriminatory power,[32] there remained full recognition of the constitutionality of reasonable and non-discriminatory police regulation.[33]

It has been ruled frequently through the years that constitutional rights of religious exercise are not absolute. There is not "an absolute right to speak or publish without responsibility whatever one may choose or an unrestricted and unbridled license that gives immunity for every possible use of language and prevents the punishment of those who abuse this freedom." [34]

The Amendment embraces two concepts, — freedom to believe, and freedom to act. The first is absolute but, in the nature of things, the con-

[30] Murdock v. Commonwealth of Pennsylvania and seven other cases, 319 U.S. 105, 110, 111, 112, 113, 117 (1943).
[31] Follett v. Town of McCormick, 321 U.S. 573 (1944).
[32] In re Frazee, 30 N.W. 72 (1886); Hague, Mayor, et al. v. Committee for Industrial Organization et al., 307 U.S. 496 (1939); Schneider v. State of New Jersey, 308 U.S. 147 (1939); Cantwell v. State of Connecticut, 310 U.S. 296 (1940); Busey et al. v. District of Columbia, 129 Fed. (2d) 24 (1942).
[33] Martin v. City of Struthers, 319 U.S. 141 (1943).
[34] Gitlow v. People of New York, 268 U.S. 652, 666 (1925).

duct remains subject to regulation for protection of society. . . . A state may, by general and non-discriminatory legislation regulate the times, the places, and the manner of soliciting upon its streets and of holding meetings thereon; and may in other respects safeguard the peace, good order and comfort of the community without invading liberties protected by the Fourteenth Amendment.[35]

Though one is not punished in these United States for his religious views and beliefs, yet one may be punished when through external conduct these views are put into practice, if such practice is fraught with clear and present danger to the safety, morals, health or general welfare of the community, and is violative of laws enacted for their protection.[36]

However, constitutional freedoms "are in a preferred position." [37] This preferred position is to be found through a study of the facts in each case,[38] and "the delicate and difficult task falls upon the courts to weigh the circumstances and appraise the substantiality of the reasons advanced in support of the regulation of the free enjoyment of the rights." [39]

In keeping with these principles, the case of Cantwell et al. v. State of Connecticut declared constitutional a requirement that strangers soliciting funds in a community be required to make proper identification with the police to guard against fraud, so long as this did not make the granting of permission to solicit a matter of discretion on the part of officials.[40] In Murdock v. Pennsylvania the court stated clearly that they were ruling against the ordinance and its license tax called in question because:

It is not merely a registration ordinance calling for an identification of the solicitors so as to give the authorities some basis for investigating strangers coming into the community. And the fee is not a nominal one, imposed as a regulatory measure and calculated to defray the expense of protecting those on the streets and at home against the abuses of solicitors.[41]

In keeping with the recognition of the need for police supervision is a decision by the Wisconsin supreme court that hawkers and peddlers may be required to secure a permit, if it is not issued on a discriminatory or discretionary basis.[42] There is also a decision that

[35] Cantwell et al. v. State of Connecticut.
[36] Baxley v. United States, 134 Fed. (2d) 973 (1944).
[37] Follett v. Town of McCormick.
[38] Hamilton v. City of Montrose, 124 Pac. (2d) 757 (1942).
[39] Schneider v. State of New Jersey.
[40] 310 U.S. 296 (1940).
[41] 319 U.S. 116 (1943).
[42] City of Washburn v. Ellquist, 9 N.W. (2d) 121 (1943).

solicitors may be required to wear a badge furnished by the police, although another decision rules that such a badge may not have to be shown.[43] A ruling of the California supreme court declared constitutional a requirement in the city of Los Angeles that those soliciting goods and funds from door to door for charitable purposes should secure a permit vouching for the character of the solicitor, in order to protect the public from fraud.[44] But a license in restraint of recognized liberties must not be required for solicitation for religious purposes.[45]

A danger to liberty of the press in municipalities requiring permits lies in the unreasonableness of some of the requirements. A federal court had occasion to rule unconstitutional an ordinance that required anyone seeking a permit to distribute literature to salute the flag. The court said:

> We are confronted with the requirement of censorship and saluting the flag in the presence of a police officer before one can distribute such literature. Such requirement runs counter to the Federal Constitution as interpreted by the Supreme Court and numerous other Federal Courts.[46]

The Supreme Court ruled expressly against the requirement of flag saluting as a condition for distributing literature two years later.[47]

City ordinances relating to freedom of the press may be of questionable constitutionality and, after running the gauntlet of the court, actually prove to be unconstitutional. But in the meantime they will have served to restrict and obstruct the exercise of inalienable rights. There is, therefore, a warning in a closing statement in Schneider v. State of New Jersey:

> Conceding that fraudulent appeals may be made in the name of charity and religion, we hold a municipality cannot, for this reason, require all who wish to disseminate ideas to present them first to police authorities for their consideration and approval, with a discretion in the police to say some ideas may, while others may not, be carried to the homes of citizens; some persons may, while others may not, disseminate information from house to house. Frauds may be denounced as offenses and punished by law. Trespasses may similarly be forbidden. If it is said that these means are less efficient and convenient than bestowal of power on police authorities to decide what information may be disseminated from house

[43] City of Manchester v. Leiby, 33 Fed. Sup. 842; Kennedy et al. v. City of Moscow et al., 39 Fed. Sup. 26, 30 (1942).

[44] Gospel Army v. City of Los Angeles, 163 Pac. (2d) 704, 712, 713, 714, 715 (1945).

[45] Tucker v. Randall, 15 Atl. (2d) 324, 326 (1940); Cantwell et al. v. Connecticut, 310 U.S. 296 (1940).

[46] Kennedy et al. v. City of Moscow et al.

[47] Taylor v. State of Mississippi and two other cases, 319 U.S. 583 (1943).

to house, and who may impart the information, the answer is that considerations of this sort do not empower a municipality to abridge freedom of speech and press.[48]

There have been revealed some unique situations in connection with certain court cases dealing with the dissemination of religious ideas through the printed page. It has been ruled that protagonists of religion may go from door to door, ringing doorbells and soliciting those within the homes, even in cases where war workers employed at night were sleeping in the daytime, but beyond that, the right to be protected against intrusion is one which antedates the right of freedom of conscience.[49] In the case of a group of religionists going through a hotel, presenting tracts and booklets and talking to the guests about their religious views, it was ruled that with the methods used such propagation was an intrusion upon private rights.[50]

However, there is a differentiation to be made in property rights, since the freedoms specified in the First Amendment are "in a preferred position." The case of Marsh v. Alabama involved a restriction in the company-owned town of Chickasaw, Alabama, against soliciting and distributing handbills and tracts. Marsh went about the town, talking to the inhabitants and selling or giving away religious tracts and books. She was arrested when she refused to desist in compliance with the company's rules. When the case reached the United States Supreme Court, the judgment of the lower courts against her was reversed. The property, though belonging to a corporation, was open to public use, with flourishing businesses on the premises and the normal flow of commercial life of a community. The court ruled that the more an owner for his own advantage opened his property for general public use, the less his rights as an owner of private property could be asserted. The appellant could not therefore be justly denied her constitutional right to disseminate her religious views on the property.[51] A similar decision was handed down in the case of Tucker, who was arrested for transgressing, in a government-owned town built for and occupied by war workers, rules against peddling and hawking, in order to distribute printed matter stating his religious beliefs.[52]

The United States mail service is a useful agency in the propaga-

[48] 308 U.S. 147, 164 (1939).
[49] Marsh v. State of Alabama, 326 U.S. 501, 505 (1945); Martin v. City of Struthers, 319 U.S. 141, 142, 144, 146, 147 (1943); Commonwealth v. Palms, 15 Atl. (2d) 481, 485 (1940).
[50] People v. Vaughan et al., 150 Pac. (2d) 964 (1944).
[51] Marsh v. State of Alabama, 326 U.S. 501 (1946).
[52] Tucker v. State of Texas, 326 U.S. 517 (1946).

tion of the religious ideas, but the rules and regulations of the Post Office Department must be heeded. The postal laws and regulations are explicit, and it was ruled years ago that

the unrestricted use of the mails is not one of the fundamental rights guaranteed by the Constitution. . . . Liberty and freedom of speech under the Constitution do not mean the unrestrained right to do and say what one pleases at all times and under all circumstances, and certainly they do not mean that contrary to the will of Congress one may make of the post office establishment of the United States an agency for the publication of his views of the character and conduct of others. The very idea of government implies some imposition of restraint in the interest of the general welfare, peace, and good order. The statute under consideration . . . is designed to exclude from the mails that which tends to debauch the morals of the people, or is contrived to despoil them of their property or is an apparent, visible attack upon their good names.[53]

In the case of United States v. Ballard et al., involving a religious sect which was charged with using the mail to defraud, the lower courts were supported in their refusal to try to adjudge the merits of the doctrines propagated, but accusation of fraud was affirmed aside from the truth or error of the teachings disseminated through the mails.[54]

In the same year, 1944, the case of a popular magazine came before the court. It had been using second-class privileges, and the postmaster general had ruled that it was not a magazine in dissemination of information within the meaning of the postal laws. It was claimed by the accused that the examination of the magazine had entailed censorship in trespass of constitutional rights. The court stated:

a censorship, except for military reasons, is the denial of the right of freedom of the press and the right of freedom of speech, and that is a denial of all those rights and privileges which are had in the enjoyment of a free government. It is the first step to a perpetuated tyranny. We feel, however, that there are safeguards against such. If the Postmaster General deals with an individual case without classifying it as a group, his act becomes capricious and arbitrary, and is subject to a review by the courts. . . . If his course becomes too general, Congress can re-write the Act that he has failed to interpret in keeping with prevailing standards and conceptions, if he has so misinterpreted it. . . . Censoring deals more with the specific article, the deleting of objectionable portions. Classifying means grouping.

The court decided that the postmaster had been arbitrary in his rul-

[53] Warren v. U.S., 183 Fed. 718, 720, 721 (1910). Public Clearing House v. Coyne, 194 U.S. 497, 24 S. Ct. 789, was cited in support.
[54] 322 U.S. 78 (1944).

ing against the magazine and the injuction against its exclusion from the mails was denied.[55]

Efforts have been made from time to time to have adopted by Congress a law which would make a criminal offense the passing through the mails of matter derogatory of any person or persons on the basis of race or religion. Such a law would be difficult to enforce in the presence of political or religious controversy.

It is evident that freedom of the press, like freedom of speech, is an inalienable right, constitutionally recognized. As expressed in the First Amendment, it applies to all the citizens of the individual states through the Fourteenth Amendment. The only limitations which can be applied to the exercise of this right is that of intrusion upon the liberties of others, and this regulation is made by the states through the police powers.

Freedom of the press cannot be taxed, and license taxes levied upon the distribution of printed matter have been declared unconstitutional. A nominal fee may be charged for a permit issued by local authorities. However, this permit can be required of those engaged in the distribution of religious literature only as a certification that the person receiving the permit is what he claims to be. There resides in the police power in this connection no power of discrimination and no exercise of discretion in granting any permit that may be required.

[55] Esquire, Inc. v. Walker, Postmaster, 55 Fed. Sup. 1015, 1020, 1021 (1944).

CHAPTER XIX

The Religious Character of
Sunday Legislation

THE question of Sunday laws and their enforcement has been an important one to all European and other Western governments ever since 321 A.D., when the first Sunday law was issued by the emperor Constantine. It was one of the chief issues during the early period of United States history. It continues to be important in our day and indications are that it will receive increasing attention in the years to come.

The law of 321 was not an ecclesiastical enactment, but a civil one. However, it was religious in character. Desiring unity in his troubled empire, Constantine evidently saw in Sunday observance an institution which he could make a point of unification. The Christians were already keeping Sunday. It was being observed by the Mithraists.[1] Constantine met the practices of both popular cults. His law mentions no god, but only "heavenly providence." It reads:

All judges and city people and the craftsmen shall rest upon the venerable Day of the Sun. Country people, however, may freely attend to the cultivation of the fields, because it frequently happens that no other days are better adapted for planting the grain in the furrows or the vines in the trenches. So that the advantage given by heavenly providence may not for the occasion of a short time perish.[2]

Thus the first Sunday law, the edict of the emperor Constantine, was the product of that pagan conception, developed by the Romans, which made religion a part of the state. The day was to be venerated as a religious duty owed to the god of the sun.

Probably at about the same time, soldiers in the army were commanded to worship on the Lord's day.[3] There followed a suc-

[1] Franz Cumont, *The Mysteries of Mithra* (Chicago, 1903), p. 191.
[2] *Codex Justinianus,* bk. iii, title 12, 3. Trans. from J. C. Ayer, *A Sourcebook for Ancient History* (New York, 1933), para. 59 (g), pp. 284, 285.
[3] Eusebius, *Life of Constantine*, bk. iv, chap. 18.

cession of laws prohibiting law suits on the Lord's day.[4] There was also a law protecting Jews from law suits and prohibiting them from bringing law suits on the Sabbath, the seventh day of the week, or on other days sacred to the Jews.[5] There were laws forbidding circus spectacles or theatrical shows on the Lord's day.[6]

Chief Justice Clark, speaking for the supreme court of North Carolina in a case involving the validity of a contract executed on Sunday, said:

Sunday was first adopted by Christians in lieu of Saturday long years after Christ, in commemoration of the Resurrection. The first "Sunday law" was enacted in the year 321 after Christ, soon after the emperor Constantine had abjured paganism, and apparently for a different reason than the Christian observance of the day. . . . Evidently Constantine was still something of a heathen. As late as the year 409 two rescripts of the emperors Honorius and Theodosius indicate that Christians then still generally observed the Sabbath (Saturday *not* Sunday). The curious may find these set out in full, Codex Just., lib. I, tit. IX, Cx. 13. Not till near the end of the ninth century was Sunday substituted by law for Saturday as the day of rest by a decree of the emperor Leo (Leo Cons., 54).[7]

There was no effort in Roman law, after the decree of 321, to enforce cessation of labor on Sunday. In fact, there is record of only one council of the church which attempted this. There was a council, not a general one, which met at Laodicaea sometime before the year 381 A.D., which ruled in its twenty-ninth canon that "the Lord's day the Christians shall especially honor, and, as being Christians, shall, if possible, do no work on that day."[8] Nor is there record of any effort made, even by the church, during the next two centuries to enforce Sunday idleness. When such a law appeared again, it was in Gaul under the Merovingian kings, who forbade Sunday labor in decrees dated 585 and 596.[9]

A number of restrictions on Sunday observance were made under the emperor Charlemagne. These required the observance of Sun-

---

[4] *Codex Theodosianus,* bk. ii, title 8, 1 (A.D. 321); bk. viii, title 1, 1 (A.D. 365); bk. ii, title 8, 18; bk. viii, title 8, 3; bk. xi, title 7, 13; *Codex Justinianus,* bk. iii, title 12, 2 (about A.D. 386); *Codex Theodosianus,* bk. ii, title 8, 19; *Codex Justinianus,* bk. iii, title 12, 7 (A.D. 389); *Codex Theodosianus,* bk. xv, title 5, 5 (A.D. 425); *Codex Justinianus,* bk. iii, title 12, 10 (A.D. 469).

[5] *Codex Theodosianus,* bk. ii, title 8, 26 (A.D. 329).

[6] *Ibid.,* bk. ii, title 8, 20 (A.D. 329); bk. ii, title 8, 23 (A.D. 399); bk. ii, title 8, 25 (A.D. 409); bk. xv, title 5, 5 (A.D. 425); *Codex Justinianus,* bk. iii, title 12, 10 (A.D. 469).

[7] *Codex Justinianus,* bk. iii, title 12, 1, 3. Quoted in Rodman v. Robinson, 134 N.C. Rep. 510 (1904).

[8] Charles Joseph Hefele, *History of the Church Councils* (Edinburgh: 1872–96), 1:316.

[9] *Capitularia Merovingica* in *Monumenta Germanica Historica, Legum Sectio II* (Hanover, 1883), 1:11, 17.

day from sundown until sundown, and were mainly directed to the forbidding of servile work[10] and the holding of courts[11] and markets;[12] the holding of markets, according to an ancient description discovered in the Balkans a century or so ago, a Roman law of Constantine's day had allowed.[13]

The Anglo-Saxon king, Ina, about 691 issued a strong decree making Sunday a day of rest indeed, as far as ordinary labor was concerned.[14] Later Anglo-Saxons attempted only to prohibit marketing on that day. Similar laws were adopted on the continent. Henry III of Engand in 1237 forbade the frequenting of markets on Sundays, and Henry VI in 1444 forbade fairs in churchyards on that day or on other holidays.[15]

In James I's day a law dated 1606 levied a fine of a shilling on anyone absenting himself from church, but in 1618 James signed a law allowing some sports after church on Sundays. However, a law of 1625, the first year of Charles I, put restraints on Sunday amusements. Cromwell enforced a Sunday law, and in the year 1676, the 29th of Charles II's reign, a very strict Sunday law was passed, which reads in part as follows:

For the better observation and keeping holy the Lord's day, commonly called Sunday, bee it enacted . . . that all the lawes enacted and in force concerning the observation of the Lords day and repaireing to the church thereon be carefully putt in execution. And that all and every person and persons whatsoever shall on every Lords day apply themselves to the observation of the same by exerciseing themselves thereon in the dutyes of piety and true religion publiquely and privately and that noe tradesman, artificer workeman labourer or other person whatsoever shall doe or exercise any worldly labour, business or worke of their ordinary callings upon the Lords day or any part thereof (workes of necessity and charity onely excepted) and that every person being of the age of fourteene yeares or upwards offending in the premisses shall for every such offence forfeit the summe of five shillings, and that noe person or persons what-

---

[10] *Ibid.*, pp. 36, 61, 69, 104.
[11] *Ibid.*, pp. 69, 174.
[12] *Ibid.*, pp. 149, 174.
[13] *Inscriptiones Antiquae Totius Orbis Romani,* 164, 2, in Robert Cox, *Literature of the Sabbath Questions* (Edinburgh, 1865), 1:359.
[14] Hefele, *History of the Church Councils,* 5:243.
[15] For judicial discussion of ancient Sunday laws see Rodman v. Robinson, 134 N.C. Rep. 510, 47 S.E. 19; Richardson v. Goddards, 23 How. U.S. 28; 16 L. ed. 412; Rosenbaum v. State, 131 Ark. 251, 199 S.W. 388, L.R.A. 1918 B 1109; Adams v. Harnell, 2 Douglas 73, 43 Am. Dec. 455; State ex rel. Temple v. Barnes, 22 N.D. 18, 132 N.W. 215, Am. Cas. 1913 E. 930; Walsh v. State, 33 Del. 353, 136 Atl. 160; Splane v. Commonwealth, 9 Pa. Cas. 201, 12 Atl. 431; Commonwealth v. Hoover, 13 Pa. Dist. 45, 25 Pa. Sup. 133; Campbell v. International Loan Association, 17 N.Y.S. 298.

soever shall publickly cry shew forth or expose to sale any wares merchandizes, fruit, herbs goods or chattells whatsoever upon the Lords day.[16]

The North Carolina court already cited, speaking about the origin of Sunday laws, said:

Even if Christianity could be deemed the basis of our government [which is denied], its own organic law [for observing Sunday] must be found in the New Testament, and there we shall look in vain for any requirement to observe Sunday, or indeed any day.

The Saxon laws under Ine (about A.D. 700) forbade working on Sunday, but under Alfred (A.D. 900) and Athelstane (A.D. 924) the prohibition was merely against marketing on Sunday, and there seems to have been no statute against working on Sunday (whatever the church may have enjoined) until the above-cited statute, 29 Car. II, Ch. 7 (1678), the first part of which is almost verbatim our statute, Code Section 3782. See 4 Blk. Com., 63. Indeed, it appears from the records of Merton College, Oxford, that at its manor of Ibstone, in the latter part of the thirteenth century, contracts with laborers provided for cessation from work on Saturdays and holidays, but it was stipulated that work should be done in regular course on Sunday. Thorold Rogers, *Work and Wages*, Chapter 1.

In Pennsylvania in the case of Commonwealth v. Hoover App., in which the defendant had been arrested for buying a cigar on Sunday, the court said:

Sunday legislation is more than fifteen centuries old, and this "historic argument" is of value in construing existing law. "All Sunday legislation is the product of pagan Rome; the Saxon laws were the product of Middle Age legislation of the Holy Roman Empire. The English laws are the expansion of the Saxon, and the American are the transcript of the English" . . . During the Middle Ages, the civil authorities exercised the right to legislate in religious matters after the manner of the Jewish theocracy. The English Reformation introduced, for the first time, the doctrine of the Fourth Commandment to the first day of the week.[17]

This analysis of ancient Sunday laws has never been questioned or overruled by our courts.

Laws regulating conduct on the first day of the week were among the first enactments of the American commonwealths.[18] At the outbreak of the Revolutionary War the seventeenth-century Sunday law

[16] *The Statutes of England, 1235–1713* (2d rev. ed., printed for Her Majesty's Stationery Office, London, 1888), Volume 1, 29 Chas. II, Chapter 7.

[17] Pa. Sup. Ct. 134 (1904).

[18] It should be noted that Rhode Island was an exception to this general rule. Even in Rhode Island, however, Sunday laws were passed at a later date, though never really enforced.

of 29 Charles II was the Sabbath law enforced in all the American colonies. It is regarded in legal circles as one of the immediate historical antecedents of our present Sunday legislation. Therefore the early Sunday laws and even some of the present Sunday laws of many of the states bear a marked similarity to this Sunday law of Charles II. Referring to the similarity to be found in these laws, the *Americana* says: "The act of Charles II (1676) was the law of the American colonies up to the time of the Revolution, and so became the basis of the American Sunday laws." [19] The present Sunday law of South Carolina reads:

No tradesman, artificer, workman, laborer, or other person whatsoever, shall do or exercise any worldly labor, business, or work of their ordinary callings upon the Lord's day (commonly called the Sabbath), or any part thereof (work of necessity or charity only excepted); and every person being of the age of fifteen years or upwards, offending in premises, shall, for every such offense, forfeit the sum of one dollar. [20]

The present Sunday law of North Carolina reads:

On the Lord's day, commonly called Sunday, no tradesman, artificer, planter, laborer, or other person shall, upon land or water, do or exercise any labor, business, or work of his ordinary calling, works of necessity and charity alone excepted, nor employ himself in hunting, fishing, or fowling, nor use any game, sport, or play, upon pain that every person so offending, being of the age of fourteen years and upwards, shall forfeit and pay one dollar. [21]

The text of the laws themselves plainly shows that the object of Sunday laws is the enforcement of religion.

The religious origin of the present Sunday statutes of many states is revealed in such religious terms as "Lord's day," "Sabbath day," "Christian Sabbath," "worldly employment," "secular business," "holy time," "Sabbath observance," "Sabbath breaking," "profanation of Lord's day," and "violate the Sabbath." [22]

[19] "Sunday," *Encyclopedia Americana* (printing of 1946), 26:32.
[20] South Carolina Code of Laws, 1932, Chapter 82, Section 1732.
[21] North Carolina Code of Laws, 1931, Chapter 75, Section 3955. This section does not apply to the county of Cumberland (except to the city of Fayetteville) or to the county of Robeson. Public Laws, 1921, Chapter 487; 1923, Chapter 506; 1925, Chapter 451.
On March 7, 1921, Section 3955 was so amended as to make the offender guilty of a misdemeanor and upon this conviction to be fined or imprisoned according to the discretion of the court, this act to apply to Cumberland County only.
[22] Instances are found in Bloom v. Richards, 2 Ohio St. 387; Carr v. State, 175 Ind. 241, 93 N.E. 1071; Commonwealth ex rel. Woodruff v. American Baseball Club, 29 Pa. 136, 138 Atl. 497, 53 A.L.R. 1027; Commonwealth v. White, 190 Mass. 578, 77 N.E. 636; Gillooley v. Vaughan et al., 92 Fla. 943, 110 So. 653; Kilgour v. Miles, 6 Gill I.J. (Md.) 268; Lindenmiller v. People, 33 Barb. 548; Moore v. Owen, 109 N.Y.S. 585, 58 Misc. 330, 22 N.Y. Cr. 58; Richmond v. Moore, 107 Ill. 429, 47 American Rep. 445, Rosenbaum v. State, 131 Ark. 251, 199

The first Sunday legislation in the area now occupied by the United States was issued by Virginia in 1610. It required that

Every man and woman shall repair in the morning to the divine service and sermons preached upon the Sabbath day, and in the afternoon to divine service, and catechising, upon pain for the first fault to lose their provision and the allowance for the whole week following; for the second, to lose the said allowance and also be whipt; and for the third to suffer death.[23]

In 1617 Virginia passed a law punishing a failure to attend church on Sunday with a fine payable in tobacco. As re-enacted by the general assembly in 1623 this law reads: "That whosoever shall absent himselfe from divine service any Sunday without an allowable excuse shall forfeite a pound of tobacco, and he that absenteth himselfe a month shall forfeit 50 lbs. of tobacco."[24] Thus Sabbath laws were placed on the statute books of the colonies at an early date.[25]

From the foregoing we see that Sabbath laws in England, especially during and after the Reformation period, and in America from the founding of the first colonies, were based upon the laws of God. They were concerned with a purely religious institution and not a civil one. No other day than the first day of the week has been regarded as having a sacred character. The Puritans, while they followed the precedent established by the law of Charles II, went even further than Charles in the stringency of Sunday observance required and in the penalties imposed. In some cases death was the punishment for breaking the Sabbath, as in the law adopted by the Connecticut Puritans:

Whosoever shall profane the Lord's day, or any part of it, either by sinful servile work or by unlawful sport, recreation, or otherwise, whether wilfully or in careless neglect, shall be duly punished by fine, imprisonment, or corporally, according to the nature, and measure of the sinn, and offence. But if the court upon examination, by clear, and satisfying evidence find that the sin was proudly, presumptuously, and with a high hand committed against the known command and authority of the

S.W. 388, L.R.A. 1918 B 1109; Siddons v. Edmonston, 42 App. D.C. 459; Specht v. Commonwealth of Pennsylvania, 8 Pa. 312, 49 Am. Dec. 518; State ex rel. Temple v. Barnes, 22 N.D. 18, 132 N.W. 215; State v. Mead et al., 230 Ia. 1217, 300 N.W. 523; Weldon v. Colquitt, 62 Ga. 449, 35 Am. Rep. 128.

[23] "Articles, Laws, and Orders, Divine, Politique, and Martial, for the Colony in Virginia: first established by Sir Thomas Gates, Knight, Lieutenant-General, the 24th of May, 1610. Again exemplified and enlarged by Sir Thomas Dale, Knight, Marshall, and Deputie Governour, the 22d of June, 1611." Reprinted at Hartford in 1876.

[24] Hennings Statutes at Large: Virginia, 1619–1660, Act 2, Volume 1, p. 123.

[25] Act 3 passed by the assembly provided "that there be an uniformity in our church as neere as may be to the canons in England; both in substance and circumstance, and that all persons yeild readie obedience unto them under paine of censure." Ibid.

blessed God, such a person therein despising and reproaching the Lord, *shall be put to death,* that all others may feare and shun such provoking rebellious courses.[26]

In Maryland a law of 1723 provided

That no person whatsoever shall work or do any bodily labor on the Lord's day, commonly called Sunday, and that no person having children, servants, or slaves, shall command, or wittingly or willingly suffer any of them to do any manner of work or labor on the Lord's day, (works of necessity and charity always excepted,) nor shall suffer or permit any children, servants, or slaves, to profane the Lord's day by gaming, fishing, fowling, hunting, or unlawful pastimes or recreations; and that every person transgressing this act, and being thereof convict by the oath of one sufficient witness, or confession of the party before a single magistrate, shall forfeit two hundred pounds of tobacco, to be levied and applied as aforesaid. . . . where the said fine shall not be immediately paid on conviction, that it shall and may be lawful for the magistrates, or other officers aforesaid, and they are hereby required, to order the offender, not being a freeholder, or other reputable person to be whipped, or put in the stocks. . . . no offender shall receive above thirty-nine lashes, or be kept in the stocks above three hours, upon any one conviction.

Section 1 of this law provided that blasphemers should be punished by being branded with the letter B and that those guilty of a third offense must suffer the death sentence:

That if any person shall hereafter, within this province, wittingly, maliciously, and advisedly, by writing or speaking, blaspheme or curse God, or deny our Saviour Jesus Christ to be the Son of God, or shall deny the Holy Trinity or any of the Persons thereof, and shall be thereof convict by verdict or confession, shall, for the first offence, be bored through the tongue and fined twenty pounds sterling to the lord proprietor to be applied to the use of the county where the offense shall be committed, to be levied on the offender's body, goods, and chattels, lands or tenements, and in case the said fine cannot be levied, the offender to suffer six months' imprisonment without bail or mainprise; and that for the second offence, the offender being thereof convict as aforesaid, shall be stigmatized by burning in the forehead with the letter B and fined forty pounds sterling to the lord proprietor, to be applied and levied as aforesaid, and in case the same cannot be levied, the offender shall suffer twelve months' imprisonment without bail or mainprise; and that for the third offence, the offender being convict as aforesaid, shall suffer death without the benefit of the clergy.[27]

---

[26] Law of 1656. William Addison Blakely, *American State Papers Bearing on Sunday Legislation* (Washington, 1911), p. 42.

[27] All the above act, consisting of fifteen sections, and those laws of Maryland that were considered applicable to the District of Columbia were taken over and made a part of the laws of

Such examples of colonial legislation[28] may be multiplied indefinitely to show that all Sunday legislation from Constantine to William Penn was based on the supposition that the Lord's day is the divinely appointed Sabbath and was enacted to preserve the day from desecration.[29]

In Massachusetts the supreme court said:

Our Puritan ancestors intended that the day [Sunday] should be not merely a day of rest from labor, but also a day devoted to public and private worship and to religious meditation and repose, undisturbed by secular cares or amusements. They saw fit to enforce the observance of the day by penal legislation, and the statute regulations which they devised for that purpose have continued in force, without any substantial modification, to the present time.[30]

These Sunday laws have been copied and perpetuated in nearly all the states of the union, and attempts have been made to have similar laws passed by the federal government.[31]

the district by act of Congress in 1801, when the district was taken over as the territory of the national capital. The above law has remained on the statute books of the district. In 1908 the court of appeals of the district set the Sunday law aside as "obsolete" and "repealed by implication." Blakely, *American State Papers,* pp. 518, 519.

[28] For colonial Sunday legislation, see *American State Papers.*

[29] The Pennsylvania act of 1794 purported to be an ordinance for the enforcement of the Sabbath as a *civil* institution.

[30] Davis v. Somerville, 128 Mass. 594 (1880).

[31] Of the numerous attempts to induce Congress to pass a Sunday law, the following, proposed for the District of Columbia, is a sample. On December 5, 1927, Mr. Lankford introduced in the House the following bill, "to secure Sunday as a day of rest in the Distrcit of Columbia, and for other purposes," which was referred to the committee of the District of Columbia and ordered to be printed.

"Be it enacted by the Senate and House of Representatives of the United States of America in Congress assembled, That it shall be unlawful in the District of Columbia for any person, firm, corporation or any of their agents, directors, or officers to employ any person to labor or pursue any trade or secular business on the Lord's day, commonly called Sunday, works of necessity and charity always excepted. It shall furthermore be unlawful in the District of Columbia for any person under employment or working for hire to engage in labor under such contract of employment or hire on the Lord's day, commonly called Sunday, except in works of necessity and charity.

"In works of necessity and charity is included whatever is needful during the day for the good order, health, or comfort of the community, provided the right to weekly rest and worship is not thereby denied. The labor herein forbidden on Sunday is hired, employed, or public work, not such personal work as does not interrupt or disturb the repose and religious liberty of the community. The following labor and business shall be legal on Sunday:

"(a) In drug stores for the sale of medicines, surgical articles, and supplies for the sick, foods, beverages, and cigars, but not for articles of merchandise forbidden on Sunday for other stores and merchants.

"(b) In hotels, restaurants, and cafes, and in the preparation and sale of meals.

"(c) For the sale of motor oil, gasoline, and accessories necessary to keep in operation cars in actual use on such Sunday, together with labor incident to such repairs.

"(d) In connection with public lighting, water, and heating plants.

"(e) For the operation of boats, railroad trains, street cars, busses, sightseeing cars, taxicabs, elevators, and privately owned means of conveyance.

"(f) For telephone and radio service.

The manner in which such legislation has been treated by the courts forms a curious and interesting chapter in our constitutional history. At the beginning of our national history Sunday observance was enforced by the original thirteen states, which simply continued colonial legslation in this respect, each of the colonies having had an established religion. Many of the court decisions, both before and after the adopting of the Constitution, speak in positive terms of the religious character, object, and purpose of Sunday laws. In the case of Brimhall v. Van Campen, in which the supreme court of Minnesota held that a note executed on Sunday was void under the Minnesota law prohibiting any manner of labor, business, or work on Sunday except works of charity or necessity, the court said: "This Sunday act can have no other object than the enforcement of the fourth of God's commandments." [32]

Some of the courts, though attempting to evade the religious purpose of the Sunday laws, have nevertheless embodied in their opinions statements showing that the intent and purpose of the law was to "advance the interests of religion" and guard the "sanctity" of "the Lord's day" as "a time-honored and heaven-appointed institution." A few more instances in which the courts have regarded Sunday as a religious institution and recognized the day as one of holiness may be noted in passing.

In New York Chief Justice Kent stated that "the statute for preventing immorality consecrates the first day of the week as holy

"(g) In dairies and in connection with preparation and delivery of milk and cream.

"(h) In connection wth watching, caretaking, or safeguarding premises and property, and in the maintenance of police and fire protection.

"(i) In connection with the preparation and sale of daily newspapers.

"Section 2. That it shall be unlawful in the District of Columbia to keep open or use any dancing place, theater (whether for motion pictures, plays spoken or silent, opera, vaudeville, or entertainment), bowling alley, or any place of public assembly at which an admission fee is directly or indirectly received, or to engage in commercialized sports or amusements on the Lord's day, commonly called Sunday.

"Section 3. It shall be unlawful in the District of Columbia for any person, firm, corporation, or any of their agents, directors, or officers to require or permit any employee or employees engaged in works of necessity and charity, excepting household or hotel service, to work on the Lord's day, commonly called Sunday, unless within the next six succeeding days during a period of twenty-four consecutive hours such employer shall neither require nor permit such employee or employees to work in his or its employ.

"Section 4. Any person who shall violate any of the provisions of this act shall, on conviction thereof, be punished by a fine of not less than $5.00 nor more than $50.00 for the first offense, and for each subsequent offense by a fine of not less than $25.00 nor more than $500.00 and by imprisonment in the jail of the District of Columbia for a period of not more than six months.

"Section 5. All prosecutions for the violation of this act shall be in the police court of the District of Columbia.

"Section 6. This act shall become effective on the sixtieth day after its enactment."

[32] 8 Minn. 1 (1858).

time." [33] The Massachusetts court gave as one reason for setting aside the day as "holy" the fact that "the legislative power or the uniform usage of every Christian state has exacted the observance of it as such." [34] The statute in Iowa sets Sunday apart as "sacred." [35] Many other statutes carry such an interpretation. [36]

In 1834 a New York judge spoke of "the public order and solemnity of the day." [37] In Pennsylvania a judge held that "the day itself is clothed with peculiar sanctity." [38] Of two Kentucky statutes one applied "exclusively to Sundays as sacred, and the other to holidays as secular." [39] In Iowa Sunday is "sacred, set apart for rest by the voice of wisdom, experience, and necessity." [40] In referring to the Sunday laws in North Carolina the court said, "All religious and moral codes permit works of necessity and charity on their sacred days." [41]

It has been said by the Georgia court that "all courts should abstain from the transaction of ordinary business on that holy day." [42] The supreme court of Mississippi, in considering the case of Kountz v. Price, in which a Sunday law was involved, said it was "intended to promote public morals, and to induce the observance of the duties of religion in society . . ." [43] The supreme court of Alabama, in considering a statute prohibiting worldly business on Sunday, made the following statement:

We do not think the design of the legislature in the passage of the act can be doubted. It was evidently to promote morality and advance the interest of religion, by prohibiting all persons from engaging in their common and ordinary avocations of business, or employment, on Sunday . . . [44]

In 1894 Judge Alvey of the supreme court of Maryland, in speaking of the Sunday laws in the different states, said: "They are substantially the same in their general scope and provision — all looking to keeping the day sacred." [45] In the same year Judge Boyd, in considering the Judefind case, said:

[33] People v. Ruggles, 8 Johns. 290 (1811).
[34] Pearce v. Atwood, 13 Mass. 324 (1816).
[35] Davis v. Fish, 1 Green 406 (1848).
[36] Johnson v. The Commonwealth, 22 Pa. St. 102 (1853); Stockden v. The State, 18 Ark. 186 (1856); Corey v. Bath, 35 N.H. 530 (1857); Varney v. French, 19 N.H. 233 (1848).
[37] Boynton v. Page, 13 Wend. 425 (1835).
[38] Jeandelle's Case, 3 Phil. 509 (1859).
[39] Moore v. Hagan, 2 Duv. 437 (1866).
[40] Davis v. Fish, 1 Green 406 (1848).
[41] Ricketts' Case, 74 N.C. 187 (1876).
[42] Gholston v. Gholston, 31 Ga. 625 (1860).
[43] 40 Miss. 341 (1866).
[44] O'Donnell v. Sweeney, 5 Ala. 467 (1843).
[45] 56 Md. 209.

Article 36 of our Declaration of Rights guarantees religious liberty; but the members of the distinguished body that adopted that constitution never supposed they were giving a death blow to Sunday laws by inserting that article. Those laws do not prohibit or interfere with the worship of God on any day other than Sunday . . .

It is undoubtedly true that rest from secular employment on Sunday does have a tendency to foster and encourage the Christian religion . . .

There are many most excellent citizens of this state who worship God on a day other than Sunday, and our constitution guarantees to them the right to do so, a right which no one can interfere with.[46]

In the case of Karwisch v. The Mayor and Council of Atlanta the plaintiff had been convicted before the mayor of Atlanta for keeping his store open on Sunday. The supreme court of Georgia said: "The law fixes the day recognized as the Sabbath day all over Christendom, and that day, by divine injunction, is to be kept holy — 'on it thou shalt do no work.' "[47]

In 1848 it was stated by the supreme court of Iowa that Sunday has been "established by laws, both human and divine, for public worship and private devotion . . . a time-honored and heaven-appointed institution."[48]

It is obvious from the statements quoted, which are only a few of the many that might be selected, that statutes dealing with Sunday legislation and court decisions in cases involving these statutes regard Sunday as a religious institution, an attitude which makes it difficult to deal with Sunday legislation as a "civil institution." This effort to "sanctify" or "consecrate" a particular time arrogates ecclesiastical functions to American legislatures which are not commonly ascribed to them in the American theory of jurisprudence.

Without exception where Sunday laws have been upheld, the "immorality," "vice," and "sin" consist not in the acts themselves but in the doing of them on Sunday. The difficulty with this is that Sunday labor must then be regarded by our secular courts just as an ecclesiastical tribunal would regard boisterous behavior in a church or an unauthorized intrusion upon a sanctuary. This attitude was expressed by the supreme court of Minnesota in considering the Sunday law statute of that state: "The law is not enforced for the benefit of either, but to prevent a desecration of the day."[49] This point of view was also well expressed by Chief Justice English of the supreme court of Arkansas when he said:

[46] Judefind v. State, 78 Md. 510 (1894).
[47] 44 Ga. 205 (1871).
[48] Green 406 (1848).
[49] Brackett v. Edgerton, 14 Minn. 134 (1869).

The object of the statute was to prohibit the *desecration* of the *Sabbath* by engaging in the vicious employment of playing *cards* on that day, which is set apart by divine appointment, as well as by the law of the land, for other and better engagements; and whether the defendent played for a wager or amusement, he is alike guilty of a desecration of the Sabbath, and consequently of a violation of the law. The playing *cards* upon *that day* is the gist of the offense, and whether the playing be for a wager or amusement is not material.[50]

The language used by Judge English is unmistakable; it states clearly that the object of the Sunday statute in Arkansas is to enforce the observance of the Sabbath. It will be noted that the offense committed is not the act of playing cards but the act of playing cards *on Sunday*. A man may be punished for committing a nuisance on Sunday, but he is not punished because of the fact of having committed it on Sunday. American law makes no distinction between Sunday and any other day when a nuisance has been committed.

The supreme court of Indiana in considering the power of the legislature of that state to enact a Sunday law summarized it in the following words:

When our existing government was created, its creators determined that there were some matters in which the majority should not control the minority; that there were some things over which the legislature should not have authority; that in some things the people should not be within the power of the legislature. Such is our organization of government — our constitution. One of the subjects withdrawn by that constitution, in the Bill of Rights, from legislative interference, is that of religion; and the writer has no hesitation in saying, highly as he individually values the Sabbath, that if the *Sunday* law is upon the statute book for the protection or enforcement of the observance of that day, as an institution of Christian religion, it cannot be upheld; no more than could a law forbidding labor on *Saturday,* the Jewish Sabbath, or on any and all other days of the week, which may be in the fulfillment of a requirement of a creed, set apart for religious observance, by any portion of our citizens, whether Christian, Jewish, Mohammedan, or pagan.[51]

A later emphasis has been placed upon the concept that the custom of observing Sunday as the Lord's day is one that has come

---

[50] Stockden v. State, 18 Ark. 186 (1856).
[51] Thomasson's Case, 15 Ind. 449 (1860); see also Melvin v. Easley, 7 Jones 356 (1860); Frolickstein v. Mayor of Mobile, 40 Ala. 725 (1867); Bott's Case, 31 La. Ann. 663 (1879); Cline v. State, 9 Okla. Crim. Rep. 50; Swann v. Swann, 21 Fed. Rep. 299 (1884); Andrews v. Bible Society, 6 Sandf. N.Y. 156 (1850); Ayres v. Methodist Church, 5 Sandf. N.Y. 351–77 (1849); State v. Powell, 58 Ohio St. 324, 41 L.R.A. 854 (1898); Slaughter-house Cases, 16 Wall. 36, 62; Bloom v. Richards, 2 Ohio St. 387 (1853).

down to us from our forefathers and that the state ought to protect customary observances.[52] It has been held that Christianity is a part of the common law of the nation and is therefore entitled to the recognition and protection of the temporal courts.[53] Courts have held through the years that the fact that Sunday has religion as its base does not render legislation concerning the observance of Sunday unconstitutional.[54]

It has therefore been argued, in keeping with the decisions cited, and as a necessity, indeed, if so religious an institution as Sunday is to be maintained by civil law, that Sunday laws are not a violation of "life, liberty, and the pursuit of happiness." [55] Sunday laws, it has been declared, are not a violation of freedom of religion.[56] If they were, they could not be enforced in that respect.[57]

However, a change has been taking place, contemporary with the issuing of these decisions. The position that it is constitutional to enforce a day of rest as an expression of national religious tradition sanctioned in common law is being presently abandoned.[58] There is only one other direction interpretation can take, and that is police power. Sunday laws are now being enforced and supported in their enforcement in the courts under the guise of police power measures.

[52] Commonwealth v. White, 190 Mass. 578, 77 N.E. 636 (1906); State v. James, 81 S.C. 197, 62 S.E. 214, 128 Am. St. Rep. 902, 16 Am. Cas. 277 (1908); Carr v. State, 175 Ind. 241, 93 N.E. 1071 (1911); State ex rel. Temple v. Barnes, 22 N.D. 18, 132 N.W. 215, Am. Cas. 1913 E. 930 (1911).

[53] State ex rel. Temple v. Barnes, 22 N.D. 18, 132 N.W. 215, Am. Cas. 1913 E. 930 (1911); Commonwealth ex rel. Woodruff v. American Baseball Club, 290 Pa. 136, 138 Atl. 497, 53 A.L.R. 1027 (1927).

[54] Specht v. Commonwealth of Pennsylvania, 8 Pa. 312, 49 Am. Dec. 518 (1848); Judefind v. State, 78 Md. 510, 28 Atl. 405, 22 L.R.A. 721 (1894); State ex rel. Temple v. Barnes, 22 N.D. 18, 132 N.W. 215, Am. Cas. 1913 E. 930 (1911); Rosenbaum v. State, 131 Ark. 251, 199 S.W. 388, L.R.A. 1918 B 1109 (1917).

[55] State v. Dolan, 13 Idaho 693, 92 Pac. 995 (1907); State v. Haining, 131 Kan. 854, 293 Pac. 952 (1930).

[56] Judefind v. State, 78 Md. 510, 28 Atl. 405, 22 L.R.A. 721 (1894); State v. Powell, 58 Ohio St. 324, 50 N.E. 900, 41 L.R.A. 854 (1898); State v. Blair, 130 Kan. 863, 288 Pac. 729 (1930).

[57] Rodman v. Robinson, 134 N.C. 503, 47 S.E. 19, 65 L.R.A. 682, 101 Am. St. Rep. 877 (1904); Carr v. State, 175 Ind. 241, 93 N.E. 1071 (1911); Pirkey Bros. v. Commonwealth, 134 Va. 713, 114 S.E. 764, 27 L.R.A. 1290 (1922); State ex rel. Smith v. Wertz, 91 W. Va. 622, 114 S.E. 242, 29 A.L.R. 391 (1922).

[58] State ex rel. Temple v. Barnes, 22 N.D. 18, 132 N.W. 215, Am. Cas. 1913 E. 930 (1911).

CHAPTER XX

Sunday Laws and the Police Power

As we have seen in many of the cases requiring an interpretation of the law, the courts have endeavored to establish that the object of Sunday laws (under the police power) is the preservation of good morals and the peace and good order of society, and not to emphasize the religious significance of the day. Some of these decisions have been based upon the necessity of physical benefits, some upon religious principles, and still others upon a strange combination of the two.

One of these strange combinations is seen in the case Moore v. Owen. It was stated:

> One of the leading features of the *Christian* Sabbath as one of our *civil* institutions, inherited from our ancestors who settled this country, is that all people should abstain from pursuing their ordinary week-day occupation of Sunday and that it should be given up to rest and *religious observances.*[1]

Police power has been defined as the inherent power of the state to prohibit all things hurtful to the comfort, safety, and welfare of society. It may be exercised to control the use of property of corporations as well as that of private individuals.[2] It may be extended to prevent needless destruction of property and to protect life.[3] It may be exercised in aid of what is sanctioned by usage or is held by the prevailing morality or strength and preponderant opinion to be greatly and immediately necessary to the public welfare.[4] However, such exercise must be carefully examined in the presence of personal and constitutional rights.

---

[1] 109 N.Y.S. 585, 58 Misc. 331, 22 N.Y. Cr. 58 (1908). The italics have been added. For other examples see Ex parte Jentzsch, 112 Calif. 468, 44 Pac. 803, 32 L.R.A. 664 (1896); State ex rel. Hoffman v. Justus, Sheriff, 91 Minn. 447, 98 N.W. 325, 64 L.R.A. 510, 103 Am. St. Rep. 521, 1 Am. Cas. 91 (1904); Carr v. State, 175 Ind. 241, 93 N.E. 1071, 32 L.R.A. (N.S.) 1190 (1911); Levering et al. v. Williams et al., 134 Md. 48, 106 Atl. 176, 4 A.L.R. 374 (1919).
[2] Town of Lake View v. Rose Hill Cemetery Co., 70 Ill. 191 (1873); Brass v. North Dakota ex rel. Stoeser, 153 U.S. 391 (1893); Budd v. New York, 143 U.S. 517 (1891).
[3] John S. Thorpe v. Rutland and Burlington R.R. Co., 27 Vt. 140 (1854).
[4] Noble State Bank v. Haskell, 219 U.S. 104 (1911).

The Supreme Court of the United States in 1905 reversed the judgment of the New York court in the Lockner case, which had been decided on health grounds.[5] The federal court held that the labor law of New York limiting the hours of labor in bakeries was not a proper exercise of the police power. The New York court had upheld the constitutionality of the law on the ground that the stipulation as to the hours of labor in bakeries was a measure for the protection of public health and a safeguard to the individuals who followed the occupation of bakers. Justice Peckham of the United States Supreme Court, in speaking for the court, said:

We think the limit of the police power has been reached and passed in this case. There is, in our judgment, no reasonable foundation for holding this to be necessary or appropriate as a health law to safeguard the public health or the health of the individuals who are following the trade of a baker.[6]

In answer to the arguments presented by the plaintiff, that the law was a health measure enacted in the interest of the state to aid in making its people strong and robust and therefore came under the police power, the court said:

If this be a valid argument and a justification for this kind of legislation, it follows that the protection of the federal constitution from undue interference with liberty of person and freedom of contract is visionary, wherever the law is sought to be justified as a valid exercise of the police power. Scarcely any law but might find shelter under such assumptions . . . The act is not, within any fair meaning of the term, a health law, but is an illegal interference with the rights of individuals . . .

It is impossible for us to shut our eyes to the fact that many of the laws of this character, while passed under what is claimed to be the police power for the purpose of protecting the public health or welfare, are, in reality, passed from other motives.

In the case of Mugler v. Kansas, the court said:

If, therefore, a statute purporting to have been enacted to protect the public health, the public morals, or the public safety, has no real or substantial relation to those objects, or is a palpable invasion of rights secured by the fundamental law, it is the duty of the courts to so adjudge, and thereby give effect to the constitution.[7]

Where the ostensible object of an enactment under the police power is to secure the public comfort, welfare, or safety, it must

[5] Lockner v. New York, 198 U.S. 45, 49 L. ed. 937 (1905).
[6] *Ibid.*
[7] 123 U.S. 623 (1887).

appear to be adopted to that end. It cannot invade the rights of persons and property under the guise of a police regulation when it is not such in fact.[8] In Eden v. State of Illinois, which was a prosecution for a violation of the Sunday law making it unlawful to do barbering on Sunday, the court in passing on the question of the relation of police regulation to health said:

How, it may be asked, is the health, comfort, safety, or welfare of society to be injuriously affected by keeping open a barber shop on Sunday? It is a matter of common observation that the barber business . . . is both quiet and orderly.[9]

The court referred to the case of Toledo, Wabash & Western R. R. Co. v. City of Jacksonville (67 Ill. 37), where it was held that if the law prohibits that which is harmless in itself or requires that to be done which does not tend to promote the health, comfort, safety, or welfare of society, it will in such case be an unauthorized exercise of police power, and it will be the duty of the courts to declare such legislation void.

The supreme court of Nebraska held unconstitutional an act defining what should constitute a legal day's work for all classes of mechanics, servants, and laborers throughout the state except those engaged in farming and domestic labor and making a violation of the act a misdemeanor, because the act attempted to prevent persons legally competent from entering into contracts.[10]

In the state of Illinois a man by the name of Steele was prosecuted for speculating in theater tickets on Sunday under a statute that had been enacted under the police power. The court held that to prevent speculation in theater tickets under this law was unconstitutional, since it had no relation to the public health, safety, morals, or welfare of the community.

The right of citizens to pursue an ordinary calling is a part of their right of liberty and property, and any law which prevents or abridges this privilege is obnoxious to the constitutions of this state and the United States.[11]

[8] Ritchie v. People, 155 Ill. 98 (1895); Town of Lake View v. Rose Hill Cemetery Co., 70 Ill. 191 (1869); Railroad Co. v. Jacksonville, 67 Ill. 37 (1873); People v. Gillson, 109 N.Y. 389 (1888); Millett v. People, 117 Ill. 294 (1886); Calder v. Bull, 3 Dall. 386 (1798); In re Jacobs, 98 N.Y. 109 (1885).
[9] 161 Ill. 296 (1896).
[10] Low v. Rees Printing Co., 41 Nebr. 127 (1894).
[11] People of Illinois v. Steele, 231 Ill. 340 (1907); see also Bessette v. People, 193 Ill. 334 (1901); Chicago v. Netcher, 183 Ill. 104 (1899); Ritchie v. People, 155 Ill. 98 (1895); Coal Co. v. People, 147 Ill. 66 (1893); Frorer v. People, 141 Ill. 171 (1892); Wice v. C. & N. Ry. Co., 193 Ill. 351 (1891); Gunning Sys. v. Chicago, 214 Ill. 628 (1905); Powell v. Penn., 127 U.S. 678 (1887).

Judge Cox, speaking for the supreme court of Indiana regarding Sunday legislation and the police power, said: "Sunday laws, which are an invasion of natural private rights, are enacted under this power." [12]

The police power, vague and vast as it is, has its limitations. It does not justify any act that violates the prohibitions, expressed or implied, of the state or federal constitution. The maxim *Sic utere tuo ut alienum non leadas* — "so use what is yours as not to injure another" — defines and exhausts the whole police power of a free American government. Under that power it may deal with action and inaction so far as they affect the relations of the citizens to each other or treason. It should not go beyond these limitations. A government that undertakes to do more than this ceases to be free and becomes paternal and despotic.

It is consciousness of the difficulty concerning the basis for and nature of Sunday laws that brought about the shift to a basis in police power. The highest New York court has stated that the one-day-in-seven law

cannot be sustained as one enforcing the religious observance of any day, but that it must be sustained, if at all, as a valid exercise of the police power of the state, for the promotion and protection of the public health and welfare. . . .

The thought of one day of rest in seven has come down to us fortified by centuries of recognition. It is true that often it has been coupled with and perhaps subordinate to the desire for religious observance. But the idea of rest and relaxation from the pursuits of other days has also been present, and whether we like it or not we are compelled to see that in more recent times the feature of rest and recreation has been developing at the expense of the one of religious observation.[13]

However, declaring Sunday laws constitutional on the basis of the police power began many years ago at the hands of no less an authority than the United States Supreme Court. A Chinese laundryman in California challenged the constitutionality of a California law, under the provisions of which he had been arrested and convicted of a misdemeanor for operating his laundry on Sunday. When the case reached the Supreme Court in 1885, the court sustained the conviction on the grounds that the law protected public health under the police power of the state.[14] In a case arising in Georgia, the

---

[12] Carr v. State of Indiana, 175 Ind. 241 (1911).
[13] People v. C. Klinck Packing Co., 214 N.Y. 121, 108 N.E. 278 (1915).
[14] Soon Hing v. Crowley, 113 U.S. 703, 28 L. ed. 1145, 5 S. Ct. 730.

United States Supreme Court sustained on the same basis a Georgia law forbidding the transportation of railroad freight in that state on Sundays. The court said:

There can be no well-founded doubt of its being a police regulation, considering it merely as ordaining the cessation of ordinary labor and business during one day in each week; for the frequent and total suspension of the toils, cares, and stain of mind or muscle incidental to pursuing an occupation or common employment is beneficial to every individual and incidentally to the community at large, the general public. . . . Short intervals of leisure at stated periods reduce wear and tear, promote health, favor cleanliness, encourage social intercourse, afford opportunity for introspection and retrospection, and tend to a high degree to expand the thoughts and sympathies of the people, enlarge their information, and elevate their morals. . . . If a law which, in essential respects, betters for all the people the conditions, sanitary, social, and individual, under which their daily life is carried on, and which contributes to endure for each, even against his own will, his minimum allowance of leisure, cannot be rightfully classed as a police regulation, it would be difficult to imagine any law that could.[15]

A few years later the highest court again ruled that Sunday laws were police measures for the common good. A barber had been arrested in Minnesota for barbering on Sunday. The Minnesota court stated:

"The object of the law is not so much to protect those who can rest at pleasure, but to afford rest to those who need it and who, from the conditions of society could not otherwise obtain it."[16] Many state courts have also ruled that Sunday is a day of rest essential to public welfare, [17] and that Sunday is therefore a civil institution.[18] As a police

[15] Hennington v. Georgia, 163 U.S. 299, 16 S. Ct. 1086, 41 L. ed. 166 (1896).

[16] Petit v. Minn., 74 Minn. 376, 77 N.W. 225, 177 U.S. 164, 20 S. Ct. 666, 44 L. ed. 716 (1900).

[17] Specht v. Commonwealth, 8 Pa. 312, 313, 49 Am. Dec. 518 (1848); Bloom v. Richards, 2 Ohio St. 387 (1853); People v. Havnor, 149 N.Y. 195, 43 N.E. 541, 31 L.R.A. 689, 52 Am. St. Rep. 707 (1896); State v. Chicago, Burlington & Quincy Railroad Co., 239 Mo. 196, 143 S.W. 785 (1912); City of Mt. Vernon v. Julian, 369 Ill. 447, 17 N.E. (2d) 52, 119 A.L.R. 747 (1938); Ex parte Hodges et al., 83 Pac. (2d) 201 (1938); Rogers et al. v. State, 4 S.E. (2d) 918 (1939); McKeown v. State, 124 S.W. (2d) 19 (1939); State v. Mead et al., 230 Ia. 1217, 300 N.W. 523 (1941); Broadbent v. Gibson, 140 Pac. (2d) 939 (1943); State v. Malone, 192 S.W. (2d) 68 (1946).

[18] Lundenmuller v. People, 33 Barb. 548 (1861). "It is a law of our nature that one day of rest in seven must be observed as a day of relaxation and refreshment, if not for public worship. Experience has shown that the observance of one day in seven as a day of rest is of admirable service to a state, considered merely as a civil institution. . . . As a civil institution, the selection of the day is at the option of the Legislature." See also People v. Havnor, 149 N.Y. 195, 43 N.E. 541, 31 L.R.A. 689 (1896); Brunswick-Balke-Collander Co. v. Evans, 228 Fed. 991, dismissed 248 U.S. 587, 39 S. Ct. 5, 63 L. ed. 434 (1918).

power measure[19] many courts have held Sunday laws to be constitutional.[20]

There were three marked characteristics of Roman law concerning Sunday observance: the forbidding of court sessions and of attending official acts; the abstention from ordinary business and labor, with certain exceptions; and the prohibition of sports and theatricals.[21] These prohibitions have carried down through early English law and particularly through the Sunday law of Charles II's reign, into our own legal system.

Sunday is a *dies non judicus*.[22] No charge may be made to a jury on Sunday,[23] and summonses may not legally be served on that day.[24] The legislature may, however, declare it a *dies judicus*.[25] Business and ordinary callings are illegal on Sundays,[26] and therefore Sunday laws have been upheld in prohibiting certain acts which are lawful at other times.[27] It is not the occasional but the repeated acts on Sunday which constitute an illegality.[28] A number of recent decisions have pointed out that when restrictions upon Sunday business are applied to all in that calling, it is not class legislation.[29]

It is constitutional to except certain occupations and businesses from the application of Sunday restrictions or to except them during certain hours. This is on the ground of public necessity.[30] Restaurants and undertaking establishments are among the businesses exempted.[31]

[19] Soon Hing v. Crowley, 113 U.S. 703, 5 S. Ct. 730, 28 L. ed. 1145 (1885); Ex parte Jentzsch, 112 Calif. 468, 44 Pac. 803 (1896); Petit v. Minn., 177 U.S. 164, 20 S. Ct. 666, 44 L. ed. 716 (1900); State ex rel. Hoffman v. Justus, Sheriff, 91 Minn. 447, 98 N.W. 325 (1904); State v. Dolan, 13 Idaho 693, 92 Pac. 995 (1907); Commonwealth ex rel. Woodruff v. Am. Baseball Club of Phila., 290 Pa. 136, 138 Atl. 497 (1927); City of Mt. Vernon v. Julian, 369 Ill. 447, 17 N.E. (2d) 52 (1938); Broadbent v. Gibson, 140 Pac. (2d) 939 (1943).

[20] State v. Cranston, 85 Pac. (2d) 682 (1938); Baird v. State, 167 S.W. (2d) 322 (1943); Ex parte Johnson, 141 Pac. (2d) 599 (1943); Broadbent v. Gibson, 140 Pac. (2d) 939 (1943); State v. Malone, 192 S.W. (2d) 68 (1946).

[21] See Chapter XIX.

[22] Guerrera v. State, 124 S.W. (2d) 595 (1939); Shaver v. Sparks et al., 277 Ky. 581, 126 S.W. (2d) 1110 (1939); Blizzard v. Blizzard, 8 S.E. (2d) 679 (1940); Pedersen v. Logan Sq. State & Savings Bank et al., 369 Ill. App. 54, 32 N.E. (2d) 644, 377 Ill. 408, 36 N.E. (2d) 732 (1941).

[23] Guerrera v. State.

[24] Pedersen v. Logan Sq. State & Savings Bank et al.   [25] *Ibid.*

[26] Ex parte Andrews, 18 Calif. 678 (1861); Gillooley v. Vaughn et al., 92 Fla. 942, 110 So. 653 (1926); Komer v. City of St. Louis, 316 Mo. 9, 289 S.W. 838 (1926); Rosenbaum v. City and County of Denver, 81 Pac. (2d) 760 (1938); State v. Thorne, 198 S.E. 632 (1938); Blizzard v. Blizzard, 8 S.E. (2d) 679 (1940); City of Harlan v. Scott et al., 290 Ky. 585, 162 S.W. (2d) 8 (1942); Forehand v. Moody et al., 36 S.E. (2d) 321 (1945).

[27] Gillooley v. Vaughn et al.   [28] Forehand v. Moody.

[29] People v. Krotkiewicz, 286 Mich. 644, 282 N.W. 852 (1938); Ex parte Hodges et al., 83 Pac. (2d) 201 (1938); Richman v. Board of Com'rs. of City of Newark, 122 N.J.L. 180, 4 Atl. (2d) 501 (1939); Ex parte Johnson, 141 Pac. (2d) 599 (1943).

[30] State v. Dolan, 13 Idaho 693, 92 Pac. 995, 14 L.R.A. (N.S.) 1259 (1907); Broadbent v. Gibson, 140 Pac. (2d) 939 (1943); Forehand v. Moody et al., 36 S.E. (2d) 321 (1945).

[31] Carton v. Shea, 45 N.E. (2d) 826 (1942); Baird v. State, 167 S.W. (2d) 332 (1943).

In general, the exceptions must relate to health, safety, morals, or general welfare.[32] Prevailing conditions are to be considered in determining the validity of claims to exception.[33] In some cases motion picture theaters have been excepted when their net Sunday proceeds have been devoted to charitable objects.[34] In other cases this has been denied, on the ground that charity does not give, but receives.[35]

The question of operating barbershops on Sunday has frequently been carried to the courts. In the Utah case of State v. Sopher,[36] which was a prosecution against Sopher for keeping his barbershop open on Sunday[37] the court held that the law was constitutional in prohibiting barbering on Sunday on the ground that it was not a work of necessity. While some states permit barbershops to be open on Sunday, at least until some designated hour,[38] the courts have held in a number of cases that the operation of a barbershop on Sunday is not a necessity within the intent of the law.[39]

In both Illinois and Missouri it has been held that a special law against Sunday barbering is unconstitutional, because it deprives barbers of property without due process of law and because it is in effect class legislation. The Illinois court said that "when the legislature undertakes to single out one class of labor, harmless in itself, and condemn that and that alone, it transcends its legitimate powers, and its action cannot be sustained."[40] In Michigan the court held valid a special law against Sunday barbering, with an exception in favor of those groups who observe the seventh day of the week as a day of rest.[41]

In California the court held that an act making it a misdemeanor to keep open and conduct a barbershop, bathhouse, or hairdressing parlor, or to work as a barber on Sunday or other holidays, is undue restraint of personal liberty and constitutes special legislation — that it is not a proper exercise of the police power and is unconstitutional.[42]

---

[32] City of Mt. Vernon v. Julian, 369 Ill. 447, 17 N.E. (2d) 52 (1938).

[33] Francisco v. Commonwealth, 180 Va. 371, 23 S.E. (2d) 234 (1942).

[34] Williams v. Commonwealth, 179 Va. 741, 20 S.E. (2d) 493 (1942).

[35] Forehand v. Moody et al., 36 S.E. (2d) 321 (1945).   [36] 25 Utah 318 (1902).

[37] The Sunday law of Utah allows livery stables, restaurants, boardinghouses, and bathhouses to be open on Sunday.

[38] The state of New York, for example, has a law allowing barbershops to be open on Sunday in the city of Saratoga until 1 P.M.

[39] State v. Frederick, 45 Ark. 347 (1885); Commonwealth v. Dextra, 143 Mass. 28 (1886); Commonwealth v. Waldman, 140 Pa. St. 89 (1891); Ex parte Kennedy (Tex.), 58 S.W. 129 (1900); Gray v. Commonwealth, 171 Ky. 269 (1916).

[40] Eden v. State of Illinois, 161 Ill. 296 (1896); for Missouri see State v. Granneman, 132 Mo. 326 (1895).

[41] People v. Bellet, 99 Mich. 151 (1894).

[42] Ex parte Jentzsch, 112 Calif. 468 (1896).

In an Oklahoma case the conviction of Johnson was sustained for barbering on Sunday contrary to a town ordinance, although barbering was not specifically forbidden in the state Sunday law. It.was ruled that it must be specifically excepted from the operation of the Sunday law.[43]

Prohibitions against grocery stores conducting business on Sunday have been sustained in the courts, sometimes with stipulations of certain hours for closing.[44] It has been pointed out, however, that restrictions on Sunday grocery business must be generally applied.[45] In California, where the state Sunday law was repealed by popular referendum in 1883, a town ordinance concerning the handling of meats was validated in that it forbade the sale of uncooked and uncured meat on Sunday as a health measure.[46]

Another class of activities that frequently comes into conflict with a particular branch of the Sunday laws includes amusements, sports, games, and exercises on Sunday. In Massachusetts it was held that Sunday law statutes, being criminal, are to be construed strictly and cannot be enlarged by implication.[47] The Massachusetts court held that a religious or Christian society may lawfully give a public vaudeville entertainment on the Lord's day if the excess of receipts over expenses is to be devoted to a charitable purpose.

In 1900 the supreme court of Missouri in construing a Sunday law forbidding the playing of "games of any kind on Sunday" used the following language:

Until the lawmakers expressly provide for such sweeping changes in the lives and customs and habits of our people, it is not proper for the courts by construction to impair their natural rights to enjoy those sports or amusements that are neither *mala in se* nor *mala prohibita* — neither immoral nor hurtful to body or soul.[48]

In 1910 the supreme court of Idaho in construing Section 6825 of the Idaho statutes, which prohibits public amusements on Sunday, in effect decided that

an amusement that is not *per se* unlawful or criminal and is not in itself immoral or dangerous or detrimental to the public health will not be

[43] Ex parte Johnson, 141 Pac. (2d) 599 (1943).
[44] State ex rel. Hoffman v. Justus, Sheriff, 91 Minn. 447, 98 N.W. 325 (1904); State v. Dolan, 13 Idaho 693, 92 Pac. 995 (1907); State v. Cranston, 85 Pac. (2d) 682 (1938); Richman v. Board of Com'rs. of City of Newark, 122 N.J.L. 180, 4 Atl. (2d) 501 (1939).
[45] Ex parte Hodges et al., 83 Pac. (2d) 201 (1938).
[46] Justesen's Food Stores v. City of Tulare, 84 Pac. (2d) 140 (1938).
[47] Commonwealth v. Simon Alexander, 185 Mass. 551 (1903).
[48] Ex parte Joseph Neet, 157 Mo. 527, 80 Am. St. Rep. 638 (1900).

included within the provisions of the statute prohibiting certain specified public amusements and other like and similar amusements on Sunday . . . [49]

It has been generally held that amusements may be prohibited on Sunday.[50]

The criminal court of appeals of Oklahoma decided in 1921 that to conduct moving picture shows on Sunday is not "servile labor" within the intent of the statutes. Section 2405 of the Oklahoma statutes of 1910, under which the following decision was rendered, is the same law that is in force in Oklahoma today, as given under Section 1825 of the Oklahoma statutes of 1921. The statute in question prohibited "servile labor" except works of necessity or charity on the Sabbath. The respondent, Clint Smith, was informed against for breaking the Sabbath by selling tickets for a moving picture performance. A demurrer to the information was sustained on the basis that the facts set forth in the information did not constitute "servile labor" as contemplated by the laws of Oklahoma. The state appealed the case from the county court to the criminal court of appeals. Justice Bessey, in delivering the opinion, said:

A Sunday law should not be a religious or an ecclesiastical act to promote religious doctrine, or religious rites or ceremonies. Ours is purely a civil government, which guarantees to every person the right to espouse and practice any religious creed he may choose, or to espouse and practice none. We therefore come to the conclusion that the operation of a moving picture show is not "servile labor," and not prohibited, within the meaning of this portion of our Sunday statute, and the order of the court, sustaining the demurrer to the information, is sustained, and the cause ordered dismissed.[51]

Some courts have held that the state may declare unlawful on Sunday what is lawful at other times;[52] that theaters may be closed on Sunday under the police power;[53] and that the courts can act only on what the legislature has enacted on the question of Sunday amusements, and may not interfere with the enforcement of just

[49] In re G. W. Hull, 18 Idaho Rep. 475 (1910).

[50] City of Bogaloosa v. Blanchard, 141 La. 33, 74 So. 588; City of W. Monroe v. Newell, 163 La. 409, 111 So. 889; Capital Theater Co. v. Commonwealth, 178 Ky. 780, 199 S.W. 1076; Ex parte Johnson, 20 Okla. Cr. 66, 201 Pac. 533; West Coast Theatres v. City of Pomona, 68 Calif. App. 763, 230 Pac. 225.

[51] State v. Smith, 198 Pac. Rep. 879; see also Blinkley v. State, 198 Pac. Rep. 884; Ramsey v. State, 198 Pac. Rep. 886; State v. House, 198 Pac. Rep. 888; Treese v. State, 198 Pac. Rep. 889 (1921).

[52] 92 Fla. 943, 110 So. 653 (1926).

[53] State v. Haining, 131 Kan. 854, 293 Pac. 952 (1930).

laws.[54] Different courts have ruled differently concerning theaters operating on Sundays for the benefit of charity.[55]

The supreme court of Ohio decided in 1898 that a law forbidding Sunday baseball was no trespass of constitutional freedoms and sustained it as a police measure.[56] But in the case of People v. Poole et al., which was a prosecution by the state of New York charging Poole with violation of the statutes prohibiting public sports on Sunday, Judge Gaynor, who gave the opinion for the court, said:

Physical exercises and games are not forbidden on the Sabbath in the Ten Commandments. Only work is there prohibited. . . . Moreover, this commandment [the fourth] relates to the seventh day of the week, and not to the first. In the New Testament there is no Sunday law at all.

And if we view the statute as a health law, we shall still not perceive any intention in it to prohibit all out-of-door games and exercises on Sunday, for to prevent them, especially in the cities, would injure the health of the community and materially increase the death rate.[57]

The supreme court of New Mexico also decided that the playing of baseball on Sunday is not a sport or labor within the meaning of the Sunday law statute prohibiting labor or sports on the first day of the week.[58]

In the case of Hiller v. State it was held that an ordinance of the city of Baltimore prohibiting the playing of baseball on Sunday — even though it took place in a secluded part of a large natural park out of sight of houses, without any reward for playing or charge for admission but merely as recreation and in a quiet and peaceful manner, without noise or conduct disturbing the public peace — was within the proper exercise of the police power and not contrary either to Article 36 of the Declaration of Rights, guaranteeing religious freedom, or the Fourteenth Amendment of the federal Constitution, protecting civil rights.[59] The ordinance was passed in 1827 and is as follows: "Any person who shall fish, hunt, pitch quoits or money, fly a kite, play bandy or ball, or any other game or sport upon the Sabbath day within the limits of the city shall for each offense pay a fine of one dollar . . ." Justice Burke, speaking for the court said:

[54] Commonwealth v. Phoenix Amusement Co., 241 Ky. 678, 44 S.W. (2d) 830 (1931).
[55] Williams v. Commonwealth, 20 S.E. (2d) 493 (1942); Forehand v. Moody et al., 36 S.E. (2d) 321 (1945).
[56] State v. Powell, 58 Ohio St. 324, 50 N.E. 900 (1898).
[57] 89 N.Y.S. 773 (1904).
[58] New Mexico v. Thos. M. Davenport, 17 N. Mex. Rep. 214 (1912).
[59] 124 Md. 385 (1914).

It is now generally held that laws and ordinances of this character are passed in the exercise of the police power, and it must be admitted that the state and the city have the power to pass all proper laws and regulations of this nature.[60]

In some places baseball playing is permitted in the afternoon, when it will not conflict with church services held in the morning; or, if church services are held at some other hour, it is prohibited during that time — thus showing the religious motives back of such laws. It is difficult to see how such prohibitions can properly come under the police power, since baseball playing is not in itself "immoral" or "detrimental" to "public health."

In 1919 the Maryland court, while sustaining the Sunday law against amusements, as a police measure, not to be weakened because "the day enjoined is the Sabbath," ruled that Sunday baseball is permissible when no admission fee is charged.[61] The Pennsylvania court has sustained prohibition of Sunday baseball.[62]

It has been recently ruled, however, that a change of activity is a form of rest,[63] and in general the tendency seems to be toward lessening the force of restrictions of recreations.

It must be pointed out that strange anomalies frequently exist in the laws dealing with Sunday legislation. The legislature of Mississippi, for instance, when it enacted Senate Bill 87 at the legislative session of 1926, prohibited meat markets in municipalities of more than five thousand people from selling meat on the first day of the week. If it was made under the police power, was it for the "health of the individual," the "welfare of the community," the "public safety," or "public morals"? Our courts have said that before enacting a law involving the exercise of the police power the legisla-

[60] The constitution of Maryland stipulates: "That as it is the duty of every man to worship God in such manner as he thinks most acceptable to Him, all persons are equally entitled to protection in their religious liberty; wherefore, no person ought, by any law, to be molested in his person or estate on account of his religious persuasion or profession, or for his religious practice, unless, under the color of religion, he shall disturb the good order, peace, or safety of the state, or shall infringe the laws of morality, or injure others in their natural, civil, or religious rights; nor ought any person to be compelled to frequent, or maintain, or contribute, unless on contract, to maintain any place of worship or any ministry; nor shall any person, otherwise competent, be deemed incompetent as a witness, or juror, on account of his religious belief; provided he believes in the existence of God, and that under His dispensation such person will be held morally accountable for his acts, and be rewarded or punished therefore in this world or the world to come." Article 36.

"That no religious test ought ever to be required as a qualification for any office of profit or trust in this state, other than a declaration of belief in the existence of God . . ." Article 37.

[61] Levering et al. v. Williams et al., 134 Md. 48, 106 Atl. 176, 4 A.L.R. 374.

[62] Commonwealth ex rel. Woodruff v. Am. Baseball Club of Phila., 290 Pa. 136, 138 Atl. 497 (1927).

[63] Broadbent .. Gibson, 140 Pac. (2d) 939 (1943).

ture must ask itself these questions: Is there a threatened danger? Does the regulation involve a constitutional right? Is the regulation reasonable? Applying these tests to the Mississippi law, one asks: If it is a health law, why not protect the health of the people who happen to live in a city or village of less than five thousand people? Why allow people who live in municipalities of five thousand or less to buy meat and prohibit those who live in larger municipalities from doing so? If meat buying is undesirable on Sunday in a municipality of more than five thousand, why is it not undesirable in all municipalities? According to this law, it is the size of the community that determines whether it is wrong to buy meat on Sunday.

In Massachusetts the court held that delivery of bread by the baker or his employee at the customer's place of business on the Lord's day is a violation of its Sunday law, which prohibits any manner of work except works of necessity and charity.[64] The court said:

> The statute prohibiting the performance of labor, business, or work, except works of necessity and charity, on Sunday, was enacted to secure respect and reverence for the Lord's day. "That the day should be not merely a day of rest from labor, but also a day devoted to public and private worship and to religious meditation and repose, undisturbed by secular cares or amusements."

In the case of Commonwealth v. Crowley the respondent was fund guilty because he sold bread on Sunday.[65] The law allowed bakers but no one else to sell bread. If the person baked the bread himself he could sell it on Sunday, but if someone else baked it and he bought it from him, he could not sell it on Sunday.

Nebraska allows bathhouses to be open on Sunday until twelve o'clock noon.[66]

In a New York case the respondent was prosecuted for fishing in a pond and was convicted.[67] The pond was private property belonging to a club of which he was a member. Section 265 of the penal code of New York stipulates that "all shooting, hunting, fishing, playing, horse racing, gaming, or other public sport, exercises, or shows upon the first day of the week, and all noise disturbing the peace of the day, are prohibited." The court held that this provision prohibits fishing, that its prohibition is absolute, forbidding fishing on Sunday anywhere in the state and under all circumstances.

---

[64] Commonwealth v. McCarthy, 244 Mass. 484 (1923).
[65] 145 Mass. 430 (1887).
[66] Nebr. 464 (1889).
[67] People v. Moses, 140 N.Y. 214, 35 N.E. 499 (1893).

Three of the judges of the highest appellate court voted that the offense consisted in the mere act of fishing, regardless of whether it interrupted "the repose and religious liberty of the community." The fourth judge concurred on the ground that the act did "constitute a serious interruption of the repose and religious liberty of the community." Three of the judges dissented. It would appear that the three judges who decided "that the offense was made out by the mere act of fishing, regardless of whether it interrupted the repose of the community" had a high regard for the religious discipline of the fish, and therefore did not wish to see them depraved on Sunday by being tempted with a delicious-looking bait.

The supreme court of Minnesota has made the following distinction with respect to what may be sold on Sunday as a necessity without violating the Sunday laws of the state.[68] The court held that the selling of tobacco was not a violation of the statute which allows necessities to be sold on the Sabbath day, but that meat, groceries, and clothing could not be sold. It is evident that the court considered tobacco a greater necessity than meat, groceries, and clothing; that the selling of tobacco was a necessity and the selling of meat a misdemeanor. If a person is required to buy his meat on the preceding day or night, might he not as well be required to buy his tobacco at the same time? These are only a few of the many opinions which our courts have expressed in an effort to uphold Sunday laws, and sometimes these opinions put them into embarrassing positions later.

Although many opinions have been cited, and many more might be cited, in which the courts have upheld the constitutionality of Sunday laws, it should not be assumed that all court decisions have upheld such legislation; on the contrary, the decisions given in a number of court cases have not upheld Sunday laws, and in others strong dissenting opinions have expressed opposition to such legislation. While an array of authorities can be marshaled in support of Sunday laws of uniform operation, they are by no means agreed on a single principle upon which to base such laws. Frequently judges carry with them to the benches religious prejudices derived from early training. Such bias has prevented the carrying out of the philosophy of perfect religious freedom. It is time, however, that the courts recognize that true religion is never advanced but always injured by enlisting in its behalf the punishments and rewards of secular powers.

[68] State ex rel. Hoffman v. Justus, Sheriff, 91 Minn. 447, 98 N.W. 325 (1904).

It is regrettable to see these anomalies which challenge the dignity of law. But it is regrettable, too, to see the danger to personal freedom residing in any laws concerning religion, for these must present a challenge to the fairness of law.

There was some early protest against the fact that Sunday laws involve a challenge to conscience. It has been decided in several cases that any statute that attempts to compel the observance of the first day of the week as a religious duty will be unconstitutional and void.[69] In an Ohio case Judge Thurman, in delivering the opinion upholding a Sunday law merely as a municipal regulation under the police power, said:

The statute upon which defendant relies prohibiting common labor on the Sabbath could not stand for a moment as a law of this state, if its sole foundation was the Christian duty of keeping that day holy, and its sole motive to enforce the observance of that duty.[70]

In Ex parte Koser the California court said:

If it once be admitted that the legislature has power to thus provide [by passing Sunday laws] for the public health and good morals, where is the limit to its exercise? And if the public health can thus be provided for, what is the objection to laws prohibiting the use or the culture of tobacco, or even tea or coffee, as injurious to health? . . . there would be just as much propriety in enacting the number of hours out of the twenty-four during which all should sleep, on pretense of compelling a restoration of exhausted energies, as in prescribing the number of hours in every week during which all must refrain from their ordinary avocations.[71]

In upholding certain Sunday laws as a civil regulation on the ground that one day's rest in seven is necessary for the health and moral well-being of the citizens, Sunday has been compared with the Fourth of July and other holidays. But it would appear that there is a difference between setting Sunday aside as a day of rest with a penalty attached for violation and setting aside the Fourth of July or any other holiday with no penalty attached.[72] Our courts have held that where infliction of a penalty for the commission of an act is imposed, this is equivalent to an expressed prohibition of such

---

[69] Swann v. Swann, 21 Fed. Rep. 299 (1884); State v. Judge, 39 La. 132 (1887).
[70] Bloom v. Richards, 20 Ohio St. 387 (1853).
[71] 60 Calif. 177 (1882).
[72] Some cases have pointed out the distinction in law between holidays and Sunday: State ex rel. Frank E. Putnam et al. v. Holmes, Sec'y of State et al., 172 Minn. 162, 215 N.W. 200, 54 A.L.R. 333; Glenn v. Eddy, 51 N.J.L. 255, 17 Atl. 145, 14 Am. St. Rep. 684; State ex rel. Walter v. Superior Court, 49 Wash. 1, 94 Pac. 665, 17 L.R.A. (N.S.) 257; A. G. Spalding & Bros. v. Bernhard, 76 Wis. 368, 44 N.W. 643, 7 L.R.A. 423, 20 Am. St. Rep. 75.

an act. In other words, if there is no penalty, then the act is not strictly prohibited. Penal statutes are construed strictly.

A court in California held that an act making it a misdemeanor to keep open and conduct a barbershop, bathhouse, or hairdressing parlor, or to work as a barber on Sunday or other holidays is an undue restraint of personal liberty and is special legislation — an improper exercise of the police power — and is unconstitutional. In passing on the questions presented in this case the court said:

In this state they [Sunday laws] have never been upheld from a religious standpoint. Under a constitution which guarantees to all equal liberty of religion and conscience, any law which forbids an act not in itself *contra bonos mores,* because that act is repugnant to the beliefs of one religious sect, of necessity interferes with the liberty of those who hold to other beliefs or to none at all.

Liberty of conscience and belief is preserved alike to the followers of Christ, to Buddhists and Mohammedans, to all who think that their tenets alone are illumined by the light of divine truth; but it is equally preserved to the skeptic, agnostic, atheist, and infidel, who says in his heart, "There is no God."

Still, it may be suggested in passing that our government was not designed to be paternal in form. We are a self-governing people, and our just pride is that our laws are made by us as well as for us. Every individual citizen is to be allowed so much liberty as may exist without impairment of the equal rights of his fellows. Our constitutions are founded upon the conviction that we are not only capable of self-government as a community, but what is the logical necessity, that we are capable, to a great extent, of individual self-government. If this conviction shall prove ill founded we have built our house upon the sand. The spirit of a system such as ours is, therefore, at total variance with that which, more or less veiled, still shows in the paternalism of other nations. It may be injurious to health to eat bread before it is twenty-four hours old, yet it would strike us with surprise to see the legislature making a crime of the sale of fresh bread. We look with disfavor upon such legislation as we do upon the enactment of sumptuary laws. We do not even punish a man for his vices, unless they be practiced openly, so as to lead to the spread of corruption, or to breaches of the peace, or to public scandal. In brief, we give the individual the utmost possible amount of personal liberty, and, with that guaranteed him, he is treated as a person of responsible judgment, not as a child in his nonage, and is left free to work out his destiny as impulse, education, training, heredity, and environment direct him.

In stating the law in regard to a man's constitutional rights and freedom, the court said:

A man's constitutional liberty means more than his personal freedom. It means, with many other rights, his right freely to labor, and to own the fruits of his toil. It is a curious law for the protection of labor which punishes the laborer for working. Yet that is precisely what this law does. The laboring barber, engaged in a most respectable, useful, and cleanly pursuit, is singled out. . . . If he labors, he is a criminal. Such protection to labor carried a little further would send him from the jail to the poorhouse.

There is no Sunday period of rest and no protection for overworked employees of our daily papers. Do those not need rest and protection? The bare suggestion of these considerations shows the injustice and inequality of this law.[73]

In the case of Ex parte Koser, which was a prosecution under the Sunday statute, the court held that there was no state religion and on this question the court said: "We have no state religion. Consequently we should not have any crimes against religion cognizable by the state." [74]

Such rulings as the foregoing have not changed the fact that those who keep no day of worship at all, and those who observe another day than Sunday, find their personal liberty in some jeopardy. Frequently, however, in states that have Sunday laws prohibiting "common labor on Sunday" an exception is made of those who conscientiously observe the seventh day of the week or some other as their Sabbath. In Indiana the court held that even if the seventh-day observers are not exempted from the operation of the Sunday laws, they do not violate such laws when they work on Sunday.[75] In rendering its opinion the court said:

The framers of the statute meant to leave it to the consciences and judgments of the citizens to choose between the first and the seventh day of the week. One or the other of these days they must refrain from common labor. Which it shall be is to be determined by their own consciences. It was not the purpose of the lawmakers to compel any class of conscientious persons to abstain from labor upon two days in every week. Without the proviso which is said to break down the law, a large number of citizens would be compelled to lose two days of labor. One day, because of their conscientious convictions of religious duty, and one by the command of the municipal law. We know that there are sects of Christians who conscientiously believe the seventh day to be the divinely ordained Sabbath. We know, too, that there is a great people, who, for many centuries, and through relentless persecution and terrible trials, have

---

[73] Ex parte Jentzsch, 112 Calif. 468 (1896).
[74] 60 Calif. 468 (1896).
[75] Johns v. State, 78 Ind. 332 (1881).

clung with unswerving fidelity to the faith of their fathers that the seventh day is the true Sabbath. If the proviso were wrenched from the statute, these classes of citizens would be compelled, in obedience to their religious convictions, to rest from labor on the seventh day, and, by the law, also compelled to refrain from common labor on the first day of the week. A leading and controlling element of our system of government is that there shall be absolute freedom in all matters of religious belief.[76]

In discussing the exemption of those who observe another day, Ernst Freund, in his work entitled *Police Power,* says: "All laws should scrupulously respect the principle of religious equality, and as experience shows that the exemption within the bounds indicated is quite feasible, it should be recognized as a constitutional right." [77]

The Ohio courts have declared that a statute without exemption for seventh-day observers would not be valid.[78] In 1894 the Michigan court ruled that exemptions in Sunday laws for those who keep another day was not discriminatory.[79] In an Oklahoma case involving a storekeeper who regularly observed Saturday as the Sabbath, the court pointed out that such a man, if compelled to close his store on Sunday, would be deprived of one day of labor out of the usual six, and since he operated his store without disturbing the peace, he should be exempt from the prohibitions of the Sunday-closing law.[80] The following year the Kentucky court handed down a similar ruling.[81]

A case in Ohio involved a young man named Kut who refused to work on Saturday because it was the day he observed as the Sabbath. He lost his employment and brought suit. The supreme court of Ohio did not sustain him in the suit. It ruled that it could not be charged that when one who from conscience worshipped on Saturday yielded to necessity and worked on that day, he was then breaking the Sunday law. But it also ruled in keeping with earlier Ohio decisions that observers of the Saturday Sabbath were exempt from the penalties of Sunday laws.[82] It may be mentioned incidentally that when Kut, having lost his employment because of refusing

---

[76] For decisions sustaining these views see City of Cincinnati v. Rice, 15 Ohio 225 (1846); City of Canton v. Nist, 9 Ohio 439 (1859).

[77] Ernst Freund, *Police Power, Public Policy and Constitutional Rights* (Chicago, 1904), p. 502.

[78] City of Cincinnati v. Rice.

[79] People v. Bellett, 99 Mich. 151, 57 N.W. 1094 (1894).

[80] Krieger et al. v. State, 12 Okla. Cr. 566, 160 Pac. 36 (1916).

[81] Cohen v. Webb, 175 Ky. 1, 192 S.W. 828 (1917).

[82] Kut v. Albers Super Markets, 76 Ohio App. 51, 63 N.E. (2d) 218 (1945).

to work on Saturday, applied for unemployment compensation, his request was refused.

There have, however, been a regrettably larger number of decisions which have ruled out exemptions for non-observers of Sunday as discriminatory on the one hand, and on the other not prejudiced to religious liberty.[83]

A recent ruling in Iowa served to protect a type of religious activity on Sunday which some claimed was disturbing to the Sunday peace. The Iowa law, Section 13227, Code of Iowa 1939, reads in part:

> Breach of Sabbath — Exceptions. If any person be found on . . . Sunday . . . or in any manner disturbing a worshipping assembly or private family, or in buying or selling property of any kind, or in any labor except that of necessity or charity, he shall be fined.

A group of religionists went from door to door in the city of Clinton, Iowa, distributing printed matter setting forth their tenets of faith and occasionally accepting small sums for their booklets. They were arrested for disturbing the peace.

On appeal, the case reached the Iowa supreme court, which ruled against the findings of the lower courts. The court said:

> It is contended by the State that the calling upon householders after 10 A.M. on Sunday for the purpose of propagandizing appellants' religious views by spoken and printed words constituted "disturbing a private family." The language of this portion of the act is "disturbing a worshipping assembly or private family." We need not here determine the exact interpretation to be given this language. The record indicates that at the time of the calls the householders were engaged in eating or other mundane activities. No disturbance of any kind is shown to have taken place. We are not prepared to hold that the calling at private homes in the middle of the sabbath day, however unwelcome the caller may be, in itself constitutes a desecration of the Sabbath.

> The State also contends the distribution of the booklets and occasional receipt of the sum of ten cents constituted "selling property" within the prohibition of the act. However, appellants were not engaged in selling booklets. The alleged sales were merely incidental and collateral to appellants' main object, which was to preach and publicize the doctrines of their order. Indicative of this was the practice of giving booklets to

---

[83] Specht v. Comm., 8 Pa. 312, 49 Am. Dec. 518 (1848); Leiberman v. State, 26 Nebr. 464, 42 N.W. 419, 18 Am. St. Rep. 791 (1889); Judefind v. State, 78 Md. 510, 28 Atl. 405 (1894); State v. Bergfeldt, 41 Wash. 234, 83 Pac. 177, 6 Am. Cas. 979, writ for error dismissed by the U.S. Supreme Court in 1908, 210 U.S. 438, 28 S. Ct. 764, 52 L. ed. 1138; Komen v. City of St. Louis et al., 316 Mo. 9, 289 S.W. 838 (1926); Xepapas v. Richardson, 149 S.C. 52, 146 S.E. 686 (1929); Kislingbury et al. v. Trees of City of Plainfield, 10 N.J. Misc. 798, 160 Atl. 654 (1932).

those unwilling to contribute. Appellants regarded the amounts received as donations, and this was frequently the thought of those who gave money. Appellants were teaching and spreading their religious views without compensation and at their own expense. All receipts from the booklets were placed in a publication fund, which it was necessary to supplement by voluntary contributions to cover the cost of publishing the booklets. The commercial aspect of sales was absent. We do not think the statute contemplates that the distribution of booklets of this nature and under these particular circumstances constitutes desecrating the Sabbath.[84]

The Delaware court has stated that "the remedy for the injurious consequences of such [Sunday] laws, if any is needed, lies with the legislature, and not with the courts." [85]

In some cases the question has been referred to the people. Invariably where they are given the opportunity to vote on the question, the Sunday laws have been relegated to the limbo of bygone days. In Oregon the United States district judge ruled that the Oregon Sunday law prohibiting the operation of certain places of business on Sunday did not violate the constitution of Oregon,[86] which prescribes that "no law shall in any case whatever control the free exercise and enjoyment of religious opinions, or interfere with the rights of conscience." [87] The district judge ruled that this Sunday law did not interfere with the free exercise and enjoyment of religious opinions or the rights of conscience, that it was purely a civil law and did not compel religious observance of Sunday. The court went to great length in its reasoning and its interpretation of the law, even stating that forbidding any secular business or labor on Sunday should be regarded as of civil instead of religious import.

The people of Oregon immediately set themselves to the task of repealing the Sunday law; by public referendum in the November election of 1916 they repudiated the verdict of the court by repealing the Sunday laws of Oregon by a large majority vote.

It might be natural to assume that Christians are in favor of Sunday legislation and that non-Christians oppose it; this, however, is by no means true. While it is a fact that such legislation is frequently sponsored by religio-political clergymen, certain organizations, and frequently ministerial associations, it is equally true that some of the stanchest Christians, clergymen as well as laymen, are

[84] State v. Mead et al., 230 Ia. 1217, 300 N.W. 523 (1941).
[85] Walsh et al. v. State, 33 Del. 514, 139 Atl. 257 (1927).
[86] Article 1, Paragraph 3.
[87] Brunswick-Balke-Colander Co. v. Evans, 288 Fed. 991 (1916).

definitely opposed to Sunday legislation. The Reverend Thomas J. Whelan, rector of the Holy Name Church in Camden, New Jersey,[88] was opposed to Sunday laws and worked for their repeal in New Jersey. This Catholic priest traveled through the state of California, which has had no Sunday laws for more than fifty years, and found that the lack of such laws did not make for decreased church attendance; on the contrary, church statistics showed that in proportion to population more people attended church on Sunday in California than in any other state of the union.

The Reverend Herman Bielenberg, a Lutheran pastor, in opposing the Pennsylvania Sunday laws and advocating their repeal, voiced not only his own opposition but that which the Lutheran church has frequently enunciated against this kind of legislation. He said:

In the first place, my appearance before the council was not on behalf of the operation of Sunday movies. I stated at the outset that I held no brief for theaters and movie houses. My appearance was meant solely to point out the dangers of religious legislation, which is class legislation, and to make clear the position of our church, which has its convictions, but has never tried to force anyone into believing as we do. It is, in my humble estimation, a deplorable situation when the churches of Christ who feel that they ought to keep Sunday, try to force everyone else to do the same thing, regardless of their conviction. It is thoroughly un-American. . . .

My plea is this: Let us respect each other's convictions. If you are so inclined, try to make your convictions my convictions by persuasion, but let us desist from forcing, coercing, legislating people into our position, if we feel that the gentle art of persuasion yields no results.[89]

Mr. Bielenberg quoted at some length from the Augsburg Confession, which was drawn up during the Reformation and presented to the emperor at the Diet of Augsburg on June 25, 1530, and which is still the official confession of the Lutheran church, to show that the church does not believe that there is scriptural authority for Sunday observance. He continued:

That is my position and the official Lutheran position on the Sunday question. But even if we felt in duty bound to keep Sunday, we would consider it a grievous mistake to legislate this fact into the laws of the land. . . .

Let no one think that our church teaches lawlessness, or places no emphasis on the evil character of sin. We do not advocate the indulgence

[88] *Courier Post*, April 11, 1933.
[89] *Oil City* (Pennsylvania) *News Herald*, January 5, 1933.

of the flesh. . . . We worship our God on Sunday, while opposing Sunday laws. Laws cannot make me worship, and laws cannot keep me from worshipping. I prize the old adage: "He governs best who governs least." [90]

In speaking for the Baptists, the Reverend Arthur C. Baldwin, pastor of the Chestnut Street Church in Philadelphia, wrote the following letter to the editor of the *Philadelphia Public Ledger,* which was published on January 31, 1933:

Sir: As a churchman and lover of the real Christian Sunday, I am hoping that the present archaic Sunday laws in Pennsylvania will be changed by the legislature.

This is not because I want an open Sunday. I consider that to be a real peril. I do not believe that this nation can give up religion, its worship, quiet, and rest without a great irreparable loss. I urge a right observance of Sunday openly, and wish to use all the influence I possess to promote the observance of a quiet, helpful day.

The right sort of Sunday, however, can only come from the development of an inner spirit. We do not do well to rely on the state for that which only religion in the heart of man can produce.

Pastor Francis D. Nichol in a public hearing before the city council of Hyattsville, Maryland, presented the views of the Seventh-day Adventists on the subject of Sunday laws:

I believe they are wrong because they violate the great principle enunciated both by Bible writers and by the founding fathers of this country —the principle of the separation of church and state. In the centuries before the United States government was established, church and state were, to a greater or less degree, united in every land. And all the hardships and persecutions to which religious minorities have been subjected through the centuries have resulted from such a union of church and state. When the religious majority in a state are able to register their beliefs on the statute books and can employ the arm of the law in support of their views, persecution, to a greater or less degree, inevitably follows. This is not a theory regarding government; it is a sad fact of history written in tears and blood in the annals of all religious minorities who thus suffered.[91]

The practice of keeping Sunday laws on the statute books, even when they appear antiquated and are not being enforced constitutes a potential danger. That fact was called to the attention of the people of Ohio by the *Cleveland News* in which an account was given of how a local committee for the enforcement of the NRA code dug

[90] *Ibid.*
[91] *Hyattsville* (Maryland) *Independent,* January 13, 1933.

up an old Ohio Sunday blue law and endeavored to bring about its enforcement in connection with the NRA. In commenting upon the situation, the *News* said:

Antiquated Ohio blue laws, that were thought to have been dead these many years, are being resurrected by Cleveland merchant associations to enforce the N.R.A.

The Buckeye Road board of trade was the first association to use the old laws as a weapon. The Fair Merchants of Central and Woodland and other groups were quick to follow.

Today the big question before the merchants of the city was how fast the movement may be expected to spread. And how many of the blue laws will be brought to life to restrict the city's Sunday trade.

Will it mean, they ask, that the full letter of the old blue laws will be enforced, making a Sabbath-breaker subject to a fine of $100 and a sentence of six months in the workhouse? [92]

It is evident that no one may ever be certain as to when or under what pretense religious laws may be resurrected. Not a few newspapers carried vigorous editorials protesting against the use of the NRA as a propaganda agency for Sunday laws or compulsory observance. In a number of communities local NRA committees linked Sunday closing crusades with the NRA movement for national recovery. In an editorial of the *Sacramento Bee* discussing the various attempts by certain people to secure the passage of Sunday laws and how the people have repeatedly shown that they are opposed to such legislation, it was said:

Yet under the guise of loyalty to the N.R.A., certain groups and classes are seeking to impose upon California what the people have declared shall not be done and which the courts have declared to be unjust and unconstitutional. [93]

There is increasing public sentiment in favor of amending or repealing Sunday legislation. The Wisconsin state legislature repealed every Sunday law upon its statute books after the people of Wisconsin had, by a majority vote of 124,650 in a popular referendum election, given a mandate to the state legislature to repeal the existing Sunday laws. The Wisconsin Sunday laws had been very drastic, although only partially enforced and only in localities where religious sentiment dominated public officials.

Several other states, including California, Oregon, Arizona, and Wyoming, have repealed their Sunday laws. In California, in which

[92] *Cleveland News*, September 20, 1933.
[93] *Sacramento* (California) *Bee*, September 16, 1933.

Sunday laws were repealed fifty years ago, steps have occasionally been taken by a group of political clergymen to have them re-enacted, but every such effort has been defeated either by the legislature or by popular referendum. In 1930 an attempt was made to have the Sunday laws placed back upon the statute books, but a referendum defeated the effort by more than 75,000 votes.

As we have seen, the Oregon Sunday laws were repealed by a popular referendum vote. The supreme court of Arizona declared the Sunday laws of that state unconstitutional. Wyoming repealed her Sunday laws in 1932 by an act of the legislature. With the exception of Arkansas, Delaware, Mississippi, South Carolina, and Virginia, all the states authorize municipalities and political divisions to modify, liberalize, or repeal a part or a whole of the Sunday laws by legislative action or popular referendum. Such action has resulted in liberalizing or repealing the Sunday laws in many of these communities. Organized efforts are afoot in Maine, Maryland, Minnesota, Tennessee, New Jersey, Pennsylvania, and there are strong sentiments in many other states for either liberalizing or repealing Sunday laws.

Where there is actually a desire to provide for one day of rest under the police power of the state without injecting the religious element into it, many people are advocating a law requiring "one day of rest in seven." The legislature of New Hampshire has passed such a law in lieu of her old Sunday law. Any person may work on Sunday provided he rests twenty-four consecutive hours during the six days next ensuing. This law aims to protect employees from seven days of work a week. California has a similar law.

The American Federation of Labor has several times gone on record as favoring a one-day-in-seven law for all employees without specifying any particular day of rest, leaving each employee to select his own day and the manner of its observance. Frances Perkins, secretary of labor in President Roosevelt's cabinet, said in her first public announcement after she was inducted into office: "While it is foolish for one person to present a program of employment relief, one constructive measure would be for all states to adopt the one day of rest in seven law. This would put many thousands back to work." Such legislation would constitute civil legislation and make for religious liberty. It would leave the religious element out of the question, and this is perhaps the logical way to dispose of the Sunday law question.

Among the most sacred heritages of man is his right of conscience.

Whatever work the state may undertake for the moral benefit of her subjects, the person's conscience should be respected. The claim put forth upon certain occasions that the design of Sunday laws is to secure liberty and health for the laboring classes does not reach the core of the question. The many cases on this subject state with unmistakable clearness that the ultimate and sole object in the minds of the Sunday-law originators was to promote the interest and influence of the church by constraining men to attend to her ordinances. In this day of enlightenment we ought not to be forced to continue work begun in the past. We live in a time when men ought to have, by reason of experience and the principles laid down by our forefathers, a better understanding and conception of religious freedom. Sunday legislation is contrary not only to the principles of American law but to the principles and precepts of Christianity itself.

CHAPTER XXI

Conclusion

SEPARATION of the church from the state was the prevailing condition in the early years of the Christian church, both from principle and from necessity. The government was hostile. The church sought to fulfill, in spite of an inimical society, what it considered a divine mission.

Not until the time of Constantine did church and state become united; for the most part they have continued so for sixteen centuries. A union of church and state has been considered the normal relationship in most of Christendom and by the great majority of peoples.

Where church and state are united, pressing issues concerning religious liberty have no opportunity to arise. Toleration may prevail, but toleration, however benevolent, is not liberty. Where toleration is not granted, the alternatives are escape by flight or utter submission with suppression of conscience.

Large numbers of colonists came to America to live in a freer atmosphere than toleration gives, or to escape some form of religious persecution. They represented a wide variety of nationalities and cultures. Except in New England, there was no area where believers in any form of religion within the Christian family of faiths were in the majority. That fact naturally aided the men who formed the national government in refusing to establish any national religion. Where states had established denominations, these were within half a century relinquished. Religion as an institution was not a concern of government as an institution.

Here in America then was the outworking of a remarkable experiment. Early Christianity had endeavored to exist and operate separate from a hostile state. It had eventually united with the state when the state became friendly. In America Christianity was asked by a new form of democratic, federal government to live separate from that government, which in turn pledged itself constitutionally to be not hostile but neutral in reference to sectarian religions.

It is noteworthy that by the middle of the nineteenth century Jeremiah S. Black, noted American lawyer and distinguished judge, gave expression to the American program in the following words:

The manifest object of the men who framed the institutions of this country, was to have a State without religion and a Church without politics — that is to say, they meant that one should never be used as an engine for any purpose of the other. . . . Our fathers seem to have been perfectly sincere in their belief that the members of the Church would be more patriotic, and the citizens of the State more religious, by keeping their respective functions entirely separate. For that reason they built up a wall of complete and perfect partition between the two.[1]

Today this enunciation is not only admitted but is a *fait accompli*. For when a social experiment has been conducted for more than a century and a half it is not premature to pass judgment. The principle of separation of church and state and the recognition of personal liberties expressed particularly in the First Amendment to the federal Constitution have been successfully applied in legislation and through litigation in the courts. American insistence upon separation of church and state has been maintained in a remarkable manner.

By 1894, upon the occasion of urging the inclusion in the New York constitution of a specific prohibition against the use of public funds for sectarian purposes, it was possible for Elihu Root to summarize a century of the nation's history in the following words: "It is not a question of religion, or of creed, or of party; it is a question of declaring and maintaining the great American principle of eternal separation between church and state." [2]

The principle of separation of church and state had become so intrenched in the American way of thinking that in 1876 Congress required every state admitted into the union to write into its constitution a requirement that it maintain a school system "free from sectarian control."

Probably the most significant recent development in this American experiment has been the application of the far-reaching principles of the First Amendment upon the states and their citizens through the Fourteenth Amendment. This interpretation, emerging within this generation, supplies what must be acknowledged as a lack in some state constitutions of a clear enunciation of the principle

[1] From "Religious Liberty" (1856) in Black, *Essays and Speeches* (1886), pp. 51, 53; see also Brigance, *Jeremiah Sullivan Black* (1934).
[2] Root, *Addresses on Government and Citizenship* (Cambridge, 1916), pp. 137, 140.

of separation of church and state. The application of the First Amendment to the states, and the passing of supplemental laws interpreted by decisions of the courts, are meeting this deficiency until the time comes when these state constitutions are strengthened by revision or amendment.

It has been proved in America that organized religions, differing markedly from one another, can exist and prosper side by side in a free society, with no effective threat to democratic government and without government support or control. It has also been proved that a government existing of, by, and for the people can govern a free society without including organized religion in its concerns.

The legal record is on the whole a happy one. Step by step, and legal item by item, the people have examined the conduct of their fellow citizens in terms of law and have evolved a pattern of freedom in human relationships. In this process, freedom of religion has been illustrated and defined.

Although the pattern has not been uniformly laid down, the progress made must be evident to all. That the teaching and maintenance of religion through public agencies is repugnant to the American people has been made clear by the exclusion, to a large extent, of religious worship from the public schools. The teaching of religion in the public schools is now unconstitutional. But instances where religious denominations have taken over and operated public schools as sectarian schools, at public expense, are not lacking. Efforts are still being made by manipulation and by proposed legislation to secure aid from public tax funds for religious institutions. The question of indirect aids, such as transportation of sectarian school children at public expense and the furnishing from public funds of free textbooks to pupils of religious schools, deserves further study.

The general trend of court decisions and legislative enactments points definitely to the conclusion that if the government is to provide the greatest benefits and privileges that a state can offer to its citizens, it must maintain a complete separation of church and state. Americans have largely outgrown the doctrines of religious tests and of taxation for religious purposes. The trend of public thought on the part of the majority is toward a complete emancipation of civil and religious agencies from each other.

Simultaneously, especially in the past quarter century, there appears to have been an attempt on the part of organized religious groups to appeal to the state for the teaching, preference, and enforcement of their dogmas. Such efforts by ecclesiastical bodies to secure the support of the strong arm of the state may be an unconscious confession of the weaknesses grown into or inherent in organized religion. It is by no means certain that organization either weakens religion or diverts it from its mission. But it is certain that any religion, organized or not, that solicits state aid or intrudes its hand into state affairs is weakened or at least is inviting the decline of its spiritual powers.

In this connection there has been a definite attempt to bolster religion by requiring Bible reading in the public schools. The incidental controversy and its significance has been one of the concerns of this study. On the other hand, along with this attempt to "place the Bible in the public schools" there has been developing in the minds of many people a greater objection to such intrusion, on the grounds that it means bringing religion into the public schools.

A public school in which no religion is taught invades the religious rights of no one. Religious instruction in the public schools is, so far as the taxpayer is concerned, an enforced support of religion, and the courts have shown a tendency to recognize this principle and to keep the schools free of doubtful practices. At first only material definitely sectarian or denominational was interpreted as being unconstitutional; there is now a definite trend on the part of the courts to eliminate entirely all instruction that might be construed as denominational. Where the laws of the state are silent on the subject of Bible reading, and practice is at the discretion of school officials, the courts are left to act only where abuse is clearly shown.

Because the American states consider that religious doctrine has no legal status, because they guarantee and promote the same citizenship for all classes without respect to race or creed, it seems reasonable to eliminate discriminatory religious material from state-supported schools. The Christian holds no civil right that the professors of another creed or of no creed do not also hold. The Mohammedan has recourse to the same remedies, civil and criminal, for wrongs inflicted that are available to the Christian, the Jew, or any other person. He may vote and he may hold public office. He may not only administer the law but he may help make it.

Litigation, court decisions covering many phases of the question, and in general all the controversy that has taken place prove that religious instruction in the public schools cannot be separated from denominational differences. Any form of sectarianism results in religious discriminations, from which our public schools should be zealously protected. Any alliance or bond joining the church and the state in their separate functions, in their separate and distinct spheres of operation, is not only injurious to both but forbodes evil to all concerned. A complete separation of church and state places Catholics, all Protestant denominations, and members of all other religions on an equal footing. Every church must grant to others its own rights and privileges and no more. Each must have a free and untrammeled opportunity to hold to its tenets and to proclaim them without state support or prejudice, so long as they are not destructive of the rights of others.

The public school is a piece of state machinery organized and supported for purely secular ends. Its function is not to make or unmake Christians, or to educate children in this or that form of religious faith. Its function is to prepare for citizenship. It eschews religious education. Its work is carried on from the point of view of utility to the state. In short, its purpose is secular education with no meddling in the province of the church.

This, the evidence clearly shows, is the basis on which a school system organized and conducted by an American state should rest. It is the one that has been reiterated again and again by the courts. The public schools should have no religious creed to teach or enforce, but should leave the teaching of religion to the home, the church, and the church school. It is only as such a position is taken that the principles and ideals upon which our government is founded can be maintained.

The public school, like the state, under whose authority it exists, and by whose taxing power it is supported, should be simply a civil institution, absolutely secular and not at all religious in its purpose, and all practical questions involving this principle should be settled in accordance therewith.[3]

The pervading constitutional principle of the various states is that the state as such has nothing to do with religion beyond affording to the people protection in the enjoyment of their religious rights and convictions. This principle enjoins upon the state the duty to afford to every citizen, so far as religion is concerned, impartial protection, but to stop there. This gives religious truth and its friends a fair and open field without patronage and without hindrance. The mature judgment of American legislatures and courts opposes,

[3] Samuel T. Spear, *Religion and the State* (New York, 1876), p. 384.

in the matter of public school organization and practice, any intrusion of religion or sectarian influences in the public schools.

An analysis of the constitutions of the states, statutes, and court decisions proves the soundness of the propositions declared by Professor Paul H. Hanus:

(1) Formal or explicit instruction in religion in the public schools is undesirable, unnecessary, and, in most cases, legally impossible; and

(2) Religious education, including detailed instruction in the Bible, is the duty of the church.

These propositions are not new; but in the contemporary transitional state of religious belief, and in view of the strong, increasing, and justifiable demand for instruction in the Bible, we need to remind ourselves often of their validity; lest, in spite of the lessons of history and of contemporary experience, we entertain unwise or even disastrous suggestions; and, failing to aid the contemporary promising, though as yet only incipient efforts of the church, we invite dissension and disaster, and so defeat our own ends.[4]

The right to preach and teach religion by free speech and a free press has been well established, and the line between the necessary exercise of the police power of the state and the enjoyment of personal liberties guaranteed by the Constitution has been rather well defined. These freedoms are vital in a democratic society, and their clear recognition by the courts is an important development.

Minority rights of conscience must always constitute something of a problem, even in a free society. Progress has been made in this respect, particularly in naturalization cases and cases involving the compulsory saluting of the American flag.

It is different in the category of Sunday laws. There is no record in recent years of a Sunday law being approved by a vote of the people. The majority of the population does not wish the unnatural restraints on a particular day made by Sunday laws. There is a latent feeling that laws essentially religious, passed under guises other than religious, are a danger to liberty. There is a danger that sumptuary laws may be adopted and enforced as necessary for economic reasons, or for reasons of public health or good order. Perhaps no area in church-state relationships needs more careful study today than the area of Sunday legislation.

The proper sphere of our government was well stated by the United States Senate when it said:

[4] Paul H. Hanus, *Beginnings in Industrial Education and Other Educational Discussions* (New York, 1908), p. 166.

It is not in the legitimate province of the legislature to determine what religion is true or what false. Our government is a civil and not a religious institution. Our constitution recognizes in every person the right to choose his own religion, and to enjoy it freely without molestation. . . . The proper object of government is to protect all persons in the enjoyment of their civil as well as their religious rights, and not to determine for any whether they shall esteem one day above another, or esteem all days alike holy. . . . What other nations call religious toleration, we call religious rights. They are not exercised in virtue of governmental indulgence, but as rights of which government cannot deprive any portion of its citizens, however small. Despotic power may invade those rights, but justice still confirms them.[5]

Occasionally we have failed to attain the ideal which our Constitution places before us in granting to every citizen fullest protection in his religious belief, but such civic inertia has been no fault of the Constitution and has been in violation of its spirit. Infringements have appeared from time to time throughout our history when individuals or organizations have endeavored, frequently under the guise of patriotism, to fan the sparks of religious prejudices. Instances may be found where individuals have been excluded from public office, from citizenship, from employment, or from attendance at colleges and universities as a result of discrimination based on religious differences or conscientious scruples. Such have been the exceptions rather than the general rule.

For religious liberty is like the air we breathe, unthought of by many until some hostile element asserts itself. Civil and religious freedom is one of the greatest privileges we enjoy. Many sacrifices have been made through dark centuries in the long and terrible struggle for liberty.

Although all the problems in the relationship of government and religion have not yet been solved, this is clear: the people of the United States believe that every man has a right to worship, or not to worship, as his conscience or reason dictates, and to disseminate his views; and that government is to protect, but not control, the exercise of these rights, without itself establishing or maintaining any form of religion. In the words of the United States Supreme Court: "We have staked the very existence of our country on the faith that complete separation between the state and religion is best for the state and best for religion." [6] In affecting this way of living, the great American experiment in freedom is proving a success.

[5] United States Sunday Mail Report, 20th Congress, 2d Session, January 19, 1829.
[6] Everson v. Board of Education, 330 U.S. 59 (1947).

Index

Academies, 27
Accredited Bible study, 91ff
Adams v. Harnell, 221n
Agnosticism, 169
Alabama
  Bible reading required, 33, 34
  court cases
    Frolickstein v. Mayor of Mobile, 230n
    Jones v. City of Opelika, Ala., and two
      other cases, 14n, 201n, 211n, 212, 213
    Marsh v. State of Alabama, 14n, 201n,
      216n
    O'Donnell v. Sweeney, 228n
    Powell v. Alabama, 201n
  statute requiring Bible reading, 33
  supreme court on Sunday as sacred, 228
Allgeyer v. Louisiana, 37
Almassi v. City of Newark, 208n
Alvey, Judge, on Sunday as sacred, 228
Amendment, First
  applied to states through Fourteenth, 14,
    90, 201, 257, 258
  flag salute, 178, 183, 186
  free transportation, 160, 161, 162, 163
  freedom of the press, 200, 208
  fundamental rights, 203, 218
  license tax, 212, 213
  preferred position of rights, 216
  religious garb not a violation, 116, 117
  restrictions on Congress, 11, 12, 36, 37
  rights guaranteed through Fourteenth,
    211
  supporting a religious establishment a vio-
    lation, 100
Amendment, Fourteenth
  due process clause, 171, 201
  First Amendment applicable to states
    through Fourteenth, 90, 161, 200
  flag salute, 183, 185
  free textbooks not a violation, 147, 148
  free transportation, 159, 161, 162, 163
  freedom of the press, 218
  license tax, 211, 214
  parental control, 134, 135, 137, 142
  religious garb not a violation, 116, 117
  Scopes case, 166
  states and religious freedom, 12, 13, 14,
    37, 200, 200n, 201

Sunday legislation, 241
American Association for the Advancement
  of Atheism, 97
American Federation of Labor and one-day-
  in-seven laws, 254
Anderson et al. v. State, 209n
Andrews v. Bible Society, 230n
Anglicans, 3, 7, 19, 23
Anglo-Saxon Sunday legislation, 221
Areopagitica, 200
Arizona
  religious test prohibited, 115
  repealed Sunday legislation, 253, 254
  statutes
    providing for nonsectarian instruction,
      60
    public funds in aid of sectarian schools,
      60
Arkansas
  Bible reading required, 33
  court cases
    Rosenbaum v. State, 211n, 223, 231n
    State v. Frederick, 238n
    Stockden v. State, 228n, 230n
  statutes
    anti-evolution law at general election,
      173
    forbidding comments, 34
    required Bible reading, 33, 34
Atchison, Topeka, Santa Fe R. R. Co. v.
  Atchison, 105n
Atkin v. Kansas, 171n
Augsburg Confession, 251
Ayres v. Methodist Church, 230n

Baggerly v. Lee, 126n
Baird v. State, 237n
Baldwin, Arthur C., 252
Baltimore, Lord, 3
Bancroft, George, 2, 25
Baptists, 3, 19, 24
Barbershops and Sunday legislation, 238, 239
Barnes v. Falmouth, 117n
Barnette case, 185
Barrington v. Missouri, 200n
Bartels v. Iowa, 132n
Barton v. City of Bessemer, 208n
Baseball, Sunday, 241, 242

263